# PRAISE FOR C

"This books makes a vital contribution to the struggles of the peoples of the Americas to defend themselves against the coups d'état that anti-democratic elites of the hemisphere have unleashed again, albeit cloaked in new garments. Paraguay in 2012, Brazil in 2016 and 2018, Bolivia in 2019 all suffered coups, with intensifying violence, revealing that slaveholding, racist, and colonial legacies are still very much alive among the wealthiest in the region. The victory of Bolivia's popular movements—courageous, heroic, and swift—resulting in the extraordinary victory of Lucho Arce and the return of Evo Morales's MAS party in 2020, serve as an inspiring example for neighboring states. Once again the lesson is clear: whenever the will of the people may be expressed freely through the ballot, proposals that lead to greater equality, more just distribution of income, and vigorous efforts to combat hunger and poverty will prevail. But this is possible only with robust popular participation in the decision-making process." —LUIZ INÁCIO LULA DA SILVA, former president of Brazil

"*Coup* tells the story of Bolivia's MAS party, the ousting of its popular Indigenous president Evo Morales, and the following wave of abuses committed by the authoritarian Áñez regime. The book is a vital contribution to our understanding of how reactionary forces leveraged a bogus claim of fraud to overthrow the elected president. It is essential reading for those committed to democracy and social justice in the Americas. *Coup* highlights the need to remain on alert in electoral times and serves as a warning about the cunning preparation of coups d'état. Today's coups are more sophisticated than those of previous decades, but they are equally ruthless and equally dangerous." —MADRES DE LA PLAZA DE MAYO–LINEA FUNDADORA, mothers of Argentina's disappeared

"Future historians will look back at the reversal of Bolivia's 2019 coup as an event equal in importance to Fidel Castro's defeat of the US-organized invasion at the Bay of Pigs. Linda Farthing and Thomas

Becker have provided us with an indispensable analysis to the sources of the conflict and how the forces of hope triumphed." —GREG GRANDIN, Pulitzer Prize–winning author of *The End of the Myth: From the Frontier to the Border Wall in the Mind of America*

"In the international media discourse that emerged in late 2019 after Evo Morales was forced into exile and Jeanine Áñez declared herself president of Bolivia, some voices remained conspicuously absent: those of the Bolivians living through the turmoil. Farthing and Becker set out to challenge this trend, crafting a narrative based on the testimony of dozens of Bolivian activists, political figures, and intellectuals. Stitched together in a compelling and lucid narrative, the insights of those on the ground—not only about the brutal right-wing repression under Áñez but also about both the advances and shortcomings of Morales's time in power—provide the clearest picture yet of what happened in Bolivia in 2019." —DR. CHRISTY THORNTON, assistant professor, Johns Hopkins University and former executive director of the North American Congress on Latin America (NACLA)

"*Coup* is a comprehensive account of the democratic disruption that Bolivia suffered in 2019. With remarkable handling of sources, Linda Farthing and Thomas Becker present a critical vision of Bolivia as well as the political, social, and democratic challenges the country faces. Captivating read!" —EDUARDO RODRIGUEZ VELTZÉ, former president of Bolivia

"Measured and methodical, Farthing and Becker's analysis of the right-wing coup d'état in Bolivia is mandatory reading for anyone attempting to come to grips with the country's recent past. Sharp, expeditious prose mirrors the often frenetic pace of political developments in recent years. Rooted in a blend of on-the-ground reportage and a mastery of the best local sources of journalism and social-scientific inquiry, *Coup* contextualizes the socio-political gains and contradictions of the era of Evo Morales, unearths the root causes of his ouster from office, and surveys the violent regime of Jeanine Áñez installed in the coup's aftermath. In a period of recurring crises of global capitalism and an attendant rise in authoritarian forms of right-wing rule, the significance of this book extends well beyond the borders of Bolivia." —JEFFERY R. WEBBER, author of *Red October: Left-Indigenous Struggles in Modern Bolivia*

# COUP

## A STORY OF VIOLENCE AND RESISTANCE IN BOLIVIA

LINDA FARTHING
THOMAS BECKER

Haymarket Books
Chicago, Illinois

Published in 2021 by
Haymarket Books
P.O. Box 180165
Chicago, IL 60618
773-583-7884
www.haymarketbooks.org
info@haymarketbooks.org

ISBN: 978-1-64259-587-1

Distributed to the trade in the US through Consortium Book Sales and Distribution (www.cbsd.com) and internationally through Ingram Publisher Services International (www.ingramcontent.com).

This book was published with the generous support of Lannan Foundation and Wallace Action Fund.

Special discounts are available for bulk purchases by organizations and institutions. Please email orders@haymarketbooks.org for more information.

Cover design by Jamie Kerry. Cover photo by Gaston Brito Miserocchi.

Printed in Canada.

Library of Congress Cataloging-in-Publication data is available.

*For my children and godchildren: Minka, Anamaya,*
*Gavriel, Luli, Clarita and Karen who support*
*and inspire me more than you know.*
—Linda

*For the brave families who lost loved ones during the 2019–2020*
*Bolivia conflicts and continue to fight for justice. La lucha sigue.*
—Thomas

# CONTENTS

# FOREWORD

The volume you have before you, *Coup*, tells the story of the ousting of President Evo Morales in rich, nuanced detail. It does so by unravelling the complex layers of injustice, exploitation, and racism that have cursed Bolivia since the arrival of Spanish *conquistadores* in 1524. The narrative in this book presents the immediate events leading to the coup, as well as the structural forces at work in the demise of the Morales presidency. The authors underscore the broader context of a deeply unequal hemisphere and world. Understanding these structural forces, as well as the proximate causes of the coup, is essential if one is to move beyond the simplistic and inaccurate narratives that dominated most English-language explanations of what happened in Bolivia in the last quarter of 2019. Indeed, the authors' implicit contention throughout (and the value of their work) is that only by understanding (at least superficially) five centuries of exploitive, racist rule by an elite minority of European descent can one begin to appreciate the intensity of the animosity of the traditional ruling classes towards Evo Morales's popular, multicultural, egalitarian project.

This animosity—as Farthing and Becker detail—animated the campaign to drive Evo Morales, the MAS (Movimiento al Socialismo or Movement for Socialism) party, and the Indigenous majority out of power. The campaign, in turn, was facilitated by a well-prepared and disproven narrative of widespread election fraud, knowingly (or unwittingly) parroted by Western observers, most media sources, and powerful states. The combination of ill-intentioned distortion with amplification and legitimation that led to the seizure of power by an unknown, Evangelical Christian zealot, Senator Jeanine Áñez, while particular in its details, followed an increasingly common outline for twenty-first century attacks on democracy.

•

Whatever may be said of the Evo Morales and MAS period in government, it must be observed that the nearly fourteen years of their rule stand in stark contrast to almost five centuries of rule by the non-Indigenous minority. As Farthing and Becker explain, for 480 years in nearly linear fashion, whether under the Spanish crown or the post-independence governments, a small minority of elites of European descent controlled Bolivia's politics, economy, and social structure. The election of Evo Morales in 2006 represented a radical departure from the status quo. While imperfect in practice, Morales sought, at least in discourse, to transform Bolivia into a popular democracy based on multiculturalism and social equality. When one appreciates the transformational nature of the promise that Morales represented, one also understands the intensity of the reaction against him personally, against the MAS party and against the nation's indigenous majority.

The authors of this foreword—the former executive secretary and former president of the Inter-American Commission on Human Rights—have been close observers of Bolivia over these past two decades. Both of us have visited Bolivia numerous times to document the human rights conditions for reports, legal actions, press releases, and the like. We have been able to observe a good part of what this book's authors detail, from the shortcomings of the Morales government to the unprecedented changes the government brought to the country.

As executive secretary, Paolo Abrão was able to document the massacres at Senkata and Sacaba, in loco, only days after the two ugliest incidents of Áñez's period of abusive rule. As director of both Harvard's and Stanford's human rights clinics,

James Cavallaro documented the slaughter of indigenous protestors during the gas wars in 2003. The book sets out in clear,
concise text the visceral sense of injustice that we were able to
experience in our time in Bolivia.

•

For too long, human rights organizations have avoided "thorny"
political issues. When is the removal of a head of state "legal?"
When does it conform to international human rights standards?
The guidelines and parameters for answering these questions
have not been sufficiently developed, in part because leading
human rights organizations have avoided these debates. Instead,
collectively, human rights organizations have prioritized questions of procedure, allowing states themselves to decide on the
legitimacy of machinations that lead to changes in leadership.
Recent examples from the Americas abound. Was the reelection
of Juan Orlando Hernández in Honduras in 2017 legitimate?
(The answer from human rights groups should have been, but
was not, a resounding "No.") And Dilma Rousseff in Brazil? Was
her impeachment and removal from office legitimate? Did it conform to internal Brazilian standards? Was procedure followed?
If so, then would no further investigation be necessary? And
what about Evo's demise in 2019? If Evo Morales stepped down
and Jeanine Añez assumed the presidency through procedures
apparently mandated by Bolivian law, would that be sufficient
under international standards? Should it matter that Evo Morales
faced threats to himself and his family, as did many other high-
level MAS authorities? Should it matter that the military—later
rewarded with money and promotions by those who ousted
Morales—"invited" him to leave the country? That Evo offered
to hold new elections, faced with the (subsequently debunked)
claim of institutionalized fraud? Should it matter than Jeanine
Añez was not the first, nor the second, nor even the third in line
to assume the presidency? Or that a cabal of international officials and powerful opposition figures met, in secret, to designate
her to be president?

The so-called human rights community divided on these questions. Those aligned with powerful Western governments went along with the electoral fraud narrative promoted by the Organization of American States. They were able to overlook threats to Morales and leading MAS figures, intervention by the military, and queue-jumping the line of succession. The greater good—as they viewed it—of removing Evo from power justified the fictions on which the "legal" ouster narrative was based.

The story of the Bolivian coup is gripping. It is worth reading on its own. But understanding the deeper narrative is absolutely vital if we are to maintain democratic rule anywhere on the planet today. The 2019 coup in Bolivia has become a blueprint for reactionary forces across the Americas and the world: Authoritarian forces contend there has been or will be fraud—a "steal" of an election. They mobilize supporters, through mass and social media, to take matters into their own hands, to take to the streets or the halls of power. Political, military, judicial, and other forces must choose on which side to align. Democratic principles suffer terribly; polarization of society into camps with parallel and utterly divergent realities ensues. Sound familiar?

All these reasons gain greater weight in light of the revelations in mid-2021 of efforts by states in the region to provide material support (weapons, munitions, and other gear) that the interim Bolivian regime sought to use against its own citizens. The Bolivian case revives the specter of illicit cooperation by military and security forces in the Americas in the 1970s and '80s to suppress dissent against the authoritarian governments that dominated the hemisphere. This cooperation, known as Operation Condor, began in 1975 and led to widespread, systematic and severe violations of fundamental rights—thousands of forced disappearances, summary executions, and wholesale use of torture.

The development and strengthening of the institutions that protect human rights in the Americas are deeply intertwined with the brutal history of Operation Condor and of the coordinated efforts by security forces to eliminate the possibility of refuge for those who dared to oppose authoritarian rule in any of the collaborating countries. Driven by this ugly history, transitions to democratic rule over the past four decades have placed human rights—both domestically and in terms of foreign policy—front and center.

The decision and action by several states in South America (and perhaps beyond) to coordinate repressive efforts thus represent profound and existential threats to human rights. These threats interrupted decades of consistently professed opposition to state terror, authoritarianism, and politically targeted human rights abuse. In this sense, the Bolivian case echoes far beyond its borders. Placed before us are renewed challenges to the core principle of international cooperation based on respect for human rights.

*Coup* is essential reading for three reasons. First, because it is the most thorough, accurate, and succinct narrative of the events leading up to and following the overthrow of the government of Bolivian president Evo Morales. Second, because it provides a deep and contextual understanding of the factors—many spanning over decades and centuries—that led to the clashes of social forces and social classes culminating in October and November 2019. And, finally, because the means by which the coup was effectuated—under the cloak of democratic discourse—provide essential lessons about the nature of processes seeking to overturn egalitarian movements in Latin America (and beyond) in the twenty-first century.

Paulo Abrão and James Cavallaro

# PREFACE

When protestors carried the coffins down from El Alto after the November 2019 massacre in Senkata, I was interviewing women in La Paz's main square. By that point, the march had moved further along the road, and the square was largely filled with women and children protestors who were avoiding an inevitable confrontation with the cops a few blocks away. Local vendors had gone back to hawking their wares. Without any warning, the plaza was filled with tear gas: thick, blinding, choking clouds of the stuff, the like of which I had never seen. We all raced to get away, and, in the midst of the fleeing crowd, I didn't spot the big hole in the pavement. Down I went. Despite the gas and charging cops, the people around me—who have mostly never experienced anything decent from people of my class and skin color—pulled me out, dusted me off, made sure I had my camera and my wits before we all raced off again. That solidarity—in this case, action that saved me—is what has always made Bolivia feel like a home to me.

That solidarity came very much to mind when Thomas Becker called me in April 2020 to propose we write a book on Bolivia's November 2019 coup. I was stuck in the United States because of COVID, and my plans and life had turned upside-down like everyone else's. The May 4th elections I was returning to Bolivia to report on and to monitor with a delegation from the National Lawyers Guild were well on their way to being postponed, and it looked like we'd all be stuck wherever we landed for the foreseeable future. After book #3, I had sworn I wouldn't do another one, but rather dedicate myself to journalism with hopes of leaving the political fray to one side for a time. Instead I hoped to write about the marvels of Bolivia's food and travel possibilities, albeit within a socially and politically conscious context.

But the trauma of the November 2019 coup—when I had reported nonstop for six weeks, at times more terrified than I have ever been—was a story I knew must be told. I had watched while my mostly male neighbors explained that they were mounting street barricades in my upper-middle-class La Paz area to keep the "hordes" (code for Indigenous peoples) at bay. I had frantically packed a suitcase when the new minister of communication threatened imprisonment for journalists she deemed subversive, a category I knew I fit into. I was hurt and horrified when middle-class friends overnight became former friends as they abandoned left politics and instead prioritized "democratic" transitions above all other values, unable or unwilling to recognize their historic class and race position in the conflict. I had barely avoided weeping when I listened to the tragic tales told in a packed bare brick church about what working-class and Indigenous protestors had suffered during the massacre in Senkata. I had seen the desperation when poor people tugged at my sleeve because no other reporters were in sight. They were frantic to register their fears that the racism that had eased during Evo Morales's fourteen years was returning full force. Usually a person not prone to tears, I had cried repeatedly during that month and a half as I watched this beloved country torn apart by racism, hatred, and intolerance.

That call from Thomas led me to realize that, especially with his help, I was uniquely positioned to write a book in English about the coup and its aftermath—with thirty-five years of living between the United States and Bolivia, close to fifteen of those years in Bolivia, as well as three books on the country under my belt. So with quarantine stretching out before me for some unspecified amount of time, I took the plunge, working to tease out the lessons from the MAS experience and Evo Morales's ouster. They are lessons that have resonance for those working for progressive social change wherever you are in the world. I have long felt that in the north, and particularly in the current world imperial power, the United States, we buy too readily into tropes of northern superiority and remain shut off to the lessons we can learn from the efforts and agency of peoples in the Global South.

That is the story we seek to bring to life here: the ongoing struggles of Bolivia's working-class and Indigenous peoples to create a more just society. It is a story that has deep roots that are both inspiring and hopeful. Despite the setbacks, such as the one in November 2019, this small country in the Andes is on a steady arc toward a more equitable society because of the enormous efforts and sacrifice of much of its population. It is in the spirit of that positive change that we offer this story in the hopes that it will inform you, move you, and inspire you to contribute to building more equitable societies wherever you live. ¡J'allalla Bolivia!

—Linda

"I have no idea where my friends are or what has happened to them," Juan Carlos Apaza told me from his hospital bed as his right eye filled with tears.[1] He touched the bandage that covered his head. His left eye was gone, destroyed after a soldier shot him in the face as he attempted to help another protestor who had been gunned down. The previous day, Juan Carlos joined thousands of *campesinos* to protest the forced resignation of Evo Morales. When the demonstrators entered the town of Sacaba, Bolivian soldiers fired on them, killing at least ten and injuring over 120.

Thanks to a courageous and adept local taxi driver, I was able to circumvent the soldiers who controlled the nearby roads and arrive at the site of the massacre. The military had just left, but the bullets and blood remained. Mothers were crying over the bodies of their sons as protest organizers dragged me to the exact locations of the killings to recount what had happened. "You see what they did to us? There's no press here. No one to tell the world that they murdered us," the demonstrators wailed.

I spent the next twenty-four hours documenting bullet holes, gathering witness testimony, and sneaking into hospitals— thanks to the closest of friends, Kathy, who distracted staff so

I could speak directly with injured victims. I will never forget the moment that Roberto Cejas's wife arrived and saw her husband's lifeless body. She collapsed when a doctor pulled back the sheet covering the bullet hole that, as she described, looked like a flower blooming from his skull. I will never forget speaking to protestors in a hidden location who were too frightened to seek medical attention because they feared the government would disappear them. And I will never forget Juan Carlos' words to me before I left the hospital: "You will see. Tomorrow they are going to say we are responsible because we are poor, because we are Indians."

At the time, I did not want to believe Juan Carlos's prediction. I had documented human rights abuses all over the world. This was a massacre. Nonetheless, the de facto government immediately crafted a narrative that the protestors were responsible for their own deaths, which the press repeated, and half the country—particularly the lighter-skinned middle and upper classes—spent the next year dismissing the victims as communists, drug traffickers, terrorists, and savages who killed themselves.

When Linda Farthing and I first discussed writing a book, we had mixed feelings about whether we were the right ones to tell the story of Bolivia's coup. There certainly is no shortage of people from the Global North who are willing to speak for Bolivians, a colonialist dynamic that neither of us wanted to perpetuate. But Linda and I felt that we not only had a unique perspective—Linda spent 2019 and 2020 covering the coup for the *Guardian* and *Al Jazeera* among others, and I documented abuses by the de facto government for Harvard's International Human Rights Clinic during that period—but we also felt that we had a *responsibility* to tell the world what took place.

After Jeanine Áñez's unelected government took power in November 2019, it arrested those who spoke out against the coup, shut down critical media outlets, and harassed witnesses of state abuses. The international community did not know how to respond, in part because those with the strongest ties abroad—Bolivia's elite—recited Áñez's narrative and white-washed her government's abuses. Linda and I wrote this book to push back on the misinformation that has surrounded the coup and to attempt to amplify the voices of the marginalized communities that were silenced in its aftermath.

We hope this book highlights the very real threat of author-itarian movements and twenty-first-century coups, particularly those veiled in democratic discourse, that have flourished in re-cent years. We also hope it forces those of us on the left to engage in self-reflection in order to identify our own mistakes that have paved the way for these reactionary takeovers. But most impor-tantly, we want this book to inspire. This is a story of resistance, and once again the world can learn so much from Bolivians' infectious revolutionary spirit and commitment to grassroots change.

—Thomas

# INTRODUCTION

# UNPACKING BOLIVIA

Bolivia has always been a land of extremes: in its history, its landscape, and its natural resources. One of the most culturally, physically, and ecologically diverse places on the planet, the country covers an area about the size of Texas and California combined (or of Ontario). The natural environment excels in superlatives: the world's largest salt flat (Salar de Uyuni in the southwest), highest navigable lake (Titicaca, straddling the border with Peru), and second-largest high mountain plateau (the Altiplano). Bolivia is considered one of the world's thirty-six biodiversity hotspots.[1] The result is a breathtaking landscape of soaring mountains surrounding windswept plateaus and deep blue lakes that tumble into temperate valleys before unfolding eastward into dense jungles to the north, and open, dry savanna and scrub forests to the south.

The Andes region is considered one of the six cradles of human civilization.[2] The Tiwanaku Empire, in what is now Bolivia, dominated the region for over fifteen hundred years, until 1150 CE, thanks to complex hydrological systems that permitted agriculture across the cold, dry Altiplano just south of Lake Titicaca.[3] Destroyed by a prolonged drought, the fragmented remains coalesced into twelve Aymara-speaking kingdoms that stretched from central Peru to northern Argentina.[4] These in turn were overrun by the better-known Inka Empire, which typically forced conquered peoples to adopt their language (Quechua), religion, and culture, although they failed to accomplish this with many

1

of the Aymaras. When the Spaniards arrived in 1532, the Inka hovered on the brink of a civil war, which hastened the collapse of their highly centralized yet fragile empire that ruled over ten million people before an invading force of less than two hundred.[5]

Unlike European cultures, in the Indigenous Andean world, space and time are simultaneous realities expressed in the same word: *pacha*. Bolivia's Indigenous peoples revere their ancestors, as the dead either actively ensure the well-being of the living, or, if not treated with proper respect, block human endeavor.

The collective wields greater weight than the individual, conferring social status on the basis of community contributions rather than individual wealth or achievement. Traditional rural Bolivia is a land of almost continuous *fiestas*—lengthy religious and social celebrations that mark the changing seasonal and agricultural cycles. Their symbolism and rituals are captured in haunting music, striking ceramics, and some of the world's finest textiles in the highlands and valleys, as well as delicate fiber weavings in the lowlands.

While most Indigenous-identified Bolivians come from highland and valley Aymara- or Quechua-speaking groups, a plethora of peoples live in the lowlands. The most numerous are the Chiquitano followed by the Guaraní. The Chiquitano are an amalgamation created from various groups by Jesuits, who Christianized them in the early seventeenth century and forced the nomadic communities into village settlements. The Guaraní, who comprise the northern branch of the much larger Paraguayan Guaraní, were not definitively conquered until 1892. Ever since, they have been dispossessed of their ancestral territories while frequently forced to labor on huge estates.[6] Some thirty-four smaller groups, among them the Guarayo, Moxeño, Tacana, Ayoreo, Chimané, Trinitario, and Ese Ejja, total another 150,000 people, many of whom were devastated by the Amazon rubber boom in the late nineteenth and early twentieth centuries.

Since the 1960s, massive migration from rural areas into the outskirts of cities has spawned an urban Indigenous culture with forty-two percent of all Indigenous people now living in cities.[7]

In the country with the lowest worker productivity in South America and little in the way of manufacturing, 69 percent of these migrants work in what is the world's largest informal economy, as day laborers or selling in markets.[8]

According to the 2012 census, 41 percent of Bolivians consider themselves Indigenous—the largest proportion of any country in the Americas—though this social and historically constituted identity is fluid. 2017 projections from Bolivia's National Statistics Institute (INE) suggest that this figure may now have increased to 48 percent.[9]

For many Bolivians, a clear border between identities of Indigenous and *mestizo*, which encompasses those of mixed European and Indigenous heritage, is illusory. Indeed, a 2012 study revealed that seven in ten Bolivians identify as belonging to an Indigenous group, while almost eight out of ten also self-identify as mestizo.[10]

Less than 10 percent of the population claim European ancestry or form part of more recent European and Middle Eastern immigration. Nevertheless, with few exceptions, this minority has dominated the country's economy and politics, constituting the core of Bolivia's ruling class and utilizing deeply entrenched systemic racism to justify the exploitation of Indigenous peoples. In a 2019 study, journalist Fernando Molina found that the ancestry of the entire Bolivian upper class remains of European origin.[11]

During the past fifteen years, an expanding economy under Evo Morales's government accelerated the growth of new Indigenous economic elites, although they still lack the economic clout that generations of entrenched privilege afford the white upper class. Their wealth stems from trucking, commerce, and informal mining, although a smattering of them profit from the illegal economies of contraband and the cocaine base trade.[12]

Three common colonial and post-colonial processes shape Bolivia: the expropriation of resources by national and international elites; Indigenous peoples' resistance; and contention between the country's regions.[13] The result is that Bolivia, with one of the lowest population densities in South America, was until recently the continent's poorest country in terms of per capita income.

These three disjunctures have bred chronic volatility in politics: there have been 190 coups d'état or unconstitutional transitions of government since the 1825 founding of the republic, and the country was under the rule of military dictatorships for eighteen years between 1964 and 1982.[14]

The Bolivian state has almost without pause prioritized elite exploitation of natural resources and the Indigenous population, fashioning an acute case of economic dependency.[15] This plunder of resources speaks to the asymmetrical and mutually interdependent relationship between poor and wealthy countries that defines the global economy. Consequently, resource nationalism—the idea that resources should benefit their country of origin—has been a consistent driver of Bolivian labor and social movements.[16] An "extractive mentality" spread among local people, according to political scientists Luis Tapia and Marxa Chávez, when Indigenous communities were exploited by the Spanish for silver and gold mining, and later intensified when tin miners consolidated into a political force.[17]

Bolivia has always been a mining country. Potosí's vast silver deposits were critical to sixteenth-century Spain and European industrialization, triggering a profound and destructive restructuring of Andean society. Uruguayan author Eduardo Galeano wrote that a popular belief in Bolivia is "that in three centuries Spain got enough metal from Potosí to make a silver bridge from the tip of [Potosí's] Cerro Rico [mine] to the door of the royal palace across the ocean."[18] Perhaps an even more apt description comes from Potosí residents who told journalist and historian Ben Dangl that the bridge could have been built from the bones of the people who died in the bowels of the mountain.[19]

As Potosí's silver became more difficult to access, Spanish colonial power declined, and with it, Spain's position as a global force. Foreign interest in Bolivia has repeatedly waxed and waned according to global commodity boom and bust cycles. And whether that commodity is silver, tin, quinine, rubber, coca, or, most recently, natural gas, Indigenous resistance has been a constant.[20] Under colonial rule, Indigenous peoples were a source of cheap labor and tax revenues—a fate that remained largely unchanged during the nineteenth- and twentieth-century republic, when elites who claimed Spanish heritage seized more native land.[21]

At the same time, Bolivia's highly centralized political system created a constant tug-of-war between the center and the periphery, resulting in a country that remains one of the least integrated in Latin America.[22] This weak state has relied more on force than legitimacy to rule, making challenges to the centralized government continual, even if they have routinely ended in compromise.

Bolivia's political transitions have been characterized by abrupt ruptures. One of the most crucial occured in 1952, when a successful revolution—steered by an ideologically diverse alliance of middle- and upper-class intellectual dissidents, miners, urban workers, and *campesinos*[23]—mobilized behind the Revolutionary Nationalist Movement (MNR), which had been thwarted from taking office by a military junta after winning the 1951 elections.

Workers founded the Bolivian Workers Central (COB) at the height of the uprising, under the leadership of the powerful left-dominated Union Federation of Bolivian Mine Workers (FSTMB) whose production accounted for most foreign exports.[24]

Faced with well-organized miners, the new government quickly nationalized most of the tin mines, extended the vote to women and Indigenous peoples, and adopted an agrarian reform that broke up the large estates, or *haciendas*, in the Altiplano and high valleys. The army was disbanded and replaced by popular militias.

With a formal sector working class that has always represented a minority of the economically active population, the COB grew to incorporate the majority of Bolivian workers—whether white- or blue-collar, private or public sector—as well as street vendors and campesino farmers. From this period until the mid-1980s, the COB played the leading role in popular resistance and promotion of working-class and Indigenous interests.[25]

During the 1950s, the newly nationalized mines struggled under poor state management, hamstrung by patronage linked to the MNR party. Agricultural production dropped because of a lack of technical and marketing assistance to the new peasant owners. By 1956, the MNR government saw little option but to borrow heavily from the United States, accepting conditions that put a brake on nationalization, as well as an International Monetary Fund (IMF) stabilization plan that slashed social programs, disarmed popular militias formed during the 1952 revolution, and reestablished the Bolivian military with closer ties to the US Army.

This fed the next significant rupture: a military takeover that would last eighteen years. While violently repressing the COB, almost all the military governments of this period shifted resources to private mining operations, foreign-owned oil companies, and large-scale agriculture in the eastern lowlands, particularly to farms owned by family and friends.

Despite continuous crackdowns, the COB led the struggle to overturn the dictatorships.[26] At the end of the 1970s, a hunger strike initiated by four miners' wives spread like wildfire, spelling the beginning of the end for the military.[27]

Popular opposition multiplied, bolstered in part by US president Jimmy Carter's human rights policy. A loose coalition of left-wing parties won office but inherited an economic crisis compounded by a severe highland drought. Within two years, Bolivia was suffering some of the worst inflation the world has ever seen, and by 1985 the coalition government was compelled to call an election.

This brought the next about-turn in Bolivia's fortunes: the new government committed wholeheartedly to a neoliberal economic model. Using a drop in international tin prices as the pretext to close most of the state-owned mines, it proceeded to fire thousands of miners, virtually destroying the COB in the process.[28] The Workers Central's downfall was accelerated by its inability to adapt its rigid structure, which required that miners always serve as its leaders, to the shifting composition of political protest brought by the growth of Indigenous and campesino organizations.[29] This sidelining of organized labor partially explains why, when the Movement for Socialism (MAS) party emerged ten years later, it was grounded in newer social movements associated with Indigenous and campesino organizations, rather than trade unions.[30]

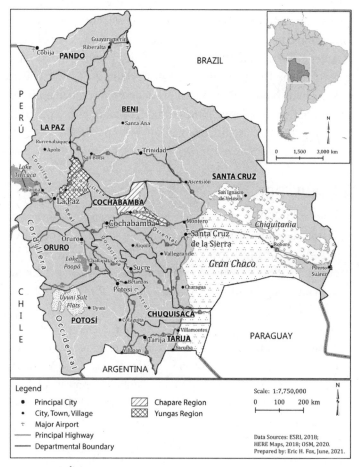

*Source: UN Bolivia*

Successive neoliberal governments from 1985 to 2005 cut services and privatized state-owned enterprises, pushing impoverished campesinos and unemployed miners to flock to the cities, turning 65 percent of the population urban, compared to 50 percent in 1985.[31] Displaced campesinos and miners also fled to semitropical lowlands east of Cochabamba to grow coca leaf as demand for cocaine in the United States soared during the 1980s.[32]

Throughout neoliberalism's supremacy, Bolivia enjoyed democratic changes of government, but inequality grew sharply.[33] This rising disparity drove popular resistance, increasingly mobilized around Indigenous rather than class identity. Groups of campesinos, urban dwellers, and unions forced the cancellation of water privatization in Cochabamba in 2000 and of natural gas exports to the United States through Chile in 2003.[34] This five-year cycle of protest ejected two presidents from office until, in late 2005, Evo Morales won the election, becoming the country's first Indigenous and self-defined as left-wing president.

## THE PINK TIDE

By the mid-2000s, elected left-wing governments governed three-quarters of Latin Americans, or 350 million people. As with so many changes that assert themselves regionally, such as import substitution economic policy in the 1950s and the military dictatorships of the 1970s and '80s, this "Pink Tide" played out distinctly in each country.[35]

In late 1998, Hugo Chávez won the Venezuelan presidential election, declaring a Bolivarian revolution to improve the lives of the poor. In Brazil, Luiz Inácio da Silva (Lula) of the Workers' Party (PT) was elected in 2002 and maintained power for fourteen years. The husband-and-wife team of Néstor Kirchner and Cristina Fernández de Kirchner governed Argentina from 2003 to 2015. Socialist Michelle Bachelet held two nonconsecutive terms in office in Chile, from 2006 to 2010 and from 2014 to 2018. All told, differing versions of self-defined left-wing governments came to power in fourteen Latin American countries.

The Pink Tide governments benefited from one of the largest economic expansions in Latin American history, driven by skyrocketing demand for commodities, principally from China. In turn, the agricultural frontier advanced and mining in remote areas mushroomed, both with devastating consequences for the natural environment and the mostly Indigenous people who rely on it.

By 2014, the boom was over, and Latin American economies contracted, while public spending ebbed. This contraction combined with the growing influence of ultraconservative evangelical movements, along with the perverse effect of the commodity boom in countries with weak institutional controls, to facilitate a right-wing return to power. Governments that had committed to ending corruption as part of their electoral platform found that soaring commodity earnings fueled bribery. Scandals, some of them manufactured, were exploited by the right wing to bring down PT leaders Lula and Dilma Rousseff in Brazil, dog the Kirchners in Argentina, and cloud the end of the Bachelet presidency in Chile.[36]

Despite the hurdles, the Pink Tide governments succeeded in transferring power away from the oligarchies, military, and churches, instead privileging the poor, women, and Indigenous peoples. For example, many women's lives were transformed through laws that promoted equal wages, condemned gender discrimination, and defended them from domestic abuse, even if these efforts were uneven and heteropatriarchal relations of power persisted.[37]

The perpetuation of these patterns reflects the failure of the Pink Tide governments to confront the underlying structures of the capitalist system beyond targeted and partial nationalizations in Venezuela, Ecuador, and Bolivia. Rather, in most countries, they introduced social democratic, welfare-state policies more akin to those of Western Europe than Cuba.

These largely served to make Latin America more inclusive and equitable. Between 2002 and 2012, Latin America's middle class (by local standards) expanded annually until it comprised up to one-third of the population.[38] Poverty shrank: from 2000 to 2014, the proportion of those living on less than four dollars a day plummeted from almost half the population to a quarter. Government redistribution efforts, such as conditional cash transfer programs that tend to deliver the greatest benefits to the poorest, impacted millions of people.

Mainstream researchers place Bolivia under Morales on the most radical end of the Pink Tide spectrum, a position most often reflected in Evo's international pronouncements and policy initiatives—for example, calls for climate change justice for low-income countries and denunciations of the United States' incessant meddling in local politics.[39] In practice, his government's economic and social policies were moderate, expanding many formal rights for Indigenous people and women while significantly bolstering social and infrastructure spending. Fiscal policies tended to be conservative and implemented only relatively minor adjustments to underlying economic structures.[40] Thus, the MAS government was fundamentally a political project, rather than an economic one.

Nonetheless, Morales and his "process of change," as the MAS program is called, were celebrated by the left and demonized by the right. US officials accused Hugo Chávez and Fidel Castro of taking advantage of Morales to create a "populist Marxist-socialist" government in the heart of South America. Morales countered by denouncing George W. Bush as a terrorist. Europeans were generally intrigued by the "process of change," although the Spanish worried that Bolivia might expropriate the holdings of their hydrocarbon giant, Repsol, which is the second-largest investor in Bolivian natural gas.[41] Activists committed to causes ranging from Indigenous rights to environmental justice heralded Morales's election as a sign that a more just and equitable world was not only possible but already under construction in the Andes.[42]

Bolivia's international influence grew during the Morales government, in part because of the 2010 World People's Conference on Climate Change and the Rights of Mother Earth, which was organized after the UN Climate Change Conference in Copenhagen had failed to reach a worldwide agreement the year before. The Morales administration funded the Cochabamba conference with the goal of providing governments and civil society the opportunity to formulate climate change proposals together. Over thirty-five thousand people from 147 countries attended, including forty-seven government delegations.[43]

The MAS government also played a critical role in generating alternatives to the region's orthodox and market-driven integration mechanisms, the Andean Community of Nations (CAN) and the Southern Common Market (Mercosur). In an attempt to break dependency, it sought to foster solidarity based on such concepts as *Vivir Bien* ("living well") and South–South cooperation, especially through the Venezuelan-initiated Bolivarian Alliance for the Peoples of Our America (ALBA) and Union of South American Nations (UNASUR) modeled on the European Union.

## STRUGGLING FOR A VOICE: INDIGENOUS, WOMEN'S, AND WORKING-CLASS RIGHTS

When Evo Morales was elected in 2005, Bolivia's social movements were among the world's most militant, with defiant resistance traditions dating from the Spanish invasion.[44] To name only the most well known, movements led by Túpac Katari and Bartolina Sisa in the eighteenth century were followed by Pablo Zárate Willka at the end of the nineteenth, before the emergence of more class-oriented resistance during much of the twentieth century.[45]

During the 1970s, highland Aymara inspired by the pro-Indigenous intellectual Fausto Reinaga formed what became an influential group. One faction (the *Indigenistas*) concentrated on resisting racism, while the other (the *Kataristas*) fused Indigenous identity with class consciousness. By 1979 the Kataristas had forged the first independent national campesino union, the highland-dominated Unified Confederation of Bolivian Peasants' Unions (CSUTCB), which affiliated with the COB. Joined in 1980 by an Indigenous women's organization known as the "Bartolinas," the CSUTCB went on to play a critical part in the 1982 restoration of democracy.[46]

Almost ten years later, in 1990, the much smaller Confederation of Indigenous Peoples of Bolivia (CIDOB) burst onto the national stage with a momentous cross-country march. CIDOB has always held a much stronger Indigenist vision than the CSUTCB, although the latter steadily shifted toward this perspective with the decline of the COB in the late 1980s.[47] In 1997, another Indigenist-oriented organization coalesced in the southern highlands, the National Council of Ayllus and Markas of Qullasuyu (CONAMAQ).[48]

Women played second fiddle to men in these movement as well as in national politics (they only won the vote only in 1952 through the concerted efforts of middle- and upper-class women).[49] But gains in representative democracy had limited resonance in highland Indigenous communities, where the predominant social structure revolved around a complementarity rooted in a balance between male and female, or *chachawarmi*. The *jilakata*—the maximum local authority—is always a man, while his partner, the *mamatalla*, replaces him when he is away or ill.[50]

While the concept of chachawarmi was later heralded by the MAS government, some scholars argue that it generally precludes women's direct participation in political decision making at the community, union, or formal political level, rather relegating women to a secondary role.[51] In practical terms, the wage gap, unequal access to education and healthcare, high levels of domestic violence, and inheritance customs and laws that favor sons have all meant that women suffer greater poverty than men.

As neoliberalism gutted the COB, US-financed repression relocated the country's principal resistance to the Chapare coca-growing region east of Cochabamba. Migrants from overcrowded valley farms joined with out-of-work miners to frame demands that mixed Indigenous identity and economic class, wrapped around respect for the millennial sacred herb, the coca leaf. By the early 1990s, the *cocalero* movement emerged as the CSUTCB's most radical wing, with Evo Morales as its leader.[52] Coca-growing women began organizing to resist US-financed policies, creating a strong female leadership that went on to play a crucial role in the creation of the MAS party and the expansion of the Bartolinas, as well as the extension of women's rights in the entire country, particularly in rural areas.

By the mid-1990s, when newly established municipal governments received funding as part of neoliberal decentralization, coca growers won elections in all five Chapare municipalities. This was the first time since the 1952 revolution that working-class, Indigenous people gained access to government funds and decision making, which convinced them to create a national "political instrument" (rather than a political party) in 1995 to speak for social movements.[53]

This "political instrument" was called the Assembly for the Sovereignty of the Peoples (ASP). Borrowing the name of a registered party, the United Left (IU), the ASP won four posts in the 1997 national elections. Morales gained a seat in the Legislative Assembly with one of the largest majorities anywhere in the country.

By 1997, the MAS had emerged from this process, marking the first instance in Bolivia's republican history that a party had been forged in a rural area.[54] It began as the electoral arm of the coca growers' union, and when it turned into a legal party in 1999, it was rooted in local social movement organizations rather than an independent entity, with campesinos as its backbone.[55] It remained rurally based until 2002, with decisions made horizontally rather than hierarchically, and little formal institutional structure.[56]

In 2000, the successful effort to thwart privatization of Cochabamba's water supply proved a needed boost for movements all over the country. Protest mushroomed in the highlands, and neighborhood associations in the rapidly growing, largely Aymara Indigenous city of El Alto became pivotal.[57] In the 2002 presidential elections, Morales came in a surprising second behind the previous president, Gonzalo Sánchez de Lozada.[58] Known as "Goni," the mining magnate had been an architect of Bolivia's neoliberalism and now planned to export natural gas to California via the country's historic enemy, Chile. In response, protestors forged a national alliance, and the next year succeeded in driving Goni from office through enormous demonstrations that ground the country to a halt. These emboldened social movements then went on to oust his politically moderate successor, Carlos Mesa, in 2005.[59]

The large mobilizations signaled the return of Bolivia's militant movements, this time without the COB at the forefront. Instead, Indigenous, nationalist, and working-class demands merged into a common cause, headed by coca growers and peasant and Indigenous federations, as well as neighborhood organizations, although regional COBs, particularly in El Alto and Cochabamba, retained an influential role.[60]

Their unity propelled Morales to victory. The social movements' program, called the "October Agenda," constituted key items of Morales's electoral campaign: the nationalization of gas, a constitutional assembly to refound the country, and an end to impunity for those (including Goni) who had unleashed state forces against unarmed protesters. The intense pressure to honor these commitments shaped MAS government policies during its early years.

As it expanded into a more urban party in 2002, and particularly after winning the 2005 election with a decisive 54 percent of the vote, the MAS started to shift away from its model of indirect affiliation (through membership in campesino organizations) to a party with more middle- to upper middle-class members independent of social movements.[61]

Morales has often been the glue that kept the MAS together.[62] As political scientist Fernando Mayorga explains, "Evo is the element that permits ideological, identity, and practical unification in the MAS."[63] His role has in this sense been an essential one, given that the groups within the MAS—rural and urban, Indigenous and Western, working class and middle class—have frequently had different political cultures, social practices, ideological traditions, and worldviews.[64]

The MAS has always been a reformist project, not a revolutionary one. Its references to socialism have been chiefly symbolic; indeed, arguably the most concrete link between Bolivia under Morales and socialism has been its solicitation of assistance from

Cuba in various fields, from a 2006 literacy campaign to a range of public health programs.[65]

Three political currents found a home in the MAS. The first sought to revive the 1952 revolution's emphasis on state dominance of the economy. The second was tied to the traditional left, with its focus on class and work-based demands. And the third represented Indigenous people, especially their demands for increased autonomy and access to land. The effort to join working-class struggles with the overlapping, long-standing demands of Indigenous people was personified in Morales, who is both a strong nationalist and a unionist with Indigenous roots.[66] Political scientist Lorenza Fontana contends that the MAS, rather than locating its origins in the Marxist ideology that had been so influential during the twentieth century, promoted "an idealized equality of the traditional community . . . opposed to the individualist, greedy spirit of modern man."[67]

The MAS is highly pragmatic, rather than ideological. Party congresses and meetings rarely involved ideological debates. Tensions have often been resolved by a time-tested technique: the allotment of party posts and government jobs to an array of factions and regional groups.[68] The outcome was a reinforced clientelism as a key modus operandi in Bolivian politics.


## TRADITIONAL ELITES

Since the establishment of Bolivia's republic in 1825, elites have often squabbled among themselves over control of the country's poorly functioning governments, usually building alliances through family relationships and friendships. Throughout changing circumstances and across generations, the conservative, racist values that underpin these upper classes have survived mostly intact.[69]

In the late 1970s, one such inter-elite melee surfaced between locally oriented companies that relied on government tariffs and credit assistance and a loose, technocratic, and transnationally oriented group whose members were predominantly European immigrants who had arrived in Bolivia after World War II. These modernizers stood behind the neoliberal model as the best option, even though it meant that multinational corporations steadily bought off local businesses, particularly in mining.[70] Today's elite are almost exclusively invested in large banks and their subsidiaries, soy agriculture, and construction companies.[71]

Bolivia's two major business centers are the administrative capital, highland La Paz, with banking, insurance companies, and construction firms, and lowland Santa Cruz, also dominated by banking, along with hydrocarbon services and agribusiness.[72] While La Paz's elite controlled Bolivia for 120 years, Santa Cruz's star has risen steadily since the 1950s, when a road linking it to La Paz was built.

The location of natural gas fields, the Bolivian state's major source of income for the past twenty years, within the Santa Cruz orbit strengthened its regional economic clout, which extends throughout the east, known as the *Media Luna* ("half moon").[73] With the Santa Cruz economy also buoyed by the rapid expansion of soy, the city is now Bolivia's largest, and one of the fastest growing in the world.[74]

With the election of the MAS, elites and their political parties faced a real loss of power. Journalist Fernando Molina argues that during the 1960s and '70s, they would have addressed this problem by deploying the military, but by the turn of the twenty-first century, with the trend toward democratic transitions, that route was no longer viable.[75] But although they lost their national political influence, the MAS government's doubling of public investment meant a sudden influx of government contracts, creating a boom for construction companies and banks.[76] For the more business oriented, the economic upswing went a long way to quiet any active resistance.

Such acquiescence was less forthcoming when it came to Santa Cruz elites, whose relationship with the national government has always been tense, the product of a weak but highly centralized state in a poorly consolidated heterogeneous country. Uprisings in Santa Cruz against the national government have occurred repeatedly.[77]

Santa Cruz's roughly forty elite families first found financial success during the Amazon rubber boom at the turn of the twentieth century.[78] Sociologist Claudia Peña Claros characterizes them as circumscribed by agriculture, "correct" family names, and control over land, much of it acquired from the Spanish Crown or as political spoils during the 1970s military dictatorships and never impacted by the 1953 agrarian reform.[79] The region's large landowners have successively grown sugar and rice, and then cotton in combination with cattle farming, followed in the 1990s by soy, which is now Bolivia's largest agricultural export.[80]

Demands for greater autonomy intensified as Santa Cruz's economic fortunes rose. Local elites, centered politically around the Pro–Santa Cruz Civic Committee viewed the centralized state as the source of Bolivia's political, economic, and social woes.[81] Their argument was often couched in language asserting the superiority of light-skinned peoples (historically more numerous in the lowlands) to what they considered the "backward" Indigenous peoples of the highlands, referencing what Molina calls their status as an ethno-class.[82]

With Morales's election, the opposition lost ground on the national stage but found refuge in their control of regional governments in the Media Luna. Political scientist Kent Eaton argues that unlike in Venezuela and Ecuador, where national governments on the left overran regional elites and reversed 1990s neoliberal decentralization, in Bolivia, the opposition toned down their inter-elite rivalries and, despite the MAS government's efforts to recentralize, convinced local people that their shared regional identity was under threat.[83] This was effective, given that poor interregional communication and the inaccessibility of government services have often resulted in a stronger sense of regional identity among both isolated Indigenous peoples and mestizo city dwellers.[84] Elites effectively convinced the population that the central government is not only dysfunctional but the principal impediment to their region's economic growth.

By the end of 2006, over a million people were demonstrating for greater regional autonomy as part of a Santa Cruz–led coalition. Threats to separate escalated in 2008 as the country stood on the edge of civil war. But the movement made a series of blunders, and these, combined with the solid backing Morales enjoyed from the majority of the population, ultimately led it to stumble. However, it still pulled off a September 2008 insurrection, which was financed to the tune of US$200,000 by Bolivian-Croatian agro-industrialist Branco Marinković and allegedly involved the US ambassador. At its height a neofascist youth group, the Santa Cruz Youth Union (UJC), attacked community groups and occupied seventy-five government offices in Santa Cruz.[85]

When local elites were discovered to be behind a massacre of seventeen Indigenous people in the northern department (state or province) of Pando, the right wing–led autonomy movement lost more steam.[86] Soon after, Marinković fled to the United States, where he was granted asylum before relocating to Brazil.[87]

By 2009, Santa Cruz elites had divided into two groups. One was aligned with a far-right political agenda centered on a shrunken Pro–Santa Cruz Civic Committee, and the other was linked to more centrist right-wing business organizations who valued the growth in public spending brought by the MAS government. This strengthened the clout of the economic-oriented elites, replacing the emphasis on separation from the rest of Bolivia with a more moderate position in support of the historic push for greater regional autonomy.

While the toxic brew of arrogance and racism led to a substantial decline in the political fortunes of the Santa Cruz–led right wing by 2010, the MAS government believed that to restore peace, it had no choice but to make concessions, particularly in land reform and in decentralization resulting in the conversion of departmental councils into assemblies with full legislative powers.

Particularly after 2014, when prices of natural gas and other commodities fell, the economic interests of the elites increasingly coincided with the MAS's determination to boost extractivism in order to fund its programs. At least six presidential decrees and four new laws accelerated the spread of the agricultural frontier.[88] In September 2019, Morales celebrated an agreement to export Bolivian beef to China with local ranchers, and these exports tripled in 2020 during the interim government of Jeanine Áñez.[89]

Politically, Santa Cruz elites did not vary their approach, even after the MAS had astutely taken advantage of their mistakes. As Molina notes, when the opportunity presented itself from 2016 on for them to reassert political power, they did it "with the same myopia" they had displayed in the 1990s.[90]

The right-wing movement was fueled by the astronomical growth of the evangelical church in Bolivia. According to a 2014 Pew Research report, 77 percent of Bolivians consider themselves Catholic and 17 percent Protestant, up from 7.6 percent in 1985. Sixty percent of these Protestants were raised as Catholics.[91]

Both conservative Catholicism and evangelical Protestantism contrast with the religious syncretism that has characterized Bolivia's Roman Catholic Church since the Conquest. These conservative Christians reject Catholic tolerance of local rituals and customs, and some consider traditional Andean rituals and religious beliefs "demonic." Indeed, graffiti such as "Evo, sent by the devil" and "Evo Satan" was scrawled across walls in several cities before the 2019 election.

Much as they have in neighboring Brazil, right-wing Christians are flexing their political muscle, instrumentalizing religion by claiming that they are carrying out God's work when they attack social welfare policies and leaders they consider socialist. They are angry that the 2009 constitution declared Bolivia a secular state for the first time since the founding of the republic 183 years before, and they reject MAS government moves to protect LGBT people and advance women's reproductive rights.

Bolivia's tormented yet rich history of Indigenous and working-class struggle reveals both the limitations levied by capitalism on struggles to create viable societies in the Global South and the stumbling blocks encountered to forge alternate paths. It provides a sharply etched example of the obstacles that low-income, resource-dependent countries experience as they seek to benefit the majority of their population, rather than foreign interests and the domestic elites who serve as those interests' junior partners. The illegal removal of Evo Morales—regardless of his flaws—is only the most recent example in a long history of the country's elites quashing threats to their hegemony.

# PART I: THE COUP

## CHAPTER 1

# THE "PROCESS OF CHANGE" CUT SHORT

A couple of hours after Evo Morales fled Bolivia's nineteenth-century presidential palace on November 11, 2019, Luis Fernando Camacho swept in with a police escort, holding a Bible and a Bolivian tricolor flag. The pastor accompanying him swore, "Never again will *Pachamama* [Indigenous Mother Earth] return here."[1]

The leader of the Pro-Santa Cruz Civic Committee, Camacho held no official position, but in little more than two weeks following the contested election on October 20, this 39-year-old right-wing Catholic zealot had mobilized a testosterone-laced discourse to seize center stage and, in the tumult, to spearhead the expulsion of the president. In the process, he had shut down the country's fourteen-year experiment with progressive politics and hijacked the longest-running democratically elected government Bolivia has ever had.

The October 20 election appeared fair, like the five previous votes administered by Morales's government since his landslide win in 2005.[2] However, a carefully cultivated narrative about fraud pushed by the opposition dominated that night. Just when Morales's closest rival in fourteen years, former president and vice president Carlos Mesa, had enough votes to force a second round, the quick vote count was suspended for nearly twenty-four hours. The Organization of American States (OAS) denounced "irregularities" at a press conference late that evening, and Mesa called for resistance, decrying "monumental fraud." Bolivia exploded.

A protest movement spilled out onto city streets, largely comprised of young people from the middle and upper classes. Every night for almost three weeks, the demonstrators alleged fraud, despite any tangible proof. Fueled by rhetoric calling Morales a dictator, their opposition was enabled by Morales's violation of the country's constitution by running for a fourth term, in disregard of his defeat in a 2016 referendum on whether he could stand again. The protestors demanded either a runoff with Mesa, or a new election. For the first time since Evo's election in late 2005, the discourse of democracy rested firmly in the hands of the opposition.[3]

Students at the nightly rallies in La Paz's upper-middle-class neighborhood of Sopocachi insisted they were demonstrating "to defend democracy, so that my vote is respected." But when pressed on how they define democracy, the answer was mostly a blank stare or some version of "getting Evo out" because "he's been in power too long."[4] As the weeks wore on, the nightly protests became more raucous and violent. Behind the scenes, Mesa and other opposition figures called for Morales to resign.

On Wednesday, November 6, Camacho announced that he would show up at the presidential palace and demand that Morales relinquish office immediately. In the face of this obvious publicity stunt, Mesa urged him to wait for the results of an audit conducted by the OAS. Camacho not only ignored Mesa, but by the end of the week had largely eclipsed him.

"I will never participate in another meeting with Carlos Mesa," Camacho told the local newspaper, *La Razón*. "I realized we were supporting a person who didn't care about the people's vote."[5] Further pleas from Mesa and the OAS to respect the constitution and allow Morales to finish his remaining time in office fell on deaf ears. Later revelations indicate that in fact Mesa played a decisive role in orchestrating the coup, leading Evo to accuse him of being its principal instigator.[6]

By Friday, the police in Bolivia's fourth-largest city, Cochabamba, had mutinied against Morales. Then they rose up in Bolivia's capital, La Paz. Later, Camacho and his supporters would openly brag that they had bribed the police with promises of increased retirement pay.[7]

Gangs supporting Camacho began to bully lawmakers from Morales's Movement for Socialism (MAS) party into resigning, including the heads of the Plurinational Legislative Assembly, leaving the constitutional line of accession vacant.[8] "They told us they would kidnap our relatives and burn down our houses," said a MAS lawmaker from the southern department (state or province) of Potosí.[9] The minister of mines, a governor, a mayor, and the head of the Chamber of Deputies, as well as some of their family members, were kidnapped or attacked, and the *campesino* union headquarters was vandalized. Morales supporters launched several assaults as well, including burning down the houses of two of their leading opponents in La Paz.

That Saturday, Camacho gave Morales a 48-hour ultimatum to leave office. The announcement took Mesa's team by surprise. Suddenly they found themselves confronting a rapid-fire and seemingly well-orchestrated unconstitutional seizure of power by Christian conservatives.

"How can he do this?" a top Mesa staffer asked. "He must have backing from somewhere," a prominent local journalist commented.[10] The usual suspect in Latin America, the United States, had provided overt but limited funding to local opposition NGOs to spread fake news, and the US supported what later proved to be a contested OAS audit of the elections. However, concrete evidence of who funded the unpredictable bully Camacho has yet to surface.

On Sunday morning, the military abandoned Morales. Six weeks later, Camacho revealed that his father, businessman José Luis Camacho Parada, had "sealed the deal" with them, which suggests that, like the police, the military had been bought off. The leaders of the armed forces successfully pressured commander in chief Williams Kaliman to "suggest" that Morales leave office. That Morales resigned hours later confirms just how much power Bolivia's military still wields.

A jubilant crowd poured into La Paz's central square in front of the presidential palace and the Plurinational Legislative Assembly to celebrate. "We've won our democracy back," said one protestor as he waved the national flag.[11]

Two hours after Evo and his vice president, Álvaro García Linera, fled to Morales's home in the Chapare, opposition leaders—joined by the Brazilian ambassador (in part as proxy for the United States), representatives of the Roman Catholic Church and the European Union, as well as Camacho's lawyer and other opposition leaders—met at La Paz's Catholic University. There, they decided that the second vice president of the Senate, evangelical Jeanine Áñez, would be Bolivia's next president. Even though Áñez's party was part of a coalition that had won only 4 percent of the vote, she proclaimed herself president two days later to a mostly empty legislative chamber. Some MAS lawmakers, who held the majority, were too frightened to show up, and those who did deliberately withheld quorum. Áñez then met with the armed forces and the police to guarantee their support before entering the palace brandishing a huge Bible as a military official pinned on her presidential sash.

Not far beneath the surface of this spectacle were Bolivia's centuries-old racism and white supremacy. The 2006 election of Evo Morales, an Indigenous leftist, had upset Bolivia's status quo like nothing since the country's 1952 revolution. Political scientist Marcelo Arequipa characterizes the movement that overthrew Morales as driven by three emotions: vengeance against uppity Indians, resentment of the supposedly preferential treatment of Indigenous people under Morales, and the fear that the white minority has held since the founding of the republic that the Indigenous majority would violently overthrow them.[12] The opposition burned *wiphalas*, the Indigenous emblem that had morphed into a second national flag under the MAS. Many police in the highlands, almost all of whom are of Indigenous origin, ripped the *wiphala* off their uniforms in the days that followed, identifying it as a symbol of the MAS. For sociologist Pablo Mamani, this desecration was "an act of hate, vengeance, humiliation, insult and human degradation."[13]

Once it was over, it became clear that Bolivia's far right had taken advantage of mass protest by largely urban middle and upper classes over Evo's unconstitutional run for a fourth term, using violence and bribes to seize the state. The outcome was a more authoritarian and undemocratic government than the one the opposition accused Morales of running.

## WHY EVO FACED A CRISIS

"How could it have happened? How did we lose our president so quickly?" wept a woman at a November 2019 march against Jeanine Áñez's takeover. On the heels of one of the longest periods of stability in the country's history, a government that had held power since 2006, and controlled the legislature since 2009, had unraveled in less than a month.

While Morales's departure from the national stage had been a long time coming, no one could have imagined such a rapid collapse. After fourteen years of inevitable errors and oversights, many voters were ready for something new. Economist Armando Ortuño describes this as "an indifference, a demobilization, an 'I don't care' attitude."[14] Damian López, a natural gas installer from Potosí, always supported the MAS, but his approval was starting to wear thin. "We want the process that Evo and his political movement started to continue," he said, "but it's time for him to go and a new generation of leaders to replace him."[15]

Their apathy was not simply on account of the tedium of the same leader; voters themselves had changed. Opposition to the MAS had mushroomed, and the social movements that had thrust them into power were, for the most part, shadows of their former selves. For political scientist Fernando Mayorga, the overthrow of Morales was, by every indication, a well-orchestrated effort to reaffirm the hegemony of the traditional oligarchy and to replace the MAS's state-centric economic model with the previous neo-liberal one.[16]

## DEMOGRAPHIC CHANGES

In the Bolivia of 2019, the Indigenous cultural revival the MAS had brought, and the drop in discrimination that accompanied it, had increasingly less relevance as rural areas were hollowed out by migration to the cities. In many highland regions, like Tahua, on the edge of the vast salt flat Salar de Uyuni, only the elderly remain—leaving ten families in a village that had once been home to one hundred. Roberto Mamani Soliz, whose parents live there, is a secondary school math teacher in nearby Potosí. "I come back several times every year to help my parents with the quinoa crop," he explained, threshing the native seed by hand. "They can't manage it on their own and it's their main food source."[17]

Some of the young, who are rapidly losing both the language and culture, only return to the countryside for festivals. Scholar-activist Félix Muruchi Poma worries that "if we don't actively work to keep our traditions alive, thanks to city living and the internet, we will completely lose them."[18]

Muruchi taught history to university students, who proved to be the most unpredictable element in the 2019 election. Half the population is under thirty-five, and they are more urban, educated, and middle class than their parents. Armando Ortuño argues: "For many older migrants, Evo Morales was someone to emulate and identify with.... For their children, Morales didn't... connect so automatically with their aspirations of becoming professionals in a culture defined by urban life and consumerism."[19]

Most of this generation had never known any government except the one led by Evo. They are more connected to the rest of the world as well: for example, South Korean K-pop is popular among some of them. Unlike their parents, who suffered economic deprivation and political struggles, their focus tends toward ensuring a middle-class standard of living.[20] In a fluid process of cultural syncretism, few of them hold a worldview that is primarily either Indigenous or European. Meeting the increased expectations of this generation in a country that is still among South America's poorest poses huge barriers, no matter what government is in power.

In an interview a few days before the October 20 election, Vice President García Linera made clear that he recognized the Morales government may have sown the seeds of its own destruction. "When the policies of a left government transform the material conditions of the poor, enabling class ascendancy, the collective imagination changes," he explained. "If we don't take this into account, those whose lives have improved can vote you out of office."[21] All the same, Ortuño argues that neither the MAS nor the opposition understood what this shift would imply for the 2019 elections.[22]

## THE 2016 REFERENDUM: THE CANARY IN THE COAL MINE

When Evo Morales won office for a third time in 2014 with over 60 percent of the vote, few Bolivians raised their voice in protest, even though the 2009 constitution clearly mandates a maximum of two consecutive terms. Morales insisted that the new constitution reset the clock on term limits. Amid the unprecedented economic boom, the population largely bought it.

The turning point came in 2016 when Evo tried to extend his tenure again, calling a referendum that would have allowed him a fourth term in office—something he was convinced would bestow his candidacy the legitimacy it sorely lacked. Up to this point, the conservative opposition had repeatedly bumbled about as the urban middle classes preferred to side with the MAS. While often pivotal in elections, the middle class are Janus-faced, routinely flipping their loyalties between the upper class and the working class. According to journalist Pablo Stefanoni, the majority of these voters never identified with the MAS political project, which they saw as too working class and Indigenous to be trusted as a reliable representation of their interests.[23] And, as political scientist Vladimir Diez Cuellar points out, "In democracies, there is no possible hegemony without middle-class consensus," which has certainly held true in Bolivia.[24]

The decision to hold a referendum proved to be a poor political calculation, but it also reflected a party increasingly inclined to rely on plebiscites to win public approval. Morales was wildly popular in the long-abandoned rural areas where he traveled by helicopter almost daily. All over Bolivia he inaugurated roads, schools, and medical facilities during a period of an unprecedented investment in the countryside.

A smear campaign in the weeks before the referendum proved effective in discrediting him. The carefully timed effort entangled one of Morales's former girlfriends, who allegedly bore a child that Morales had not recognized as his, along with accusations of influence peddling involving Chinese investors. The child proved nonexistent, and Evo was exonerated from corruption charges, although his ex-girlfriend, Gabriela Zapata, received a ten year sentence for benefiting from the Chinese contracts.[25]

However, the mud stuck, and on February 21, 2016, a slim majority (51.3 percent) voted against changing the constitution in Evo's favor. Although he initially announced respect for the results, Morales soon changed his tune, insisting that "the people" had demanded he stay on. In fact, his role as the authority that bound the MAS together meant there was no viable replacement in the wings. He promised he would leave definitively by 2025, but to many, this assurance rang hollow. The MAS embraced the message that he should remain: at a La Paz rally in November 2017, a backdrop read, "Evo: You will always be president."

Later that November, Bolivia's Plurinational Constitutional Tribunal (TCP) ruled that all elected officials could run for office indefinitely. The tribunal justified its decision with the claim that to prohibit Morales from running would violate the American Convention on Human Rights. By the time of this decision, 68 percent of city residents opposed him campaigning again: the urban elite and non-Indigenous overwhelmingly disapproved, but many working-class and Indigenous communities also shunned another Morales presidency.[26] In a country with long periods of authoritarian rule, the possibility of Morales's reelection made many nervous. According to one 34-year-old telecommunications clerk in Cochabamba, "If Evo runs for office, that's the end of democracy."[27]

The referendum and subsequent tribunal decision handed Morales's opponents the very tool they had lacked. Even though these adversaries were fractured by constant infighting, they were buoyed by the onslaught of negative public sentiment toward Morales and managed to cobble together an opposition. Known as 21F, the coalition spanned the gamut from traditional right-wing parties, to regions convinced the Morales government had shortchanged them, to environmentalists angered by the government's extraction-heavy model.

## CONFLICTING CONCEPTIONS OF DEMOCRACY

Liberal democracy emphasizes term limits and a revolving political leadership, prioritizing individual rights and the private over the public or the collective. This model is complicated in countries like Bolivia, where resource dependency has created a state that lacks checks and balances, colonialism and patriarchy enable authoritarian male leadership, and traditional Indigenous decision-making structures emphasize community consensus.

The MAS and Bolivia's social movements equate democracy with economic and social justice, while the middle and upper classes prioritize formal Western democratic mechanisms such as the secret ballot and the rule of law.[28] Anthropologist Carol Conzelman found that coca farmers in the semitropical Yungas, east of La Paz, consider it their leaders' obligation to address their economic interests. "This more holistic livelihood orientation differs sharply from the Western model of democracy that requires 'free and fair' elections," she writes.[29]

Indeed, working-class Bolivia has always had tenuous ties to representative democracy, whose occasional appearance has never brought them much benefit. A driver in the Yungas expressed it this way: "Making sure I have a stable job is more important to me than respecting the constitution. Since Evo came to power, I haven't had to migrate to Argentina to work anymore. That's why he has my vote."[30]

Those wedded to representative democracy as the ultimate measure of democratic participation might find it improbable, but although formal democracy contracted under Morales, participation by groups long excluded from politics grew. As Jonas Wolff of the Peace Research Institute in Frankfurt argues, Bolivia's "[i]nstitutional controls tended to deteriorate, while political participation, integration, and substantive equality . . . improved."[31]

## THE PERSISTENCE OF RACISM

Since the days of the Conquest, no rationale for structural exploitation has been deployed more pervasively, or more perniciously, than the social construction of race. Bolivians know this all too well. In the 1980s, one of us called Bolivia's race relations "apartheid without the pass laws." To take one example of the ways these norms structured everyday interactions, an Indigenous peasant, unless they were a union leader, would always walk a few paces behind a white person. Over the subsequent decades, social relations have transformed dramatically, and in our experience, this overt gesture of deference has faded. But make no mistake: whites still control most of the wealth, own the most fertile land, and have access to the best education.

As Indigenous leader Felipe Quispe wrote, "White power and mentality constitute the negation of the Indian."[32] White people are thus normalized, in the sense that they have never generally been perceived as a racial group. Indigenous peoples, on the other hand, are explicitly marked by racial classification. And yet, once whites perceived that their supremacy was threatened by the Morales government, many of them pivoted from a denial of racism in Bolivian society to the claim that a form of "reverse racism" was being directed toward them.[33]

As an organizing dimension of Bolivian society, racism still rears its ugly head in moments of conflict.[34] When Morales was first elected, racist graffiti proliferated on city walls, and it ebbed and flowed during subsequent years, depending on the degree of conflict between elites and the central government. During Morales's overthrow in 2019, virulent anti-Indigenous racism was evident everywhere. "There's a lot of fear among the white population because of all the old stigmas that Indians are savages," said Juan Tellez, a MAS mayor in the southern town of Betanzos.[35] "For people who look like me," said an Indigenous professional, "the election of MAS, even if we didn't agree with them politically, meant an expansion in what was possible. For the white ruling class, it represented a contraction of the privileges they have held for hundreds of years."[36]

In his writings on racism, journalist Fernando Molina concurs with sociologists Andrés Calla and Khantuta Muruchi that the MAS's fight against racism was not as effective as it could have been.[37] While eradication of racism was never cast by the MAS as more than a secondary goal, certain daily discriminatory practices diminished during Evo's time in office.

Here, an example is illustrative. One afternoon in a bakery in the upper-middle-class neighborhood of Sopocachi, one of us stood behind two women dressed in urban Aymara clothing. In years past, the white shopkeeper would most likely have moved immediately to assist the white customer first. That she did not was noteworthy. It was for the women, too: as they turned to leave and realized that a white woman was waiting, they behaved sheepishly at first, as the old rules of deference kicked in. But then their countenance changed, and their wide smiles revealed that they were pleased, if somewhat surprised, at the change we had all just experienced. Many indigenous people linked this change to the Morales presidency: after his resignation, at a pro-Morales rally in La Paz, a street vendor named Isabel said through tears, "We don't want to go back to the racism of the past."[38]

## CORRUPTION

The opposition routinely condemned the Morales government as more corrupt than its neoliberal predecessors, even though this claim was not borne out by the available evidence. The accusation was hammered incessantly, frequently with the additional unproven contention that the government was financed by drug trafficking.[39] Since high levels of corruption are endemic to countries with extractive economies, as well as to those affected by the drug trade, the opposition's narrative proved persuasive to many.

Though corruption was not unique to the MAS, it certainly pervaded Bolivia, and the MAS followed other Pink Tide governments in making one of its core commitments the eradication of this rampant problem. Ultimately, this promise would prove impossible to fulfill, especially in the face of the deluge of money that accompanied the commodity boom. "We had expected we could get rid of the awful corruption that plagues our country once and for all," said former minister of justice Casimira Rodríguez, "but too many of the people who went into government sought their own personal interests over the good of the country."[40]

Scandals mounted in number as the Bolivian government expanded in size. The most damaging was the 2015 theft from the Indigenous Fund, which had been mandated to invest in Indigenous communities.[41] The case involved MAS insiders of Indigenous origin, including government ministers, and occasioned a disillusionment that would strengthen the opposition's hand against the MAS.

Corruption was widespread across different levels of government. Administrators complained of patronage jobs to which employees clocked in without working.[42] "I saw bribes going on in my ministry," said a government official who preferred to remain anonymous, "but when I said something about it, I lost my job."[43]

As in many countries with a colonial legacy of paternalism, the custom of giving gifts to government officials is understood as a display of courtesy and respect, but the line between showing deference and offering bribes is precarious in Bolivia. Betanzos mayor Juan Tellez complained, "Business here is all done through payoffs." He continually encountered people seeking local contracts who were "confused and disoriented by my refusal to take a bribe."[44]

In 2006 the MAS created a Ministry of Transparency and the Fight against Corruption (Ministerio de Transparencia y Lucha contra la Corrupción), which exposed several major scandals involving government officials—something that had never happened before. "When I went to work at the Ministry of Transparency," recalled Vicky Ayllón, "we were so overwhelmed by the extent of government corruption, we didn't know where to begin."[45]

The MAS government passed a sweeping anticorruption law in 2012, which also allows for retroactive enforcement. Aside from a tool to control bribery, it proved a powerful weapon against its critics, including some who criticized the MAS from the left. "Knowing they might go after you with a bogus legal case certainly made you think twice about making your criticism public," said a prominent intellectual who preferred to remain unnamed.[46]

Known as autocratic legalism, the government's pursuit of corruption cases against its enemies was a tactic that became a source of increasing worry among opposition leaders. For instance, the Morales administration brought what were likely spurious legal cases against its chief electoral rival, former president Carlos Mesa. Mesa told the local press in 2019 that there were ten legal processes underway against him, three of which were initiated after his decision to run for the presidency.[47]

The new law brought other complications. An anonymous interviewee in the vice president's office explained, "Despite the eleven steps required by law, corruption is still not controlled. Unfortunately, the law generates inertia: it's better to do nothing because if you don't act, it's less likely to get you into trouble further down the line. We have a lot of micro-corruption involving a few hundred dollars. It's just the way business is done."[48]

In order to carry out programs, administrators have often opted to skirt the onerous requirements of the anti-corruption regulations. Another impediment is the ease with which a rival or enemy can be brought down by corruption accusations: the assumption is almost always that the charges are true.

## CO-OPTATION?

In the early years of the MAS, it was routine to hear the slogan "Now it's our turn." The phrase was not merely rhetorical. Union leaders and government employees alike assumed they would share in the spoils that participation in Bolivia's government has always brought. Such clientelist relationships are an enduring legacy of Spanish colonization and widely accepted in the deployment of political power, including among left organizations and unions.[49]

Morales continuously decried this deeply entrenched pattern, but the MAS never formally developed a professional public administration. In a country with an often-stagnant private sector, a state job is the best and frequently the only means of advancement, which helps explain the persistence of *pegas*. These patronage jobs have existed since the Spanish invasion, and during the Morales government were bolstered by social movements' demand that public administration be diversified. For the MAS, making this type of appointment furnished an easy path to broadening class, race, and gender composition, as well as to provide material rewards to key supporters.[50]

By November 2004, a Unity Pact of Indigenous peoples had consolidated, merging the three Indigenous peasant organizations that comprised the original MAS—the highland Unified Confederation of Bolivian Peasants' Unions (CSUTCB), the Bartolina Sisa National Federation of Bolivian Campesina Women (FNMCB-BS), and the Bolivia's Union Confederation of Colonizers (CSCB), made up of highland and valley peoples who migrated to the lowlands—with two others: the highland Indigenist National Council of Ayllus and Markas of Qullasuyu (CONAMAQ), and the lowland Confederation of Indigenous Peoples of Bolivia (CIDOB).[51]

The Unity Pact was a coalition in the best sense of the word: it respected the autonomy of its individual members at the same time that the collective formed something greater than the sum of its parts. These five organizations were, in their own words, "committed to a profound change in the structures of the Bolivian state" and called for the formation of a plurinational, pluricultural, and plurilinguistic state to reflect the country's Indigenous ethnic diversity.[52]

However, the incorporation of social movement leadership into government, while exerting influence, in many ways undermined the independence of Bolivia's social movements. This proved particularly unfortunate given that the MAS was in a better position than any of its Pink Tide contemporaries to build a government directed more explicitly from the grass roots. After 2009, the right wing had been pushed to one side and the MAS dominated the legislature, but by then the social movements were well on their way to being integrated—or, some would argue, co-opted—into the MAS, or worse, marginalized from the process.[53]

Political scientist Santiago Anria insists that the social movements were never totally under the sway of the MAS, contending that they were always able to push the government to back down, and, often when least expected, to behave autonomously.[54] Fernando Mayorga agrees, warning against pigeonholing relations between the MAS and the social movements solely in terms of the polar opposites of autonomy and co-optation. For him, the "unstable and flexible coalition" the relationship encompasses involved "moments of collaboration, occasions of subordination to the MAS, and situations of autonomy."[55]

Similarly, sociologist Anna Krausova's interviews with social movement leaders show that all five of the original Unity Pact organizations believe they had won important aspects of their agenda with the MAS, which makes it difficult to speak of straightforward co-optation. The CSUTCB and the CSCIOB (formerly CSCB), in particular, told her in 2016 that to become part of the state's bureaucratic apparatus was a major victory: for campesino leaders, such access to policy making was unprecedented, even if they had less impact on those decisions than they had hoped.[56]

The case of the Bolivian Workers Central (COB) is illustrative of the complexities and contingencies of these relationships between the state and social movements. While the MAS had informal ties to the COB, the union central never held a favored position within the MAS government. Rather, it was often treated as just another interest group with which to negotiate. In fact, most MAS policy innovations were oriented toward informal sector workers rather than organized labor, with improvements for workers won not through collective bargaining but rather through state-designed stipends for the elderly, school children, and pregnant women.[57]

Despite a three-year break in their alliance between 2010 and 2013, union leaders moved back and forth between positions in the government and the COB. This split the COB between pro-MAS factions and more radical ones that, often in isolation, pressed for maintaining independence. The upshot of this push-pull relationship, in which the COB was sometimes an ally, at other times an adversary, was that the interests of capital often took precedence over those of labor in extractivist and infrastructure projects, to the detriment of Bolivian workers.[58]

After the collapse of the 2008 right-wing uprising in Santa Cruz, the political landscape shifted, reducing the MAS government's dependence on its social movement bases to maintain political stability. The government then formed the National Coordinator for Change (CONALCAM), consisting of all the principal rural and urban organizations, including individual trade unions, but not the COB per se.[59]

CONALCAM was to comment on proposed laws, train a new generation of leaders, and sanction any movement militants who created conflict. Leaders attended a series of government-organized summits, often chaired by Evo himself, where the MAS chose the invitees, set the agenda, and wrote the final report.[60] CONALCAM's recommendations for ministerial appointments or replacements were largely overlooked, while technocrats with no grassroots links were appointed to key positions.[61] Freddy Condo, who worked as an advisor to the Unity Pact as well as a vice minister, confirmed this, saying that "with CONALCAM, the social movements steadily lost their capacity to participate in the government, and were pressured to merely rubber-stamp its initiatives."[62]

The government increasingly treated the once-critical social movements as its foot soldiers rather than as partners, a process characterized by political scientist Moira Zuazo as "a domestication of social organizations."[63] Anthropologist Nancy Postero takes this a step further, contending that because the MAS failed to implement a more radical alternative to the liberal nation-state, its actions represent a new form of policing social movements.[64]

CONALCAM fell even more tightly under MAS control when Indigenous organizations across the country split over proposed road construction through the Isiboro Sécure National Park and Indigenous Territory (TIPNIS) in 2011. The most Indigenous-identified organizations broke with the government, although some sectors of them remained allied with the MAS. These received significant injections of government funds, while those opposing the MAS were increasingly impoverished and isolated.[65] The three remaining Unity Pact organizations (the CSUTCB, the Bartolinas and the CSCIOB), known as the "triplets," became the most ardent government supporters, echoing a state–Indigenous relationship similar to that between campesino unions and the Revolutionary Nationalist Movement (MNR) government after the 1952 revolution.[66]

In the process of reinforcing traditional party and state patronage, social movements were left with a diminished capacity to pressure the government effectively. As Oscar Olivera, a leader of the 2000 water privatization protests in Cochabamba, put it: "This government makes me twice as angry as previous conservative ones because it was brought to power through the sacrifice of the people. . . . It has failed to live up to what we put it in power to do, which was to radically change our society."[67]

## THE CHIQUITANIA FIRES

Two months before the October 2019 elections, the government's belated reaction to wildfires that were raging out of control in

Bolivia's southeast handed the opposition more ammunition. The blame was placed squarely, if somewhat unjustly, on Morales's doorstep.[68] In July 2019, his government had relaxed restrictions on one of the fires' causes—slash-and-burn agriculture[69]—which is practiced throughout Bolivia by the small farmers who make up much of Morales's base. But the biggest culprits were large-scale soy and cattle producers, many of them Brazilian, who have successfully acquired vast tracts of land despite the 2007 agrarian reform law.[70] Expanding cattle production is the Amazon's greatest driver of deforestation, and since 2015, Bolivia's woodland destruction has doubled.[71] Mechanized agriculture, further south in Santa Cruz, mostly for soybean production, is responsible for about 30 percent of the total, while small-scale agriculture accounts for roughly 20 percent.[72]

Hundreds of thousands of Bolivians marched in protest over what they perceived as the government's inept response to the fires, with the right wing professing a newfound concern for the environment and lowland Indigenous peoples. At the forefront of this movement was a savvy anti-Morales activist named Jhanisse Vaca Daza.[73] For the younger generation, particularly those in the urban middle and upper classes, Vaca Daza's use of glossy infographics and memes, as well as hashtags like #SOSBolivia, made environmentalism chic. The veracity of her message was less relevant than the packaging. The result was misinformation about Chiquitania that spread as quickly as the fires.

"I support the protests, but the leaders are saying that Evo sent people from the highlands to start the fires," said Juan Rivero, a hotel worker in Santa Cruz. "I don't believe that."[74] But it seems others did: a late September poll found that electoral support for Morales had slipped by just over 5 percent.[75]

## THE LOOMING ECONOMIC MELTDOWN

Almost none of Morales's opponents disputed that the country was better off during the MAS government's fourteen years than it had ever been. Indeed, Bolivia enjoyed the longest period of economic prosperity in its history, recording the highest growth rates in South America, even after commodity prices dropped in 2014.[76] Government investment grew threefold, thanks to a huge infusion of funds after Bolivia signed its most favorable natural gas contracts ever with foreign multinationals in 2006–7.[77]

But by late 2019, the country faced a growing budget deficit that approached 8 percent of GDP—the region's highest after Venezuela and Suriname. Its international reserves had plummeted with a drop in natural gas sales, and financial reserves were halved to maintain government spending levels.[78] In 2019, the gross domestic product (GDP) of the three departments most dependent on extractive industries fell into negative territory.[79] Gas exports continued to nose-dive, worth 35 percent in 2020 of what they earned in 2018.[80]

This ushered in an increase in public debt, as well as a currency held artificially high against the dollar. In an interview just before the 2019 election, then finance minister and now president Luis Arce brushed aside these concerns. "It's really very simple," he insisted, "we can fix it."[81]

Other analysts were unconvinced. "The next government will be unstable, precarious, and with no clear mandate," Fernando Mayorga predicted the same week. "It will lack a majority in the Legislative Assembly, and with an unfavorable economic situation, any government is going to be hard-pressed to move their priorities forward."[82] A government economist agreed, remarking, "The current level of expenditure is unsustainable."[83]

## EMPOWERING ECONOMIC ELITES

By 2011, the MAS government and eastern economic elites had reconciled. As long as their wealth continued to grow, many among these elites in both La Paz and Santa Cruz accepted an Indigenous person in political power. For the MAS government's part, it had always contended that the intensification of natural resource extraction would be the only way to pull South America's poorest country out of centuries of hardship. These intertwined interests married the MAS government's extraction-based economic policy to the private sector's goal of enlarging the eastern agricultural frontier.[84]

The outcome was that Bolivia's economic elites—in banking, construction, soy, and cattle ranching—all did very well under the MAS government, even if it periodically attempted to rein them in. For example, Bolivia's mostly family-based banks objected vehemently to financial sector reforms after 2009 that sought to increase public ownership and control over investment. But as continual economic growth led to record bank profits, their objections steadily fizzled.[85]

By 2013, autonomy leader and Santa Cruz governor Rubén Costas was meeting with Evo Morales and participating in government-sponsored events, and the government maintained regular contact with almost all of the country's business organizations.[86] In 2013, Morales proclaimed Law 337, which legitimized converting land that had been illegally cleared for agriculture. Three years later, Vice President García Linera stated unequivocally that the government would be neither a rival nor a competitor of Santa Cruz business, but rather its ally in fomenting economic growth.

But while they tolerated the MAS for pragmatic reasons, the traditional elites never embraced its project. Although many of them had parted company with the rabidly right-wing Pro–Santa Cruz Civic Committee, soon after the contested 2019 elections, with pockets bulging with cash, they abandoned Morales. The MAS colluded with these elites, both to keep them quiet and strengthen the economy through extractivism, but it was flirting with a dangerous beast—one that would eventually come back to bite them.[87]

## STRATEGIC ERRORS

After fourteen years of repeated electoral wins with unprecedented majorities, the MAS saw its victory in 2019 as inevitable. This overconfidence and triumphalism would prove an Achilles' heel, flying in the face of evidence that the party's popularity had waned due to corruption scandals, voter fatigue, and anxiety about Morales's unconstitutional extension of his mandate. The MAS had also fallen short on out the necessary political education to keep voters in their corner through the changes in perspectives and values inevitably brought by rising economic status.

Political-ideological education, according to sociologist Atilio Borón, was essential to counteract apathy and to ensure the political participation and commitment of Bolivia's social movements, as well as their protection of the "process of change" in the streets. Thus, as the right wing dominated both mainstream and social media, the MAS's inability to win the war of words exacerbated their steady decline in popularity.[88]

Another misstep that cost the government prestige was its failure to recognize the flimsiness of its 2018 case against Chile in the International Court of Justice in the Hague, which demanded an exit to the sea for Bolivia. Because the narrative of Bolivia's right to the sea is so firmly entrenched in the public psyche, the loss in the Hague further discredited the MAS.[89]

Clearly, the MAS's decision to call the 2016 referendum had been a mistake: the party would likely have avoided the entire electoral crisis if they had figured out how to have Morales stand down for one cycle. Once again, overconfidence had betrayed them. On one hand, they had underestimated the damage the Organization of American States (OAS) was capable of inflicting, and the power of the right-wing forces arrayed against them from Washington to Brasilia to Santa Cruz; on the other, they had overestimated the loyalty of the military.

# CHAPTER 2

# SETTING THE STAGE FOR AN OUSTER

By the October 2019 election, pro-Morales election billboards promised "a secure future," a message that foregrounded stability rather than the profound change originally pledged by the MAS. In contrast, various strands of the opposition called Morales a dictator, warning that electoral fraud was certain. In fact, they directed the bulk of their efforts to these tactics, while failing to develop coherent policy platforms.

"There is a movement toward the center by all the candidates," said political scientist Fernando Mayorga during the campaign. "Why? Because they all fundamentally agree with the principal economic and social accomplishments of the MAS government."[1] At a MAS campaign rally, for instance, a 62-year-old woman explained why she was there: "When I was a child, I didn't have any of the opportunities that poor children now have thanks to Evo."[2]

The odds that Morales would win the country's tenth election since the return to democracy in 1982 remained high: the MAS had built a formidable base incorporating large swathes of the country's Indigenous, peasant, and neighborhood organizations. Many working-class Bolivians continued to support Morales's policies, even though they expressed ambivalence about Morales himself. A Sucre fruit vendor expressed worry "that Evo is staying in power so long."[3]

Bolivia is a country not only of weak institutions but also of flimsy political parties, which political scientist María Teresa Zegada argues only function well when they have a strong base in unions, community organizations, or territorial movements. She notes that parties suffer not only from declining membership, but also from an absence of strong ideology.[4] Moreover, Bolivia's political parties tend to coalesce, above all, as vehicles for charismatic leaders. For both these reasons, it is unsurprising that Bolivians express the third-lowest confidence in political parties in Latin America.[5] It also noteworthy that the opposition to Morales was comprised largely of constantly squabbling configurations, ensuring that the opposition remained divided between warring egos. Had they united, they likely could have defeated Morales in the first round.

In spite of these shortcomings, the opposition had steadily gained momentum over the preceding months. The National Committee for the Defense of Democracy (CONADE), which had not functioned since the end of the dictatorships in 1982, was revived, incorporating the country's principal human rights organization, the Permanent Assembly for Human Rights, La Paz's public university (UMSA), and two Catholic social organizations.[6] CONADE proceeded to organize huge opposition *cabildos*[7] in La Paz, while local civic committees held rallies of their own in Cochabamba, Santa Cruz, and Potosí.

At the cabildo in Cochabamba on October 10, 2019, a large crowd of middle- to upper-class residents poured into the streets waving the Bolivian tricolor flag. The Indigenous *wiphala* was nowhere to be seen. "I'm here because there is corruption everywhere," said one 32-year-old, the owner of a small pharmacy. "Democracy is important to defend because it makes us all equal."[8]

The composition of Evo's campaign rallies contrasted starkly. Almost everyone was darker skinned and working class. In his final campaign rally in El Alto on October 16, which was attended by tens of thousands, the atmosphere was akin to a street carnival, but commitment to Morales remained fierce. "Under Evo, respect for me as a woman who wears a *pollera*[9] has grown," said one attendee. "Before, we were hated. Now, thanks to our president, we are valued as women of Indigenous origin."[10]

## THE FRAUD NARRATIVE

While accusations of corruption and impending dictatorship won adherents to the opposition cause, it was the rhetoric of fraud that would prove most salient in the effort to overturn the Morales government. To understand how this was deployed, it is vital to comprehend just how imprecise the term "fraud" is. As political scientists Michael Alvarez, Thad Hall, and Susan Hyde observe, "There is still no widely accepted definition of election fraud because the applied understanding of fraud depends on the context: what is perceived as fraudulent manipulation of the electoral process differs over time and from country to country."[11]

Such imprecision makes the term an easy one to manipulate. In Bolivia's case, the inevitability of fraud entered the opposition's discourse at least three years prior to the election and was diffused through social media (known as *plataformas*), at large demonstrations, and at cabildos.[12] By the time of the 2019 elections, an extensive groundwork had been laid, with ample force to propel this narrative to the fore. According to anthropologist Bret Gustafson, "[t]he civil disobedience that accompanied the election was a chronicle foretold, as the opposition planned to react in the event of any Morales claim to victory, fraudulent or not."[13]

The engine fueling much of the fraud accusations was social media, and when Morales criticized its role in distorting the election, the opposition immediately screamed censorship. Social media was particularly influential among the young.[14] "Most of us are utterly dependent on social media for information.... A lot of it is not true, and few of us know our history," said twenty-three-year-old Ana Maria Copeticón, who works in a textile workshop in El Alto.[15]

Just like in recent elections in other parts of Latin America—Peru, Mexico, and Colombia—massive disinformation shaped the campaign and heightened polarization. Fake news, trolls, and bots all played a role, the bulk of which were mobilized by the opposition.[16] A report by the Inter-American Commission on Human Rights (IACHR) later revealed that in the lead-up to the election, thousands of fake Twitter accounts linked to the opposition were created.[17] Similarly, an *AJ+* analysis of information shared on social media pre- and post-elections found that 66 percent was false, while an additional 20 percent was used in misleading ways.[18]

## THE OPPOSITION CANDIDATES

At the time of the election, Carlos Mesa had been a fixture in Bolivian politics for over twenty years. After gaining national recognition as a television journalist, he served as vice president under the neoliberal president Gonzalo Sánchez de Lozada (Goni). When Goni was ousted during the so-called Gas War in 2002, Mesa assumed the presidency, only to be ejected himself two and half years later. In a country where most people are young and dark-skinned, Mesa is older and white, symbolizing the political elite that lost power when Morales took office in 2006.

His lackluster 2019 candidacy was backed by a moderate coalition called the "Citizens' Community" (CC) that demanded the 2016 referendum be respected and Morales step down. His campaign relied on slogans and memes filled with loaded signifiers like "democracy," "dictatorship," and "drug terrorist," as well as accusations of rampant government corruption. "I think these are the most important elections of recent times, perhaps since the restoration of democracy in 1982," said his campaign coordinator José Antonio Quiroga, "because what is in play is the future of democracy itself."[19]

At Mesa's campaign finale in La Paz's Plaza San Francisco, a 24-year-old CC campaign worker and law student explained her support. "I'm voting for Mesa because we need to recover the rule of law," she said. "We all know that once you've been in office a long time you want to stay in power forever."[20]

Mesa's campaign projected a strong environmentalist message, while keeping Santa Cruz agribusiness at a distance. As Quiroga put it, "We want to change the current development pattern to an environmentally friendly one." Mesa promised to accomplish this by not changing MAS social redistribution policies. "We won't devalue the currency or take away stipends," the campaign coordinator confirmed.[21]

The other main opposition candidate, right-wing senator Óscar Ortiz of the National Unity party, headed the "Bolivia Says No" coalition, an alliance of conservative parties and civil society groups. The biggest surprise during the campaign was the strong showing of Korean-born evangelical Chi Hyun Chung, who railed against LGBT rights and accused the MAS government of communism.

## THE ELECTION DEBACLE

Bolivians headed to the polls on October 20 under clear skies and along quiet roads: vehicles are banned from the streets on election day. Food and drink stalls popped up around the voting stations, lending the day a festive atmosphere. Inside, election officials unfolded and held up each voter's blank ballot to show them it was unmarked, under the watchful eye of observers from the major political parties. "I'm really hoping for a transparent, fair process today," said one voter, who had pushed her son's wheelchair to her voting place.[22] Just under six million Bolivians, who are required by law to vote, joined her at over thirty thousand polling booths—an 88 percent participation rate.[23]

But that evening, when 83 percent of the vote was in, the computerized quick results systems abruptly switched off. Morales led with 45 percent of the total, followed by Mesa with 38 percent, comfortably within the 10 percent threshold needed to require a second round under Bolivian law. When the next set of numbers was announced by the electoral commission some twenty-four hours later, Morales had a 10.56 percent lead—just enough to avoid a runoff.[24]

With accusations of fraud growing by the hour, the MAS government insisted that the quick count system was designed to shut off at this juncture in the official tally process. But it was too late: whether due to a trigger built into the system, a glitch or deliberate fraud, the shutdown provided ammunition for the opposition campaign to undermine public confidence in the electoral process. Morales remained convinced that he would win because the bulk of the remaining votes were rural, constituencies that had overwhelmingly backed him in past elections. "We're going to wait until the last vote is counted," he told supporters in La Paz's Plaza Murillo that Sunday night. "We're going to win again."[25]

By then the Organization of American States (OAS) had tweeted their concerns about vote tampering, insisting that the Supreme Electoral Court (TSE) explain why it had interrupted transmission.[26] The European Union joined them in calling for answers. "The expectation of fraud was only worsened by the electoral commission's lack of transparency and failure to realize how their actions were impacting public opinion," explained Kathryn Ledebur of the human rights group, the Andean Information Network.[27]

By October 24, only seventy thousand votes remained to be counted, all of them in Chuquisaca (Sucre), where the local electoral commission office had been burned by anti-MAS protestors. "It's clear that the results and the electoral commission cannot be trusted," Mesa told a press conference.[28] "Our current priority is to demand a second round," said Miguel Roca, a newly elected deputy from Mesa's coalition.[29] It would have been the first runoff in Bolivian history.

## PROTESTS AGAINST EVO

In what became twenty-one days of intense demonstrations in nine city centers and upper-middle-class neighborhoods, protestors, known as *pititas*,[30] clashed with police. On October 23, civic committees across the country organized an indefinite general strike. This furnished a rationale for public university officials to close universities, which made it easier for students to participate in the demonstrations. In Santa Cruz, the strike was rigorously enforced except in poorer neighborhoods loyal to the MAS. Every night protestors gathered around the Christ the Redeemer statue in an upper-middle-class neighborhood to hear reports from civic committee leaders, as musical performances and prayers led by evangelicals and Catholics called for success. The notable exception to the anti-Morales upheaval was the calm that prevailed in Bolivia's second-largest city, the Aymara and working-class El Alto.

Economic elites took a marginal and cautious role, only gradually joining the opposition movement, and rather late in the process.[31] But by the end of October, Santa Cruz's major business associations, which had kept a low profile since signing a pact with the MAS in 2011, began to openly finance community meals for the demonstrators.[32]

In an upper-middle-class neighborhood in La Paz, close to the national electoral commission offices, a nightly ritual unfolded during the first week. The police demonstrated remarkable restraint against mostly middle- and upper-class protestors until 9:20 p.m., almost on the dot, when they unleashed tear gas and everyone scurried home. The degree of restraint exercised by the police began to fray as the weeks wore on, but Morales never called out the military to clear the streets because, he said, of his own history of suffering military repression.[33]

But as the protests moved into the commercial and governmental heart of the city, more Molotov cocktails and expensive gas masks appeared, and the scene became more violent. As William Wroblewski, who was filming for Agence France Presse, recalled: "Suddenly I was surrounded by a group of guys accusing me of working for the government. . . . I showed them my press card, but they kept threatening to beat me up and destroy my equipment. Fortunately, a group of young women demonstrators intervened, and I got away."[34]

By this point paramilitary thugs had arrived from Santa Cruz to, as one bragged one night when we were dodging tear gas, "help bring the government down."[35] A tense stillness settled into the country's major cities, whose downtown streets were deserted except for protestors. In wealthier neighborhoods, vigilante groups kept a watchful eye against the threat of looting.

Bolivia's deep-seated racism, never far from the surface, predictably erupted. "Indians out of the university," read graffiti in front of La Paz's public university a week after the elections. Morales's supporters were quick to point out the demonstrators' hypocrisy. "The protestors and the opposition talk about democracy all the time," said Brígida Quiroga, a MAS deputy from El Alto. "But it's clear that they don't think poor people and Indigenous people should have the same rights as them. Is that democracy?"[36]

A morning walk in upper-middle-class La Paz now meant traversing makeshift barricades of stones, tires, and bits of rope strung across local intersections. Most of the blockades were managed by middle-aged, upper-middle-class people, but those trying to get around the barricades were more often working-class. "You are stealing our daily bread," an elderly woman named Carmen shouted at the blockaders. She said she was going to sell cosmetics in a market that was at least a kilometer away, and there was no public transport.[37]

"They accuse us of being pro-Evo when we take down the barricades," said one minibus driver, "but no, we just want to be able to work. Last week I didn't make any money at all. Today, because it's Sunday, there are fewer blockades, and I can take a bit home."[38]

On October 27, Morales announced that if the OAS preliminary report showed fraud, he would agree to a second round of voting.[39] His intent was to calm the increasingly violent protest, but the pronouncement instead emboldened those clamoring for his resignation.[40]

In contrast to the mass protests promoted by the opposition, large demonstrations in support of Morales were nonexistent. Each day, the MAS expected huge marches from El Alto like those that had characterized the political upheavals of 2003 and 2005.

They never came—instead, smaller groups of MAS supporters rallied in the city center and less affluent neighborhoods. "El Alto will save me," Morales is reputed to have said more than once. But the social movements had been effectively demobilized—some distracted and others demoralized. By now, many *Alteños'* focus had shifted to their latest consumer purchase or the success of a small business venture.

## RESIGNATION AND RESISTANCE

On Sunday, November 10, Evo Morales and his vice president, Álvaro García Linera, fled to the Chapare, where thousands of coca growers blocked roads to protect them. It was there that Morales gave his resignation speech, saying he was leaving office in order to stop the onslaught of threats and violence which MAS officials and their family members had endured. "Mesa and Camacho continue to persecute us, kidnapping our ministers, union leaders, and their families," he charged.[41] He told journalist Ayelén Oliva that he had resigned to avoid a massacre, and that he and García Linera had feared arrest, or worse, before they were whisked out of the country by a plane sent by the Mexican armed forces.[42] The move reflected Mexico's history, since the 1930s Spanish Civil War, of providing safe haven to progressive refugees fleeing repression. In this case, the Mexican foreign minister had feared Morales's life was in danger.[43] Later, Morales would charge that a price had been put on his head, and that his ouster was nothing less than a coup.[44]

Once Morales and García Linera had left, like a sleeping giant, the people who had most benefited from fourteen years of MAS government flooded into the streets. Most of them were from neighborhood and rural Indigenous organizations, rather than unions, even though the working class had grown during the MAS years relative to the size of the *campesino* population. Some working-class and Indigenous sectors who had quarreled with Morales joined the marches, including Yungas coca growers who had resisted a new coca law in 2017 and some mining cooperatives from

Bolivia's poorest department (state or province), Potosí, who had clashed with Evo over what they perceived as inadequate government investment.[45] Although for many of them Morales's legacy was tarnished, they feared the return of the white oligarchy.

The police and military attacked them mercilessly. In one telling incident in La Paz, a young middle-class woman saw the police gassing indiscriminately. "Stop!" she called out. A police officer nearby responded: "Just you watch lady. After us, the military will come and clean up the streets. If you are complaining, stupid, you must be from the MAS."[46]

Pro- and anti-MAS groups clashed in cities and towns, resulting in at least nine deaths over the next several days.[47] More than a week before Morales's resignation, on October 30, violent confrontations in Montero, just north of Santa Cruz, had left two members of the neofascist Santa Cruz Youth Union (UJC) dead and six wounded.[48] And on the day Evo left office, caravans of miners, civic committee members and students from Potosí on their way to La Paz to demand his resignation were attacked by MAS supporters, leaving sixty wounded.[49] Groups affiliated with the MAS were accused of burning city buses and looting businesses. Morales supporters burned and looted police stations in different parts of the country, as well as the houses of university chancellor Waldo Albarracin and journalist Casimira Lema.[50] These actions became the perfect excuse for the middle and upper classes to lump poor people marching together as MAS militants and opportunistic vandals. They dubbed them "hordas," a veiled racist term for low-income Indigenous peoples.[51]

Anti-MAS groups also carried out attacks in the days following the election, ransacking and burning homes of MAS officials and their family members as well as attacking Indigenous women in the streets.[52] In the southern town of Betanzos, a combined police and military force fired on pro-MAS demonstrators killing one and driving the mayor into hiding.[53] By the night after the election, anti-MAS protestors had set fire to local electoral commission headquarters in Sucre, Potosí, Tarija, and Santa Cruz.[54] "It hurts us that they burned down our offices. They burned documentation from the past, so we have lost this part of our history forever," lamented the head of the TSE, María Eugenia Choque.[55]

The next three officials constitutionally in line to replace Evo, including the vice president of the Chamber of Deputies and the presidents of the Senate and Chamber of Deputies, all MAS members, resigned because they received death threats. "Withdrawing from office . . . is to protect the life of my brother, who was taken hostage. My family has nothing to do with these problems," stated the former president of the Chamber of Deputies, Victor Borda.[56] At least forty more MAS officials left shortly after, and the country went without a president for two days.

Morales's rival Carlos Mesa described the president's resignation as "the end of tyranny." But even among those who opposed Morales, such a claim hardly appeared credible. Cochabamba feminist activist Maria Fernández, for one, remarks, "Evo's last two terms in office were marked by corruption, arrogance, and a disregard for the people who put him into power. . . . But I'm not celebrating his resignation, because this is a takeover by religious extremists who are anti-women and racist."[57]

## THE POLICE AND THE MILITARY

Bolivia's 40,000-strong national police force is characterized by a repressive, highly bureaucratic, and militarized structure as well as scarce professional training, which results in an informal work structure and high rates of bribery and corruption. "When I wanted to join the police academy," Luisa Ayala said, "they asked me for five thousand dollars just to take the exam, which was a huge amount of money for me and my family. They just said, 'Oh don't worry. You'll get it back soon once you start patrolling the streets.' I didn't join because we couldn't come up with the money."[58]

If you want the police to respond to or investigate a crime, you must pay them. Six in ten Bolivians do not trust the police—South America's highest disapproval rating.[59] One La Paz street seller we spoke to insisted that the police she sees "cause more problems than they solve."[60]

The police and military are historical enemies, as the police have always resented the superior pay and benefits granted the military by the government. The MAS was no exception, and from the beginning the party worked hard to ensure the loyalty of the military, providing them with a 16 percent pay raise in 2006—twice as much as any other sector.[61]

While the MAS bolstered police salaries by 150 percent between 2005 and 2016, they also attempted to curb police corruption by firing and arresting more commanders than ever before in the institution's history.[62] The effort was met by a violent mutiny in 2012, which forced the government to back down. Seven years later, Luis Fernando Camacho and his supporters built on the police's residual resentment to successfully bribe them with promises of raises to their retirement pay, one of their unfulfilled demands during the Morales government.[63]

On November 10, 2019, the police were joined by the military, up to that point committed to Morales, even though they had grumbled when he had pressured them to include more women and Indigenous officers in their highest ranks. But they no longer backed him: their commander recommended that Morales resign, in clear violation of Bolivia's constitution.

With the renewed involvement of the military in politics—an option political scientists María Victoria Murillo and Steven Levitsky call succumbing to the "the military temptation"—came an enormous risk to democracy. "When the military alternative is closed," they write, "the political system is strengthened because its protagonists are obligated to find solutions to social conflicts through negotiation and democratic compromise."[64] Both negotiation and compromise were sorely missing in Bolivia in November 2019.


## INTERNATIONAL INTERFERENCE

During the 2019 electoral campaign, impact from the predictable meddling of the United States (and likely Brazil as well), went largely unnoticed. This changed dramatically after the election.

From Brazil's right-wing president Jair Bolsonaro to Donald Trump, the impunity of the far right and the interference of the OAS made it abundantly clear that right-wing governments throughout the region wanted the left wing's last man standing gone.

The US-based National Endowment for Democracy (NED) spent close to $1 million per year in Bolivia between 2016 and 2019, almost exclusively to fund groups supporting the opposition.[65] But more damning are sixteen leaked recordings that divulge conversations among coup plotters who appeared confident of US backing and mention frequent contact with senators Marco Rubio, Bob Menendez, and Ted Cruz.[66]

The Trump administration praised the military for "abiding by its oath to protect not just a single person, but Bolivia's constitution" and confidently predicted that "we are now one step closer to a completely democratic, prosperous, and free Western Hemisphere."[67] From the *Wall Street Journal* to the *New York Times*, the US press hailed the coup as a victory for democracy.[68] Bolivian philosopher Rafael Bautista, for one, believes that the downfall of Evo Morales was orchestrated by the US government. "This was premeditated from Washington," he asserts, "and conceived, not just a year ago, but ever since Evo became president."[69]

Some US Democrats pushed back. More than a dozen members of Congress, including representatives Ayanna Pressley, Alexandria Ocasio-Cortez, and Ilhan Omar sent a letter in November 2019 condemning the Trump administration for supporting the ouster of Morales "that bear[s] the hallmarks of a military coup d'état," and "contributing to an escalating political and human rights crisis."[70] A July 2020 letter by seven Senate Democrats to State Department Secretary Mike Pompeo sought to encourage prompt, free, and fair elections in Bolivia.[71] They expressed concern for human rights violations and curtailments of civil liberties meant to intimidate political adversaries.

Concrete proof of Brazilian involvement has yet to surface. But circumstantial evidence suggests it—such as Jair Bolsonaro's rapid recognition of Jeanine Áñez's interim government, Camacho's meeting with Bolsonaro's foreign minister a few days after Morales's ouster,[72] Camacho's public expression of gratitude to Bolsonaro for help,[73] flights by Bolivia's presidential airplane to Brazil immediately after the Áñez takeover,[74] and the participation of the Brazilian ambassador to Bolivia in the meeting that chose Áñez as president.[75] Not only do Bolsonaro and his allies have an ideological affinity with the Bolivian far right; they also have substantial economic interests in the country—from soy in the eastern lowlands to gold in the northeast. Most of Bolivia's coca paste and refined cocaine goes either to or through Brazil.

A scandal erupted in late July 2021 when Minister of Foreign Relations Rogelio Mayta revealed newfound evidence that Argentina's conservative President Mauricio Macri had sent ammunition and other forms of "less-lethal" weapons to Bolivia just after Áñez's seized power in November 2020. Similar arms shipments by Ecuador and allegations of interference by Brazil and Chile prompted Mayta to denounce them as reflecting a new Operation Condor (the US-backed terror campaign by rightwing dictatorships in the 1970s against leftwing opponents).

## THE OAS

The 35-member Organization of American States is 60 percent financed by the US government, giving Washington disproportionate leverage over its actions. Throughout the organization's history, it has consistently acted in accordance with whatever the United States perceives as in its interests.[76]

After Morales lost the 2016 referendum, the OAS head, Uruguayan Luis Almagro, initially told him that he should respect the voters' decision. Then, in an about-face in May 2019, Almagro gave him the green light, arguing that it would be discriminatory to block Morales from running for a fourth term. The move enraged Bolivia's opposition.

When the OAS jumped to express concerns about vote tampering in October 2019, the Bolivian minister of foreign relations, Diego Pary Rodríguez, officially requested an OAS audit. The OAS agreed with the proviso that the results be binding, which the government accepted. Three weeks later, they released the audit's preliminary report, which suggested there had been "serious irregularities," and which became instrumental in the rapid-fire process leading to Morales's resignation.[77]

The final report argued there was a manipulation of results and the use of hidden computers.[78] Electoral commission officials rejected these claims outright. "We have nothing to hide," insisted commission president María Eugenia Choque at a press conference. "How can we be accused of fraud? We were inspected by the OAS, and they approved our process."[79]

In late December, the European Union Mission, which had observers on the ground during the election, pointed out deficiencies similar to the ones highlighted by the OAS, such as the MAS's use of state resources in their campaign, but stopped short of calling them deliberate fraud.[80] Instead, they called for additional trained national observers and for measures to combat disinformation.[81]

Subsequent analysis by statisticians also threw the OAS conclusions into question. A study by the Washington, DC–based Center for Economic and Policy Research (CEPR) rejected the OAS findings;[82] four members of US Congress questioned the OAS,[83] and 133 economists denounced the OAS in the press.[84] Statistician Walter Mebane of the University of Michigan presented "evidence that fraudulent votes in the election were not decisive."[85] However, others, including political scientist Calla Hummel, supported the conclusion of significant fraud,[86] as did economists Diego Escobari and Gary A. Hoover.[87]

Later, researchers from the University of Pennsylvania, Tulane University, and MIT's Election Data and Science Lab (published in the *Washington Post*), threw the fraud accusations further into doubt.[88] A *New York Times* investigation identified problems in the OAS methodology, and a July 2021 University of Salamanca report also questioned whether the alleged flaws could have swayed the outcome.[89] While these reports do not negate possible irregularities, such conclusions undermine the notion of of OAS impartiality.

In July 2020, a letter from members of the European Parliament added further criticism.[90] And in September two dozen members of US Congress called on the State Department to pursue a "full, independent review" of the OAS actions, which had "contributed to a major deterioration of human rights and democracy."[91] The OAS responded with denunciations of the critiques, including the accusation that the *New York Times* was exercising "its right to lie, distort, and twist information, data, and facts,"[92]

Wherever the truth lies, when the OAS denounced errors on election night without providing a shred of evidence, it fueled the opposition's narrative, shaped news stories locally and internationally, and propelled the scenario that motivated Morales's resignation. Whatever Evo's misdeeds in running for a fourth term, Almagro's approval of his candidacy in May 2019 looked like a setup so that Morales would later fall, and fall hard.

## COUP OR NOT: THE DEBATE

The day after Luis Fernando Camacho took over the presidential palace, Carlos Mesa announced, "Let's be clear: there has been no coup d'état in Bolivia, but rather a legitimate and massive citizen mobilization, a real Bolivian democratic spring."[93] Ever since, debate has raged over whether the events in October and November 2019 constitute a coup, both inside and outside Bolivia. The discussion is particularly emotional given that the country holds one of the world's highest rates of coup d'états since the Second World War.[94]

What happened in November 2019 certainly was not the classic coup involving an (often brutal) military takeover—sadly too well known throughout Latin America. Of the eighty-seven coups in Latin America during the twentieth century, Bolivia and Ecuador registered the highest number overall, and most coups were led by the military, instigated by the right wing and frequently linked to US interventionism.[95]

Political scientist José Luis Andia argues that what happened in Bolivia was merely a more sophisticated version: one that used modern technology to create a narrative that masked unconstitutional action under the guise of popular will.[96] In such a "coup lite" or "soft coup," as it is sometimes called, unconstitutionality is not so glaring that it becomes intolerable to a large percentage of the population.

Others disagree. Political scientist Franz Barrios argues that what occurred was not a coup, because the constitutional order had already been broken by Morales when he ran for a third term in 2014.[97] Another political scientist, Jonas Wolff, contends that what makes the transition from Morales to Áñez look undemocratic is that it openly contradicts the popular will as reflected in the composition of Bolivia's legislature. However, he argues that, in terms of procedure, the fact that the Constitutional Court approved the transition grants it legitimacy.[98]

In the view of Eduardo Rodríguez Veltzé, former president of Bolivia and its Supreme Court, the Constitutional Court illegitimately endorsed Áñez's self-proclamation, ignoring strictly regulated constitutional procedures and failing to provide a formal decision with legal reasoning.[99] This reflected what he see as the most serious outcome of the 2019 process: "a derailment of our constitutional order."[100] In Bolivia, a president's resignation only becomes valid if it is accepted by the Plurinational Legislative Assembly. In the events leading up to Morales's 2019 departure, a rush session was called that excluded most MAS officials from the process. Then, after all those in the presidential chain of succession were terrified into resigning, opposition leaders and external agents illegitimately decided who would become president, rather than permitting the Legislative Assembly to choose Moraels's successor.[101]

Murillo and Levitsky insist that a coup took place. They caution that military involvement during undemocratic power transitions exacerbates political conflict and generates greater persecution, even where the ousted government has demonstrated authoritarian tendencies. In Bolivia's case, they contend that the transition became a coup when the police and armed forces abandoned their constitutionally mandated subordination to an elected president and forced him to resign.[102] US Senator Bernie Sanders made a similar point and was very direct about it: "[A]t the end of the day it was the military who intervened . . . and asked [Morales] to leave. When the military intervenes . . . that's called a 'coup.'"[103]

For feminist activist María Galindo, speaking at the Women's Parliament on November 16, 2019, in La Paz, "a profound crisis that went far beyond whoever won the elections led to a coup." She identified four levels to this crisis: Bolivia's colonial legacy, economic dependence on natural resource extraction, persistent racism, and enduring patriarchy.[104]

In our view, what took place in October and November 2019 was indeed a coup: far-right forces with military and police backing hijacked a protest, ostensibly driven by Morales's disrespect for the country's constitution, although in fact largely created by the opposition's successful manipulation of young people. Morales and other officials were directly threatened and suffered violence, leading to resignations under duress. Following these resignations, unelected officials and foreign diplomats chose a new president, circumventing constitutional procedures and ignoring precedent. This group chose the second vice president of the Senate, Áñez, arguing that after the presidents of both chambers resigned, the succession should pass to the next-highest-ranking official. Beyond the fact that this group had no constitutional power to make this decision, they did not apply their own reasoning: they skipped over the first vice president of Chamber of Deputies, Susana Rivero, a MAS official who has testified that she resigned before the position was given to Áñez, who was constitutionally "lower" in the chain than Rivero.[105] These events mark what took place in November 2019 as a coup d'état.

A forerunner of what happened in Bolivia is Brazil, where non-military means were marshaled to oust President Dilma Rousseff of the Workers' Part (PT) to bar Luis Ignácio (Lula) da Silva from running for president in 2018, served as the blueprint for the Bolivian coup, and parallels can also be found in the overthrows in Honduras in 2009, Paraguay in 2012, and Haiti in 2004.[106] In each of these cases, complex domestic factors coupled with international interference resulted in the expulsion of a legitimately elected leader.

## CONCLUSIONS

The illegal seizure of power in Bolivia in 2019 followed on the heels of 14 largely successful years of MAS governance, which the study of Bolivian history strongly suggests was the best government the country has ever had—especially when measured across dimensions of improved health, education, incomes and stability. While the wealthy benefited from the economic boom driven by high commodity prices, the real winners were working class and indigenous peoples, with the economic, educational and health status of Bolivia's poorest - rural indigenous women - rising more than any other group. The following two chapters tell the story of what the MAS accomplished and where it stumbled in its work to build a more equitable society. This provides a backdrop that makes the tragedy of November 2019 even more disturbing.

Bolivians march through the Altiplano to protest Jeanine Áñez's rise to power and attacks on indigenous people. Copyright 2019, Marcelo Pérez del Carpio

Indigenous women demonstrate in La Paz's city center. Copyright 2019, Thomas Becker

Police gas protestors following the 2019 coup. Copyright 2019, Marcelo Pérez del Carpio

Above: Jeanine Áñez poses with Arturo Murillo and a Bible after she declares herself president. Copyright 2019, Marcelo Pérez del Carpio

Right: Protestor gives the Nazi salute at a march against Evo Morales. Copyright 2019, Radoslaw Czajkowski

Opposite page, above: Military patrol the streets following the coup. Copyright 2019, Marcelo Pérez del Carpio

Opposite page, below: Opposition protestors march through the streets of La Paz accusing Evo Morales of fraud, drug trafficking, and tyranny. Copyright 2019, Marcelo Pérez del Carpio

Evo speaks at his closing campaign rally before the 2019 elections. Copyright 2019, Marcelo Pérez del Carpio

# PART II: FOURTEEN YEARS OF THE MAS

## CHAPTER 3

# GROWTH AND SUCCESSES

Early each morning, Juanita Flores walks ten minutes down a newly paved road to climb into a sparkling new cable car that whisks her to her job selling vegetables in a renovated market in downtown La Paz. "I get here in half the time it used to take me," she says, "and in the rainy season I don't have to slosh through mud anymore." On her walk she passes a refurbished school and several new multistory buildings, all with sewage systems and running water. She and her husband, who owns a minibus, are gradually buying their own home. "I never dreamed we would be able to buy a house," she adds.[1]

Such striking improvements are evident everywhere, financed by profits from the commodity boom that the MAS government invested in infrastructure and social programs. The flood of funds has particularly impacted rural areas, where poverty rates when Morales took office were among the world's highest.[2] Social programs, new and improved roads, public buses, cable cars, modern hospitals and clinics, and upgraded schools and universities provide physical evidence that nearly fourteen years of MAS government have transformed almost every corner of South America's poorest country, even if some of the infrastructure investments have proven to be white elephants.[3]

Economically and politically, the Morales administration lent Bolivia unparalleled stability, with Evo the longest-serving president since the country's 1825 founding. With low inflation, an

annual growth rate of over 4 percent since 2008, and a currency
held steady against the US dollar, the middle class grew by 10 percent, turning Bolivia into a lower-middle-income country by World
Bank criteria. The population transformed from being classified
as predominantly poor, to mostly middle income (58 percent)—
that is, between US$1,026 and $3,895 per capita in 2019.[4] It also
shifted Bolivians' perceptions: almost half the population identifies
as middle class (46.6 percent), significantly more than in wealthier
countries like Mexico, Chile, the United States, and Brazil.[5] The
new middle class is largely urban and includes formerly impoverished Indigenous people, particularly the Aymara.[6]

As a profoundly pragmatic party and government, the MAS
achieved more than any other administration in Bolivia's history.
A government that had been stripped to the minimum during neoliberalism grew threefold to accomplish this feat, with the number
of public sector employees ballooning 70 percent between 2005
and the end of 2018.[7]

## SOCIAL PROGRAMS
### CASTING A WIDE SOCIAL SAFETY NET: THE BONOS
The reduction of extreme poverty was a MAS priority from the
start. The country that Morales inherited had an overall poverty
rate of 51.9 percent, with an inequality (Gini) index at an alarmingly high 0.58.[8] Lacking any social safety net, such as a welfare
system or unemployment insurance, the MAS government joined
other Latin American countries in financing small payments to
alleviate extreme poverty. These conditional cash transfers reach
as much as one-fifth of the population and constitute one of the
most significant innovations in social policy in Latin America
over the last twenty-five years.[9] While conditional cash transfers were adopted by both the left and right across the region,
what distinguishes the left-wing programs is that they are often
accompanied by expansions in pension systems, improvements
in healthcare, and land reform.[10] Common criticisms leveled at

these programs are that they fail to tackle structural issues such as wage inequality and wealth redistribution, and that they are demobilizing, serving to reinforce clientelism.[11]

Bolivia's three programs include an annual stipend for children who stay in school, an old-age pension payment, and a supplement for women who attend pre- and post-natal care. The bulk of these *bonos*, as they are known, go to fund the *Renta Dignidad* (dignity pension) for people over sixty, an extension of a program that began in the late 1990s. "It isn't enough to live on, but it pays for staples for most of the month, so it's a big help," said an elderly man in Cochabamba. "With my wife receiving it too, we always have enough food."[12] Under Morales, the retirement age dropped from sixty-five to sixty, and minimum benefits were extended to self-employed people. By 2010, bucking the global trend, Bolivians became eligible to retire at fifty-eight.

The "Bono Juancito Pinto" provides an annual payment, equivalent to about twenty-five US dollars; initially, it was given to children during their first five years of school, and by 2014 it covered public school students at any educational level.[13] The program proved successful at reducing dropout rates, although it did little to prevent children, especially teenagers, from working.[14]

Another bono, named after nineteenth-century Indigenous leader Juana Azurduy, gives pregnant and nursing mothers a subsidy for attending pre- and post-natal checkups. While some feminists have critiqued this program because it reinforces traditional gender roles, maternal mortality dropped by almost 40 percent between 2005 and 2017.[15] A 2016 impact evaluation found that babies have more checkups, are more likely to be fully vaccinated, and are less likely to be anemic. However, difficulties persist with access, especially for isolated rural women.[16] "It takes me a long time to get here, which means I can't work that day," complained Florinda Vallejo, as she waited to pick up her stipend in a long, hot line in the Chapare lowlands. "But the checkups are good for me and my baby. The money isn't much, but it's a help."[17]

Particularly for the poorest, these small stipends, taken together, are game changers. Combined with increases in the minimum wage, official figures put the drop in extreme poverty from 38 to 15 percent between 2006 and 2017, while overall poverty tumbled from 61 to 35 percent during the same period.[18] In terms of the Human Development Index, a more holistic indication of well-being that combines life expectancy and access to knowledge with per capita income, Bolivia experienced a steady and significant increase during Morales's government.[19] Perhaps even more noteworthy was the dip in inequality: by 2018, the Gini index had plummeted from Latin America's second highest to its fifth lowest among eighteen countries, at 42.2.[20]

## RECONCEPTUALIZING EDUCATION

Being strapped with one of the region's weakest educational systems has slowed economic and social development in Bolivia for decades. In 2016, according to a United Nations study, education levels ranged from 13 years on average among wealthier, lighter-skinned male students to only 2.5 years of schooling for highland Indigenous women.[21]

When Morales took office, women were three times as likely as men to be unable to read and write, particularly in rural areas, where the illiteracy rate was double that in cities. The new government moved quickly to increase literacy with its "Yes, I can" campaign, launched in 2006, that reached over five hundred thousand people. The results were remarkable: illiteracy dropped from 13.3 percent in 2001 to 3.8 percent in 2014.[22] "Not being able to read and write is like being blind," recalled Margarita Pérez from Cochabamba. "Now I feel like a real person for the first time."[23]

Education policy was initially conceived as a key element in the effort to decolonize society, incorporating Indigenous knowledge within a community-based and participatory system. Named after the founders of the Altiplano village of Warisata, where a pioneering effort to provide Indigenous education began in the 1930s, and inspired by the liberation pedagogy of Paulo Freire, a new education law passed in December 2010.

The law, which requires every child to learn an Indigenous language and culture in addition to Spanish and Western subjects, has faced stumbling blocks in both urban and rural areas. As rural Cochabamba teacher Marcelo Martina explained, "The new law is quite difficult to understand. There are a lot of bureaucratic requirements and too much paperwork."[24] Igor Ampuero, director of the nongovernmental educational organization FUNDE in Cochabamba, explained that the law's "transformative aspects were weakened because we continued with the same educational system, where we have both public and private schools and where we have two unions—one for rural teachers and one for urban."[25] Additionally, former MAS government minister Rafael Puente has noted that the new law is too Andean-centric in its orientation.[26]

Sociologist Mónica Navarro argues that the education system remains management-led, centralized, and monocultural. What is missing is a capacity for schools to respond to local realities and needs: for example, administrators have failed to tie the school cycle to the agro-festive calendar in rural areas, where communities are closely linked, culturally and productively, to the rhythm of agriculture.[27]

Wilson Ogeda, who teaches languages in the Cochabamba town of Capinota, believes that the new law has made education "more ideological and less scientific. We need more practical training in classroom teaching."[28] This speaks to a lack of professional development and ongoing support for teachers.[29] The MAS vice minister for higher education, Jiovanny Samanamud, acknowledged that "one of our biggest tasks is to improve teacher quality."[30] To accomplish this, the government set up a training institute, but, according to Igor Ampuero, "It was not very effective. It had the goal of training 150,000 teachers but lacked the necessary resources."[31]

Social scientist Joëtta Zoetelief found that obstacles to ongoing teacher training were partly connected to the long-standing distrust of government by teachers' unions, particularly in La Paz.[32] "The unions place little value on continuing education and helping teachers improve their classroom teaching," said Ampuero.[33] The unions are hierarchical and male dominated: 58

percent of Bolivia's classroom teachers are women, and most of the teachers' union leadership is male.[34] Overall, the teachers' unions supported the MAS reform, in contrast to their fierce rejection of a neoliberal effort in 1994. However, they struggled with the Ministry of Education, principally over teachers' working conditions and wages.

Education researcher Mieke Lopes Cardozo argues that while the MAS government carved out some spaces for teachers to exercise agency in their classrooms, conservative teacher training and school administrators, coupled with continuing low wages, have given teachers "limited space . . . to actually take up roles as actors of change."[35] Guaraní educator Marcia Mandepora pointed out that "we are still working with a model of educational administration contaminated by the logic of the global market, where students worry about getting good jobs rather than serving their communities, and teachers keep quiet so as not to lose their salaries."[36]

MAS efforts to strengthen curriculum quality were lacking in substance.[37] For the administrators who headed two of the three new Indigenous universities launched in 2008, the changed curriculum failed to zero in on the differences and complementarity between Indigenous and Western epistemologies and the need for dialogue between the two ways of knowledge.[38] "The conception of interculturality has often been trivialized as folkloric presentations of local Indigenous cultures," observed Mandepora.[39]

The Indigenous Universities (UNIBOLs) are designed to address the needs of rural students who are far less likely than city dwellers to go to university. With varying degrees of success to date, their goal is to equip Indigenous young people to flourish in both the Indigenous and western world.

Located near highland Huarina, Chimoré (in the Chapare), and Cuevo (in the southeastern Chaco), the universities are intended to serve Aymara, Quechua, and lowland Indigenous peoples respectively. Students receive backing from their local organizations as well as government subsidies. Nineteen-year-old Leni Machis, who studied textiles in Huarina, explained, "Being here is both an amazing privilege and opportunity because nowhere else would I be given a full scholarship that covers everything, and without it I couldn't possibly go to university."[40]

The university programs focus on strengthening the communitarian economy, emphasizing subjects such as forestry management, veterinary medicine, and fisheries. At UNIBOL Guaraní, in the Chaco, they also study oil and gas technology. Mandepora, a former rector, argues that this type of training is to "help our peoples monitor, mitigate, and participate in gas extraction with more awareness of its environmental and social impacts."[41]

UNIBOL Guaraní currently sponsors 650 young people, mainly Guaraní, but also other lowland students. They study their group's language—which many arrive unable to read or write—as well as Spanish and English. "We were chosen through our community organizations, and we have made a commitment to go back and work there," says forestry student Juan Rodríguez, who is from the small Chiquitano community of Fátima. "I want to work to restore our forests that once had precious species like *cedron* and *tajibo*, but these are all gone now. We need to encourage replanting and start a nursery."[42]

Despite the drawbacks, the MAS commitment to education had paid off by 2015, when 8.7 percent of Bolivia's GDP was invested in education—3 percent more than the regional average.[43] School dropout rates plummeted from 6 to 1.2 percent from 2005 to 2015; the proportion of temporary and untrained teachers plunged from 25 to 2.5 percent in the same period; and over three thousand new schools, ten new technical training institutes, and fifteen hundred distance learning centers were built.[44] Teachers' salaries doubled, while rural instruction of Indigenous languages grew.

## REVITALIZING AN AILING HEALTHCARE SYSTEM

"Healthcare should be available to all Bolivians. Not just the privileged few," the vice minister of land, Juan Carlos León, told a crowd in the high valley town of Cotagaita, south of Potosí, the day after the March 2019 launch of the Unified Healthcare System

(SUS). Overnight, the program had extended free healthcare coverage to 51 percent of the population, or five million people.[45]

"People say we are in no position to do this," León continued, "but we have to take the first step in creating universal healthcare, otherwise it will never happen."[46] The medical associations in the country railed against the SUS, arguing that the resources were not in place to execute it. They also saw the new law as a threat to privileges they had fought tooth and nail to maintain.

The Morales government worked hard to reform Bolivia's disjointed and incompetent healthcare system. In 2006, only 20 percent of rural people had access to both basic sanitation and drinking water. By 2020, that figure had risen to 36 percent.[47] In 2006, the country sat close to the bottom of the region's health indicators. "Seventy-seven percent of the population is excluded from services in some manner," explained Morales's first health minister, Dr. Nila Heredia.[48] That number saw a dramatic improvement over the subsequent decade and a half.

A remarkable amplification of healthcare services occurred based on an intercultural, intersectoral, and integrated primary healthcare (PHC) system, which was praised by the World Health Organization as a model for other lower-income countries.[49] Conceptually, it incorporated community participation in health planning and implementation and a recognition of the social determinants of illness.

However, there were both theoretical and operational obstacles to implementation. For example, local health committees were slow to form, and many members failed to understand their roles and responsibilities.[50] In many places, inadequate equipment and poorly trained personnel hindered effective service delivery.

According to the Pan American Health Organization, by 2016 Bolivia had 3,857 primary care clinics, providing health services to 25 percent of its most vulnerable population.[51] This was combined with a Zero Malnutrition Program that operates in the municipalities most susceptible to food insecurity and risk of malnutrition among children under five.

The government also set up the continent's first-ever vice ministry of traditional medicine.[52] It was most successful in Oruro and Potosí, where central hospitals offered postgraduate degrees in intercultural health as well as certification for traditional healers. However, inadequate funding kept traditional medicine mostly on the fringe, guaranteeing the abiding dominance of Western medicine.[53]

In 2006, the Morales government contracted a Cuban medical brigade to come to Bolivia. Cuba deployed about nine hundred doctors and eight hundred paramedics, supplying medical services to over six hundred thousand people, including cataract surgery for the Bolivian soldier who had killed the last Cuban doctor he had met—Che Guevara.[54]

Five thousand low-income and Indigenous Bolivians studied medicine in Cuba, ten times more than under previous administrations. Bolivia tried to copy Cuba's socialist healthcare model, but its system is entirely Western in orientation, doctor-centric, and hierarchical.[55] "We need to figure out how to integrate traditional medicine into our health programs," said Dr. Daniel Flores Quispe from an Indigenous family in Tarabuco, in the southern department (state or province) of Chuquisaca, who won a scholarship to study in Cuba. "Because people really believe in it; it plays a critical role in curing all kinds of illnesses."[56]

Many Bolivian doctors resisted what they saw as the imposition of Cuban socialism and often expressed disdain for traditional medical practitioners. Medical students objected to the expectation that they work for three years in a rural health facility, while faculty resisted any efforts to revise the medical school curriculum.[57]

In 2012, when the government demanded that doctors in public facilities work the eight hours a day for which they were paid, rather than the accustomed six, doctors and medical students poured into the streets in protest. The shortened hours meant that "sometimes, you see people waiting hours in line just to get an aspirin," said physical therapist Hernan Vallejos Calle, who works in the northeastern department of Beni.[58] After fifty-two days of often-violent disruption, the government scrapped the effort.

A second major clash came with the government's proposed penal reform in 2017, which aimed to pare down prison over-crowding and Bolivia's astronomical rate of preventive detention, the region's highest.[59] Within the law was a stipulation that doctors could be sued for malpractice. Forty-seven days of protest later, the government saw no choice but to abandon the reform.

## AN UNPRECEDENTED BOOM

The economic situation improved dramatically under the MAS, especially for the country's most vulnerable populations. For fourteen years, Bolivia enjoyed the longest and most sustained period of growth in its history, although the structure of the economy itself remained largely unaltered.[60] This blessed one of the region's historically most volatile countries with unheard-of stability. And even though financial reserves dropped with a decline in commodity prices, in 2018 they still stood at the highest in South America as a percentage of GDP.[61]

Luis Arce, then finance minister and now president, largely relied on a strategy of stimulating internal demand through increased government investment, which bolstered spending capacity. From 2006 to 2018, GDP per capita more than tripled.[62] These advances were propelled by a quadrupling of the minimum wage (even though the MAS government was unable to enforce it), with annual raises above inflation in all but three years, and a second government-mandated Christmas bonus (instead of the usual one), with the stipulation that 15 percent be spent on goods made in Bolivia.[63] Conditional cash transfers also helped boost local demand.[64]

On the other hand, the focus on disbursing benefits to informal workers meant that unionization rates declined, further weakening the Bolivian Workers Central (COB) and stripping the working class of its power vis-à-vis capital. Political scientist Angus McNelly argues that informality in Bolivia

> entails the growing precarity that cheapens labour and touches every area of working-class lives, from where people

live and send their kids to school, what and where people eat, to how people access social services and their relationship with the state. . . . Informalisation has increased the working-classes exposure to the vicissitudes of the market, even as dependence on market relations increases, producing a social formation vulnerable to even the slightest exogenous shock.[65]

Notably, the percentage of informal workers did not shrink under Morales.[66]

Political scientists Jorge León Trujillo and Susan Spronk maintain that the COB remained influential, even as it vacillated between friend and foe of the government.[67] Much of the economic growth was concentrated in sectors that do not produce many formal jobs, such as hydrocarbons and commerce. Moreover, many Bolivians work in small family businesses or informally, which means they fall below the threshold for union formation (twenty workers).[68]

# THE OCTOBER AGENDA

The pressure to fulfill the social movements' "October Agenda," which had solidified after the 2003 Gas War, was intense during the first years of the Morales government. The Agenda had coalesced around three demands: the nationalization of natural gas; the creation of a Constituent Assembly to write a new and more inclusive constitution; and ensuring the former president, minister of defense, and others who held office during the Gas Wars stood trial for the deaths and injuries that had occurred during their watch.

## *NATURAL GAS NATIONALIZATION*

On International Workers' Day, May 1, 2006, surrounded by soldiers and banners proclaiming, "Property of all Bolivians," Morales announced natural gas nationalization at the country's largest gas field, San Alberto in the southeastern Chaco. Even if the move stopped shy of the full expropriation demanded by many social movements, in a country whose export economy has provided natural resources at disadvantageous prices to the world for over five hundred years, this was the best deal a Bolivian government ever cut.

Morales's approval rating shot up to 81 percent,[69] demonstrating how deeply linked the national sense of dignity and sovereignty are to control over resource wealth.[70] The move built on a tradition on the Latin American left that perceives nationalization both as the answer to economic ills and as critical to national dignity.

Despite vociferous protests from multinational corporations, Northern governments, and Western media, Bolivia's new gas law was not, in fact, a classic nationalization; there was no expropriation of assets, and all the foreign companies negotiated new agreements. Private multinational firms still extract most of the country's natural gas and minerals, although the share of profits transferred to the state shot up dramatically. Critics such as political scientist Vladimir Diez-Cuellar argue that "nationalization" became nothing more than a euphemism for a new relationship between the state and multinationals, divesting the term of any meaning.[71] Nonetheless, the income generated by this move significantly ameliorated the fortunes of Bolivia's poor majority.

## THE CONSTITUENT ASSEMBLY

Any discussion of the new constitution approved in 2009 must include the caveat that Bolivia has always been more successful at writing constitutions than following them.[72] Despite this checkered history, the desire to write a new and more inclusive constitution was widespread, originating as a demand in 1990 with the first national lowland Indigenous March for Territory and Dignity.[73]

The organization of the Assembly was an ambitious undertaking for the newly elected government. The MAS won 134 of its 255 seats, shy of the two-thirds needed to circumvent compromises that would ultimately curb how radical the document could be.[74] The Assembly's chief protagonist was the peasant and Indigenous movement, despite the fact that ethnic minorities had been unsuccessful in their call for representation to be distributed by social sector rather than geography. The MAS government decided that constituents would be elected through party lists, which led to women occupying 33 percent of the total seats and comprising 47 percent of the MAS delegates. [75]

The constitution the Assembly created has often been counted among the most progressive in the world for its emphasis on Indigenous, women's, and environmental rights. However, political sociologist Miguel Centellas cautions against this enthusiasm, arguing that it fundamentally perpetuated the 1950s state model of prioritizing a strong government role in national development, inevitably creating conflicts between the state and local Indigenous communities.[76]

The Constituent Assembly that convened in August 2006 elected Silvia Lazarte, a Quechua-speaking coca grower, as its president. "The Constituent Assembly was the most exciting and most important thing I have ever been involved in," said longtime Chiquitano/ Guaraní organizer Marisol Solano.[77] For the first time in Bolivian history, women in Indigenous dress sat as equals beside white men in business suits formulating the country's framing document.

Consultations were held throughout the country, and twenty-one committees convened to formulate the text. "The size of the Assembly was unwieldy—at some points there were as many as fifteen hundred people involved," said Assembly representative Raúl Prada Alcoreza.

"The right wing did everything possible to prevent any real reinvention of the country," Prada Alcoreza continued.[78] For the first seven months, the conservative opposition rejected a simple-majority approval of each article, instead insisting on two-thirds agreement. This stalled the Assembly until the MAS finally capitulated in March 2007.[79]

Not satisfied with this concession, the opposition and conservative sectors used every maneuver available to block, undermine and delegitimize the Assembly. One of their most successful tactics was the resuscitation of deep-seated resentment in Sucre over the 1899 transfer of the administrative capital to La Paz, leaving Sucre with the judicial branch. A right-wing inter-institutional committee successfully convinced a majority of the city's residents that returning the capital to Sucre would boost the local economy.[80] As a result, the Constituent Assembly ground to a halt for more than a month, with frequent conflict in the streets.

By late November 2007, three people were dead and two hundred wounded.[81] The conservative opposition then boycotted the Assembly, which meant the new constitution was approved without their participation, generating more clashes and three more deaths, with the opposition calling the proposed document illegal and invalid.[82] Anthropologist Salvador Schavelson recounts that the conflict was so intense that Morales told Lazarte: "Dead or alive, you will give me a constitution by December."[83] Despite considerable odds, she pulled it off. But the document then was subject to a reconciliation process in Legislative Assembly, where conservative control of the Senate undercut its provisions on land redistribution, environmental safeguards, and Indigenous rights.[84]

As sociologist Oscar Vega Camacho reflected, "The constitution is simply not the groundbreaking and foundational document the Assembly wrote at considerable personal sacrifice."[85] The Unity Pact had failed in its attempt to establish a different kind of state from the liberal democratic model. What was adopted, argues political scientist Fernando Garcés, was "a moderate or domesticated plurinationality that threatens neither to destructure the state nor to undo liberal institutionalism. This is then, a kind of plurinationalism that establishes the limits of self-determination of Indigenous peoples ... it is a plurinationalism tamed and controlled by the already constituted powers, not determined by the ... foundational powers of Indigenous peoples."[86] Political scientist Martín Mendoza-Botelho adds that although "the Bolivian experience became an extraordinary example of democracy at work in a heterogeneous nation that still struggles to embrace its Indigenous roots ... pragmatic considerations and short-term political objectives were favoured over painstaking institution-building efforts grounded on democratic values."[87]

Political scientist Jonas Wolff argues that while this may be true, the emerging regime has modified representative democracy by adding heterodox and non-liberal conceptions of democracy, participation, and governance through expanded citizenship, government accountability, direct democracy, self-governance, and citizen participation in resource allocation.[88] Bolivia offers a counter-paradigm with respect to liberal democracy and development models for political scientist Lorenza Fontana, who argues that its constitution belies the argument that communitarian values are inevitably overcome by modernization.[89]

When put to a national referendum in January 2009, the new constitution was approved by 61 percent of the voters.[90] Overnight, Bolivia transformed into a plurinational state, acknowledging Indigenous groups as separate nations with autonomy and self-determination, including rights to consultation on projects proposed for their lands. This radically changed the notion of a unitary Bolivian nation, turning ideas of race, identity, and territory on their head.[91] It also advanced women's rights significantly.[92] Collective and state rights now trumped those assigned to private capital, in a mixed public–private economy.[93] The new constitution promised judicial pluralism and equal rights for all religions, stripping Roman Catholicism of its role as the country's official faith. Water became a human right, and coca leaf gained protection as part of national cultural patrimony.[94]

The constitution's articles also provide for public oversight of state contracts, government spending, and policy, expressed through the concept of "social control."[95] Although the opposition fought any corruption-control initiative that empowered citizens, social control has been applied to a range of areas, from health program quality to restrictions on coca cultivation.[96]

Two decisions had serious implications for the upheaval over the 2019 elections. The first was the inclusion of a compromise to limit presidential office to two terms, which was pushed by the opposition and rejected, even then, by the MAS.[97] The second was the avoidance of confrontation with the military and police by opting not to modify articles related to security and defense that were laid out in the previous constitution.[98] Atempts to decentralize the police and strengthen them vis-à-vis the military also stumbled, signaling just how difficult police reform would prove to be.

The 2009 constitution contradicts itself repeatedly, often appearing closer to a laundry list of immediate concerns than a vision for the future. Overlapping departmental, municipal, provincial, and Indigenous autonomies created confusion over which level of government was responsible for particular services and policies.[99]

While environmental protection is front and center, the constitution sidesteps how this can be reconciled with the industrialization of Bolivia's natural resources. "Very often the constitution is disregarded by the government to the detriment of the environment," said Marcos Uzquiano, director of lowland Madidi National Park.[100]

The MAS made every effort to control the process. "We had the MAS trying to dictate what we did," complained representative Prada Alcoreza. "They were afraid of anything real, participatory, and independent."[101] Critics contend that the 2009 constitution favors direct rather than representative democracy, concentrates power in the executive branch, and undermines checks and balances.[102] For Chiquitano leader José Bailaba, "The MAS's biggest accomplishment was the constitution. Its biggest failure has been its inability to carry it out."[103]

## BRINGING GONI AND SÁNCHEZ BERZAÍN TO JUSTICE

At least seventy people were killed during the Gas War uprising, which erupted in October 2003 over President Gonzalo Sánchez de Lozada's plans to export natural gas. Goni, as Sánchez de Lozada is known, fled to the United States, where he has lived comfortably ever since in a wealthy Washington, DC, suburb. There, he cultivated his ties to high-level Democrats, which paid off in June 2008 when the United States granted political asylum to his former minister of defense, Carlos Sánchez Berzaín.[104]

A case in Bolivia against Goni, his ministers, and his military high command reached a unanimous verdict in August 2011 that led to the imprisonment of two ex-ministers and five military commanders.[105] Goni, Sánchez Berzaín, and the other ministers who fled before the trial were not sentenced, because defendants cannot be tried in absentia in Bolivia. The head of the families of the victims association, Juan Patricio Quispe, told the press: "We think it is an important step. . . . The sentence sets an example, so that no government will ever again feel it has the right to murder its own citizens."[106]

Since 2003, Bolivian governments have lobbied the United States to extradite Goni and his collaborators. The calls for accountability are particularly strong in El Alto, where the bulk of the killings took place. Evo once joked to Thomas Shannon, then the US assistant secretary of state for Western Hemisphere affairs, "If you send Goni back, you'll be made mayor of El Alto."[107]

In 2012, the United States rejected Bolivia's extradition request for Goni, Sánchez Berzaín, and another former minister, Jorge Berindoague Alcocer. The reason given was that the Bolivian accusations of genocide do not conform to the terms of the 1995 extradition treaty between the two countries; however, critics contend that Goni is being protected by the US government.[108] Vicky Ayllón, who worked closely on the case, complained, "The US government, through the Department of State and the embassy, blocked us at every turn." She added, "Because of Goni's high level political connections, the chances of succeeding were always slim."[109] A second application presented in early 2016 has received no response to date.

At the same time, a team of US attorneys (including one of this book's co-authors) from Harvard Law School, the Center for Constitutional Rights, and private firm Akin Gump worked on a civil case for the victims. The landmark case was brought under the 1991 Torture Victim Protection Act, one of the world's most far-reaching human rights laws. The act permits civil suits within the United States for extrajudicial killings and torture committed by officials of a foreign government once possible remedies in their home country have been exhausted. This case marked the first time an ex–head of state was forced to face his accusers in a US court for human rights abuses.

In April 2018, a Fort Lauderdale, Florida, jury found Goni and Sánchez Berzaín liable for extrajudicial killings and awarded damages of $10 million, a decision that broadened the possibilities for employing US human rights law against foreign government officials.[110] A day later, the normally deeply divided Bolivian Chamber of Deputies issued a unanimous statement praising the decision and demanding that Goni and Sánchez Berzaín return to Bolivia to stand trial. Then, a month later, in a highly unusual move, the presiding judge, James Cohn, reversed the ruling. In July 2020, the Eleventh Circuit Court of Appeals overturned Cohn's decision, returning the case to his court, and further granted a new trial for a second claim, wrongful death, proffering an opportunity for the victims to win twice. In April 2021, Cohn upheld the jury verdict in favor of the families that he had originally reversed. Goni and Sánchez Berzaín have appealed the ruling.

## INDIGENOUS RIGHTS

Evo Morales arrived in office with almost unanimous backing of the country's Indigenous people and their organizations. He proceeded to fill fourteen of the sixteen cabinet posts with Indigenous people, ten of whom were from social movements, although this number would drop in subsequent governments.[111] Social inclusion under the Morales government was striking. Signs proclaiming "All of us are equal under the law" now hang in many businesses and public spaces. One successful professional, who is Indigenous, spoke to this shift: "When Evo was elected, the world got better for people like me. For the light-skinned upper class in this country all the advantages they had accumulated were suddenly threatened."[112]

Splits between Indigenous groups aligned with the MAS and those in opposition took their toll on the advancement of Indigenous rights. Unity frayed as well because of highland and valley migration to the lowlands, which revived historic distrust between highland and lowland groups.

Despite these tensions, thirty-six Indigenous languages were officially recognized for the first time under the 2009 constitution. Government-funded institutes promoted local language and culture for twenty-nine of them.[113]

Indigenous people also made significant gains in the redistribution of land.[114] Groups added to territory they had won in the 1990s, reflecting a profound and historic transformation— twenty-three million hectares, 22 percent of all Bolivian national territory, is now held collectively by Indigenous peoples under the status of Native Community Lands (TCOs).[115]

The new constitution also validates Indigenous justice systems, although it affords no clearly defined interface between the existing system (based on Western models) and community justice. Despite this shortfall, Dr. Liberio Uño, director of an Indigenous justice program at La Paz's public university, believes that "the 2009 constitution generally strengthened Indigenous justice. After all, this is what is used in 85 percent of our national territory and by about 30 percent of our population." According to Dr. Uño, the Indigenous justice system attends to an estimated three thousand cases a year.[116]

Indigenous justice favors a restorative approach. "We believe the best solution is not to punish people, but to emphasize resolution," said Indigenous justice student Hermógenea Calderón Laura. "We want people to reflect on what they did wrong and why, and accept the punishment as part of paying their debt to the party who was harmed and to society."[117]

## WOMEN AND SEXUAL MINORITIES

Bolivia presents a paradox when it comes to women's rights. It made history in 2014 when it elected the third-highest number of national women legislators in the world (after Rwanda and Cuba), a considerable accomplishment in a country where women won the vote in 1952.[118] In 2010, half of Morales's ministers were women.[119] But at the same time, seven of every ten

Bolivian women are survivors of sexual or physical violence, the second-highest rate in the region.[120]

Women's newfound social, economic, and political rights are thanks to organizing by the indigenous women's organization the Bartolinas and middle class feminists. Together they collaborated during the Constituent Assembly to achieve the constitutional enshrinement of gender equality and legislative parity for women at every level of government—a first in Latin America. "The political parties agreed to parity without realizing what it actually meant," explained Monica Novillo of the Women's Coalition, a broad alliance of feminist organizations.[121] Following the 2019 national elections, women held 52 percent of the seats in the national legislature—a figure that had skyrocketed from 4 percent just thirty years prior.[122]

But at the municipal level, the struggle to achieve parity has been fraught with violence. "The threats women councilors face are constant," said Sofia Silvestre, who served as city councilor in the highland town of Achacachi.[123] Men have presented themselves as women (crudely describing themselves as "transvestite candidates"), and male-dominated parties sponsor women candidates they can control.

"Often there is participation, but no representation, because women follow men's lead as they have been taught to do since childhood," explained Jessy López of the Association of Women Councilors. "Many are also terrified of violence and threats. Women face having their houses burned down, their kids beaten up, their husbands lose their jobs, and being physically assaulted—such as having cement thrown in their eyes."[124]

It has also led to murder: Juana Quispe Apaza, from a highland Aymara community, asked for police protection after publicly denouncing corruption in her municipality. "My life is in danger, and I can't afford bodyguards," she told the Bolivian press before she was found strangled on a riverbank in March 2012. Three months later, at the other end of the country, Daguimar Rivera was killed when three men shot her in the face. She too had denounced influence peddling and the misuse of municipal funds.[125]

Women in politics are not the only targets of femicide and violence. Despite the 2013 passage of one of the region's strongest laws condemning violence against women, the country still struggles with an alarmingly high rate of femicide.[126] The legislation promises women protection from sexual assault, domestic violence, femicide, and forced sterilization. "Our laws, even if they are in the vanguard, unfortunately are not obeyed and [are] often completely unknown to both authorities and citizens," said councilor Sofia Silvestre.[127] Almost every week there is another story in local newspapers about a woman, usually young, who has been murdered by her partner, often in front of her children.

In a packed university auditorium one evening in early 2019, the mostly student crowd grew hushed as women described how their daughters, sisters, and mothers had been murdered. "Families are ashamed of having a daughter killed by femicide. We live in a *machista* society that says she must have done something to deserve it. She was a drunk, she was disobedient, she was a loose woman, she shouted too much, she was a bad mother, she wanted to study or work, so what do you expect?" said one of the speakers. "Femicide is a disciplinary measure of the patriarchy, a warning to other women to obey men."[128]

Women fear being separated from their children if they denounce abuse or believe that they have brought on the mistreatment by their own actions. Teen pregnancy remains alarmingly high, labor discrimination against pregnant women is rampant, laws that guarantee equal pay for equal work remain unapplied, and sexual harassment in the workplace is common.

Every day in Bolivia's public hospitals, ten women need emergency medical care because of a botched abortion.[129] Most of them are under the age of twenty-five. For women like Mónica, who works as an office cleaner, the options are few. "I already have three children and my husband left right after he found out I was pregnant again," she said. "I just can't afford any more children."[130]

Two-thirds of the country's abortions take place in rural areas, even though less than one-third of the population lives there. In Aymara communities, rather than triggering the type of moral judgement common in Western cultures, researchers Ineke Dibbits and Ximena Pabón found that abortion creates a dilemma because necessary death rituals are not performed. This can provoke a disequilibrium with nature.[131]

Julia Mamani, who worked for several years on an Aymara health project, found that "women try to abort themselves with herbs or blunt instruments. If it fails, they start hemorrhaging and often we had to pay extra to convince drivers to take them to the city because they didn't want them bleeding on their bus."[132] Middle- and upper-class women obtain safe abortions routinely at a cost of about five hundred dollars.

Current law only allows abortion in the case of rape, incest, or to save the life of the mother. A 2017–18 effort, backed by Vice President Álvaro García Linera, to decriminalize abortion in the first eight weeks of pregnancy failed after it met fierce resistance from medical organizations, the Roman Catholic Church, and evangelical Christians.

Bolivia has experienced a slow but steady advance in LGBT rights since the mid-1990s, when activists began organizing, and it accelerated during the Morales administration, even though, as in so many other areas, law and practice remained disconnected.[133] The 2009 constitution banned all discrimination on the basis of sexual orientation and gender, one of few in the world to do so.[134] Longtime activist David Aruquipa noted that "the new constitution that the MAS supported created the space to advance LGBT rights."[135] This was reinforced by the 2010 Law against Racism and Discrimination that criminalized hate crimes on the basis of sexual orientation and gender identity.

A decree issued in October 2011 officially declared the commemoration of the International Day against Homophobia, Transphobia, and Biphobia. In 2012, state recognition of LGBT rights expanded again with an LGBT television show, *Transformando*, on the state channel.

In 2014, José Manuel Canelas Jaime became the first openly gay man to serve as a legislative deputy for the MAS party, later becoming minister of communications in the last year of the

Morales government. Then, Carlos Parra Heredia, better known as Paris Galán, became the first drag queen elected to La Paz's departmental assembly. In 2016, a law passed permitting gender on identity cards to be determined by the bearer, in recognition of transgender people.[136] Unveiling the new law, Vice President García Linera said it would put an end to the "social hypocrisy" in which many Bolivians had previously refused to acknowledge the existence of the LGBT community.[137]

When Jeanine Áñez came to power with the Bible in hand, dread seized the LGBT community. "It was a real setback," said David Aruquipa. "It generated tremendous fear of repression."[138]

In late 2020, once the MAS had returned to power, Aruquipa and his partner, Guido Montaño, had their civil union recognized by the Bolivian state after a two-year struggle. "It gave us and the community a real boost," said Aruquipa, "and I think it taught us to push for all our rights, and not settle for compromises."[139]

## LAND REFORM

By 2015, the country's most significant land reform in decades had benefited over a million individuals, more of them women than ever before, and 1,283 communities (incorporating almost half a million people). This was accomplished by increasing the rate of title clearance by over 300 percent and reallocating land, mostly in the eastern part of the country, where the 1953 agrarian reform had never been implemented.[140] One-third of this land is held collectively by Indigenous and peasant organizations, with another 22 percent owned in individual or family plots by small farmers.[141] Geographer Penelope Anthias cautions that land titling in Guaraní territory in the lowlands is not a magic bullet to solve racialized dispossession and discrimination, as it can generate disputes within and between communities.[142]

When it took power, the MAS government inherited a hodgepodge of haphazardly applied agrarian reform efforts. As highland landholdings shrunk with each succeeding generation,

many impoverished *campesinos* fled eastward, where colonization schemes allotted them parcels of government-owned land.
During the same period, between 1964 and 1982, dictators
transferred a hundred million acres to some six thousand family
members, friends, and political associates.[143]

The 2006 Agrarian Reform Law had passed thanks to seven
months of sustained peasant demonstrations. While it limited
private ownership to 12,500 acres, it could not be applied retro-
actively, legitimizing huge expanses of illegally acquired land.[144]
Few estates have been expropriated, and campesino farmers
only control about a third of good arable land, perpetuating a
significant degree of inequality in landownership. Most of the
land granted to peasant farmers was already under state control,
and, reminiscent of the 1953 reform, technical assistance to the
new owners was almost nonexistent.[145] But the new law allowed
for seizures of property where owners employ forced labor or
use debt peonage, which has particularly caused hardship for
Guaraní peoples.

For the first time since the Spanish Conquest, smallholders
control 55 percent of all land. Forty-six percent of the new titles include women's names.[146] Nonetheless, the average peasant
landholding is 16 hectares, while larger farmers (who benefited
under the law in far smaller numbers) gained an average of 996
hectares apiece.[147]

The government has done little to control what is an unruly and
chaotic process of settlement by campesinos, often impoverished
and desperate, who migrate from the highlands and valleys, and
who make up a critical part of the MAS rural base. Guaraní activist Marilyn Carayuri complains, "We are still being colonized—
this time by people from the highlands."[148] These settlements are
accelerating all over eastern Bolivia. Biologist Saul Arias showed
us places within the boundaries of Amboró National Park, three
hours west of Santa Cruz, where settlers from Potosí were clear-
ing land without any government sanctions.

"There needs to be planning—it's not enough to just give
people fifty hectares and tell them to survive as best they can.

They begin to cut trees down they shouldn't, hunt animals they shouldn't, and sometimes are involved in illegal coca production, and even drug trafficking. It becomes a real social problem," said Marcos Uzquiano, director of Madidi Park.[149]

Land reform slowed considerably after 2010. By then, the Morales government had moved toward eastern agribusiness and split with the lowland Confederation of Indigenous Peoples of Bolivia (CIDOB). Pressures from the MAS's highland base, including those who migrated east, meant that for the first time since 1996, more land was titled individually than collectively.[150] The preference for individual title was evident in rural Potosí in February 2019, when Vice Minister of Land Juan Carlos León emphasized to a large crowd, "We're here today handing out titles to 2,527 people," with no mention of communal holdings.

## COCA: BOLIVIA'S SACRED AND CONTENTIOUS LEAF

Coca has been integral to Andean culture for thousands of years. This history opened the door to the leaf serving as a potent organizing symbol for the MAS party, as it is used across the country and in every social class, although middle and upper classes tend to drink it in tea rather than suck on it, as working-class and Indigenous peoples often do. Bolivia has long been the world's third-largest coca producer, after Colombia and Peru.[151]

But most of the world knows coca as the principal ingredient in the drug cocaine. "Coca has always been a part of our lives," said Jorge Chambi, who sells coca leaf in one-pound bags on the street in the highland city of Oruro. "We never had a problem with it until the drug traffickers showed up and turned it into cocaine."[152]

In 2013, Bolivia gained international recognition of its right to consume the leaf from the UN through an exception to the 1961 UN Single Convention on Narcotic Drugs.[153] "I use coca when I have to work at night," said Wilson Bernal, a 60-year-old taxi driver in El Alto. "It helps me to stay alert. Cocaine is something else, something we don't know."[154]

US-financed interdiction programs, in place until 2005, generated conflict and human rights violations while failing to stem cocaine's flow to the north. Forced eradication was unsuccessful at reducing coca crops overall.[155] Instead, it shifted where coca is grown, generating extensive replanting that has aggravated deforestation.

In the search for alternatives to the violence, corruption, and institutional instability fueled by these policies, the MAS government committed to a novel and previously untried program. Based on a 2004 accord with the Mesa government that permitted coca farmers to cultivate a restricted amount of leaf and known as "social control of coca," compliance was monitored by local growers' unions themselves.[156] The accord lowered violence in coca-growing regions almost immediately. "Things are much tougher than under the United States," said grower Emilio Flores. "Before, you just had to avoid the anti-drug police. Now your neighbors can turn you in."[157] Forced eradication with military units still takes place in zones not authorized for growing and in national parks.

In areas where unions are strong, the community control model proved more effective at reducing coca acreage than police and military repression,[158] and it successfully extended social and civil rights. Government investment as well as gender equity policies have encouraged economic diversification away from coca. The program has been recognized as a "best practice" by the Organization of American States,[159] and the United Nations Development Programme stated in 2019 that "the [Bolivian] government has helped stabilize household incomes and placed farmers in a better position to assume the risk of substituting illicit crops with alternative crops or livestock."[160] In contrast, the United States was highly critical of the initiative, labeling Bolivia one of the world's least-compliant countries in controlling drug exports.[161]

Attempts were made to grow the legitimate market for coca leaf by developing alternative uses, from toothpaste to medicines. "Coca is a marvelous gift of nature, offering a moderate stimulant like coffee—but one full of vitamins and minerals," said Ricardo Hegedus, the manager of Windsor, Bolivia's largest tea producer.

"We have dreamed of exporting coca tea legally for the thirty years I have worked here. Coca farmers' incomes would improve, and while it wouldn't eliminate drug trafficking, it would make it harder and more expensive for traffickers to get coca."[162]

But finding a legal market has proven complicated. Government officials admit that they underestimated international resistance. "We thought it would be easy because we all know the benefits of coca," said Felipe Cáceres, former vice minister of social defense and controlled substances. "We really didn't realize that so many people think that coca is the same as cocaine."[163]

In 2017, the MAS government passed a new coca law that had been a decade in the making. The law raises the 12,000 hectares (29,640 acres) limit legally recognized in a 1988 law to 22,000 hectares. As Bolivia consumes 14,700 hectares of the leaf according to a 2014 European Union study, this leaves 7,300 hectares of "excess" coca.[164] Kathryn Ledebur of the drug policy watchdog Andean Information Network contends: "This law offers real advantages over those in place in Colombia and Peru because it is negotiated with growers, which makes its goals more achievable."[165]

Coca farmers have not given up the dream of selling their leaf legitimately. "We want to sell the coca worldwide," said Lucio Mendoza, who is from a growing family in the Yungas, east of La Paz. "This would be good for the world, which will benefit, as we do, from our sacred coca leaf."[166] Christian Oporto, supervisor of international sales for Windsor Tea, agrees. "We have a star product that is stuck sleeping in our country," he said.[167]

## CONCLUSIONS

The MAS embarked on one of the most ambitious efforts at social, economic, and political inclusion in Bolivia's history, and in the history of the region as well. Despite the mixed results, the contradictions inherent in a dependence on fossil fuels to improve lives, and the limited options faced by a dependent, peripheral country, the initiatives transformed the country almost beyond recognition and improved the lives of most Bolivians. To herald these accomplishments is to salute the enormous effort made by Bolivians, from social movements to government bureaucrats to MAS party militants, who collectively worked without pause to bring a different vision to life.

## CHAPTER 4

# CHALLENGES
# AND MISSTEPS

When the MAS took office in January 2006, their goals were ambitious and inspiring, but the party struggled with political rivals, who strove to hinder them as much as possible. In a country like Bolivia, with a flimsy state and even less substantial party system, these obstacles, as well as the MAS's inexperience, contributed to the conditions that paved the way for the 2019 coup. Structural constraints framed the options available and impeded how successful the MAS could be in transforming Bolivian society.

## LEARNING ON THE FLY

"At the beginning, there was a lot of euphoria that we could change everything," said Freddy Condo, then vice minister of lands. "But groups affiliated with former political parties had more knowledge about government operations than we did. Often their jobs passed from father to son to grandson. Perhaps it would have been a good idea to throw them all out—but how could we have managed all the contracts dependent on foreign funding that were already in place? Our hands were tied."[1]

The MAS deputy for El Alto, Brígida Quiroga, also recognized why the party retained many of the technocrats from previous governments. "I think that our biggest error was that when Evo first took power, we just didn't have people adequately trained to run the government, so we had to keep the people already there in their positions," she said. "Over time they began to undermine the government and control institutions."[2]

The state apparatus that the MAS took over was, as political scientists Miguel Centeno, Atul Kohli, and Deborah Yashar describe for much of the Global South, an "incomplete, distorted and malformed" system brought from Spain, and then over time reshaped by local elites.[3] As historian Rosanna Barragán puts it, Bolivia has always had more territory than state.[4] That state has been characterized as a "fragmented presence," or as a "state with holes."[5]

Bolivia has had, and in many ways continues to have, what legal scholar Koldo Echebarría and sociologist Juan Carlos Cortázar call a clientelist bureaucracy with a high degree of politicization in processes of hiring, firing, and promotion.[6] When a new government takes over, it often brings in new staff, frequently party loyalists who enter offices swept clean of files and plans, as their political rivals strive to impede them as much as possible.

Personalism plagues public service, hindering progressive bureaucrats. Government employees find themselves torn between public service, personal interests, and party loyalty, a tension that absorbs a great deal of time and energy. Sociologist and writer Claudia Peña Claros served as minister of autonomy from 2011 to 2015. "The concept of personal loyalty is critical. If someone gets a job somewhere else, it is seen as a betrayal," she said. "In many ways, the project you are working on takes second place to these relationships."[7]

With 10 percent of the workforce in the public sector in 2005, and public servants better paid than those in private business, working in the state is one of the best, and sometimes only, path to social mobility. That focus gives the state a low performance capability, little autonomy from political parties, and a capacity for service provision fluctuates depending on Bolivia's boom-and-bust commodity export cycles.[8]

Although the MAS party was poorly consolidated when it took office, it steadily became more clientelist and hierarchical. But it was not just the party: many top government appointments came from social movement leadership, conferring their organizations' internal structures significant influence on state operations, especially in the first MAS government. Not only did social movements have high expectations of "their" government, but they also tended to be heavily shaped by patronage relationships that reinforced the already existing clientelism in public administration.[9]

Twenty years of neoliberal policies prior to 2005 left a deeply etched imprint. "We have not managed to separate ourselves from the considerable legacy that neoliberalism left us," contends former vice minister of planning Alberto Borda.[10]

State efficiency and performance have never been a priority in Bolivian government or politics. Rather, the focus is on extracting benefits and retaining power. In the absence of a concerted effort to change the political culture, these historical antecedents significantly constrained the goals of creating a more egalitarian society.[11]

Part of the challenge was to strengthen the state, not only by extending its reach and capacity, but also by making it better reflect Bolivia's diversity and heterogeneity.[12] On this front, the MAS had considerable success: by 2013 Bolivia's public service was younger, more female, and more Indigenous than ever before.[13]

Nonetheless, discrimination persisted. An Indigenous man with a PhD from a European university reported that he was blocked at every turn in his ministry—no one could stomach that he was better educated than they were. "The racism on the left in Bolivia is horrendous," said one foreigner who worked in the MAS government.[14] Women described an atmosphere in which sexist jokes were constant and their opinions seldom taken seriously. The government paid little heed to addressing the impacts of this bigotry.

The inattention on the process, rather than only the outcome, frustrated planning, and with it the effort to deepen a social and economic justice agenda.[15] In many ways, the MAS administration reflected what anthropologist Mark Goodale describes as "ideological, historical and institutional fragments that were often in tension with one another."[16] This revolution in fragments led to often uncoordinated, overlapping, or isolated programming.

Borda recounted that as planning was sidelined by the MAS government and decisions concentrated at the top, "the ideologues and intellectuals in the Planning Ministry left in frustration, and slowly professionals and technocrats were incorporated who lacked political clarity and commitment."[17] Former minister of justice Casimira Rodríguez Romero recalled how technical staff in the ministry made proposals that differed little from the highly dysfunctional justice system already in place. "It was completely traditional. This was a warning to me that it would be an uphill battle to institute change."[18]

This was echoed by Peña, the former minister, who said that "technicians became a problem for us because often they didn't understand the ideological/political focus of our proposals and most of them came from previous governments. They just weren't prepared to accept the radical changes we proposed in rural areas—many of them had never even been to a rural community in their lives."[19]

## DECONSTRUCTING TRADITIONAL FRAMEWORKS

The MAS prioritized conceptual frameworks of governance that broke away from neoliberal economic and social models. Based on Indigenous practices, pluralism, and a sustainable relationship with community and earth, its ambitious goals encompassed decolonization, Vivir Bien, ("living well"), and "leading by obeying."

### DECOLONIZATION

According to Alberto Borda, "colonization has permeated all of our social structures." The commitment to dismantle that legacy led to the incorporation of the concept of decolonization into the 2009 constitution as key to the construction of a plurinational state. A further step was taken that year when the government created the Vice Ministry of Decolonization.[20] And in 2010, a Unit of Depatriarchalization was added as the two struggles were increasingly understood as linked, especially by Indigenous women, who argued that patriarchy is a colonial inheritance that needs to be dismantled during decolonization.[21]

Though a common understanding of the term "decolonization" has proven elusive, a strong contender comes from Guaraní educator Marcia Mandepora: "'Decolonization' means we need to stop valuing what is foreign and focus on what is ours. In practical terms, we have to confront racialized class inequalities, dismantle the patriarchal logic of colonial rule, and rethink the state itself, as it was designed to control Indigenous peoples and lands for resource extraction and labor."[22]

In 2010, the Vice Ministry promoted the Law against Racism and Discrimination, which designated October 12 as National Day of Decolonization. In 2012 it proposed a Law of Decolonization and Depatriarchalization, which was never enacted. Its ambitions were to decolonize education, healthcare, the justice system, the police, and the armed forces. For Vice Minister of Decolonization Félix Cárdenas, the goal is clear: decolonization does not involve a romantic return to the past, but rather a recuperation of ancient epistemologies. As he puts it, "The task is to make the state an expression of our identity and our traditions."[23]

Social psychologist Jenny Ybarnegaray Ortiz argues that MAS government orientation idealized pre-Colombian society, particularly that of the Andes.[24] This resonates for Guaraní activist Marilyn Carayuri. "We find that what is being offered as decolonization by the government is an increase in Indigenous perspectives from the highlands, rather than a focus on our own heroes and stories," she said.[25]

## VIVIR BIEN

"We live in a world that thinks that well-being stems only from economic well-being," said sociologist Jaime Zambrana. "*Homo economicus* is how modernity is conceptualized."[26] Vivir Bien ("living well")—Suma Qamaña (in Aymara), Sumaj Kausay (in Quechua), or Uxia siborikixhi (in Chiquitano)—is an attempt to craft an alternative to this worldview by integrating an Indigenous perspective into notions of well-being.[27] Juan Tellez worked to formulate the indicators for "the Vivir Bien paradigm" in the Ministry of Planning. He believes that Vivir Bien is based on "harmony, consensus, good governance, the prioritization of community values of self- and mutual respect, redistribution of wealth, and elimination of discrimination of all kinds within a framework of valuing diversity."[28] For Marcia Mandepora, Vivir Bien is also closely "bound to the ties Indigenous people have with their natural environment."[29]

With similarities to Bhutan's Gross National Happiness Index,[30] Vivir Bien is mentioned (but not defined) in Bolivia's 2009 constitution. It draws on the International Labor Organization's 1989 Convention 169 on tribal and Indigenous rights and the 2007 UN Declaration on the Rights of Indigenous Peoples. Renouncing capitalism, war, imperialism, and colonialism, Vivir Bien recognizes basic services as a human right and prioritizes local consumption and moderation.[31]

"Decolonial thinking questions the bases and purposes of knowledge production," writes Mandepora. "In the case of extractive activities, the challenge is the search for new economic models that lead to Vivir Bien . . . , rather than the endless commodification of people and nature."[32]

## LEADING BY OBEYING

Perhaps the thorniest of the alternative conceptual frameworks embraced by the MAS is the idea of "leading by obeying" (*mandar obedeciendo*), adapted from Mexico's Zapatista movement in Maya Indigenous communities in the southern state of Chiapas. It encompasses seven principles: serve others, not yourself; represent, don't replace; construct, don't destroy; obey, don't dictate; propose, don't impose; convince, don't conquer; descend, don't rise.[33] Writing about the Zapatistas, social scientist Shannon Speed sees this leadership style as one that "downplay[s] the role of the leaders themselves, and highlight[s] collective decision making and the subjection of individual leaders' power to the collective will."[34] This perspective was echoed by Petronila Mamani in El Alto during the 2019 election campaign when she said, "Evo isn't running for office, we are running him. It's us, the people, who make the decision that he will be president again."[35]

In highland Bolivia, leadership based on collective decision making and rotational leadership is prevalent in Indigenous communities and local peasant unions. The turnover of leadership is often annual, as governance is seen as an honor but also an onerous obligation and responsibility. For many lowland peoples including the Guaraní, leaders should act as representatives of the collective will.[36]

Anthropologist Thomas Grisaffi has observed that in Chapare coca-growing unions, the most salient aspect of local democracy is that leaders must respect the decisions of the grass roots. He describes how at monthly union meetings the doors are locked so no one can leave until consensus is reached, meaning that members can spend up to ten hours in discussion to arrive at a collective decision. Because of dense relationships of shared residence and/or kinship, leaders have little choice but to respect community decisions.[37]

However, while this local decision-making mechanism has been scaled up to the level of groups of communities (historically through the *ayllu*,[38] and more recently through regional *campesino* configurations) with varying degrees of success, it has always proven difficult at larger scales.[39] As a result, other influences such as historic patterns of patronage have cast a long shadow at departmental (state or province) and national levels, where power tends to be concentrated in leaders' hands.

This is not to say that the process is undemocratic. Leadership is accountable to the grass roots, which can overturn or push them out of its way if it disagrees strongly enough, as happened in El Alto during the 2003 Gas War.[40] As a result, political participation is deeply personalist, based on a more direct relationship and communication between ruler and ruled. In Evo's years as president, he was repeatedly asked to personally resolve disagreements involving his supporters; a delegate just would not do, even if she or he was a government minister.

Initial discussions about how to translate "leading by obeying" and social movement expectations of a participatory democracy (rather than a Western-style representative one) discarded the co-governance model that was in place for four years after the 1952 revolution between the Revolutionary Nationalist Movement (MNR) government and the Bolivian Workers Central (COB).[41] In the recently nationalized mines, worker control and comanagement had blossomed but quickly succumbed to clientelism because mining union leaders lacked the necessary technical knowledge to operate the mines and could be appointed only by the MNR, which then co-opted and controlled them.[42]

CONALCAM, the coalition set up by the MAS government during the 2006–7 Constituent Assembly to channel social movement input, fuctioned within the framework that Morales "ruled by obeying." In practice, however, argues political scientist Fernando Mayorga, Evo never accepted its recommendations for ministerial appointments or replacements.[43] The Unity Pact proposed its own social control mechanism during the Constituent Assembly that conceived oversight as a fourth branch of government, monitoring the other three.[44] Justice Vice Minister Rafael Puente described social control as "a central theme of our constitution, the birth certificate for the new country we want."[45] By the time the constitution was watered down by Legislative Assembly, citizens had lost their right to "participate" in decisions. Instead, they were to be "consulted."[46]

In 2013, the Law of Participation and Social Control passed. Ostensibly, grassroots organizations would now exert oversight for municipal, departmental, and national governments. In practice, participation was largely managed by government ministries or state entities. They decided which organizations were "recognized" as participants and then invited them to meetings with predetermined agendas.[47] Funding to operationalize the law was not mandatory, so entities such as the Central Bank fulfilled their obligations largely by making public presentations describing their operations.[48]

The concepts of decolonization, Vivir Bien, and leading by obeying gradually faded from most MAS discourse after the 2011 TIPNIS conflict that divided the country's Indigenous movements into pro- and anti-MAS factions. They were steadily replaced by a rhetoric that focused on the economic and political stability the MAS had brought. Ultimately, many elements of decolonization and Vivir Bien ran up against Bolivia's enduring role as a site of resource extraction in the global economy.

## INDIGENOUS AUTONOMY: PLURINATIONALISM'S BIG TEST

One of the 2009 constitution's most innovative features was its offer of increased autonomy to the country's Indigenous population. Unfortunately, of the estimated 140 of Bolivia's current 339 municipalities that contain more than 90 percent Indigenous people, only about two dozen have sought autonomy under these terms.[49] Of these, three—Charagua Iyambae in Santa Cruz, Uru Chipaya in Oruro, and Raqaypampa in Cochabamba—achieved full autonomy after years of clambering through considerable bureaucratic hoops. By 2019, five others had their autonomy statutes recognized, and an additional two were waiting for final approval.[50] It has been an uphill climb.

"What we want is to use these autonomy efforts together to reconstruct the Guaraní nation," explained Milton Chacay Guayupan, Vice Rector of the Indigenous University in the Chaco. "To do that, we're focusing on the municipal level for now, but with the vision that we will eventually construct an autonomous Indigenous region. It may take twenty years, but that is our goal."[51]

"The struggle is always about land and territory," said National Director of Indigenous Autonomy Gonzalo Vargas in 2017.[52] Since colonial times, Indigenous peoples have yearned for independence from governments who seized their lands. But as autonomy raises questions about national sovereignty, most efforts in Latin America have focused on a type of self-determination that fits within the juridical and political confines of the current liberal state.[53]

Autonomy requires a reconceptualization of the state as a complex of nations, a process that in Bolivia has occurred only at the most superficial of levels. While legally, autonomy can occur through three routes—municipal, ancestral territorial, or regional—the Morales government always emphasized conversion into municipalities. However, in a state that has been profoundly centralized since its founding in 1825, this shift is no small feat. But it is essential according to political scientist José Luis Exeni. "Without indigenous autonomy, there is no Plurinational state," he asserts[54]

"Indigenous people were always semi-autonomous in a political sense because there was so little state presence in rural areas. Indigenous people always say that they don't want to give up that autonomy, nor do they want to be subject to the state, but they do want a link with the government so that they can access resources. . . ," added Vargas. "So, what we are really constructing is a governmental administration. The challenge comes in training people in how to manage these resources."[55]

In 2017, the municipality of Charagua became Bolivia's first autonomous Indigenous campesino community, in no small part thanks to the efforts of the overarching Guaraní organization, the Guaraní People's Assembly (APG), which formed in the 1980s to represent Bolivia's fourth-largest Indigenous group.[56] Lowland Charagua is the country's largest municipality in terms of land area, a mostly flat scrubland with little rain and fierce sun.

Approximately 10 percent of Charagua's residents are Indigenous peoples from Bolivia's highland and valleys, who have migrated there since the 1950s, largely to work in commerce and transportation. "We're all a big mix around here," laughed Charagua's urban zone executive, José Fernando Menacho Amosquivar. "My father was a Quechua speaker from Sucre, but on my mother's side we're all Guaraní."[57]

For Vice Rector Chacay Guayupan, "Our biggest challenge is how we will articulate the Indigenous people with the non-Indigenous. We are contemplating undertaking a project of Guaranization—that means introducing collectively oriented ideas into the non-Guaraní population. We have lost a great deal of this perspective within our own communities as well, so we need to reeducate ourselves away from the increasing tendency toward individualism and verticality."[58]

Charagua's process began in mid-2009, when a referendum approved the switch. But it would take years to write the autonomy statutes, negotiate them with the central government, and hold another referendum to approve them, meaning Charagua did not declare autonomy until January 2017. As the first in the country, its process and experience is the most advanced to date.

Decision making in Charagua is realized through the Ñemboati Reta Assembly, which emphasizes collective decision making. It has twenty-seven members, half men and half women. In accordance with Guaraní tradition, there is no ultimate authority or leader, or even a rotation of power, but rather power is decentralized.

Charagua's position in the middle of Bolivia's gas belt makes issues of consultation and free, prior, and informed consent guaranteed by the 2007 UN Declaration of the Rights of Indigenous Peoples central to local autonomy.[59] While the 2009 constitution discusses consultation, it does not mention the right to consent. Nor do other laws. "The state doesn't want us to have this control over who can exploit our resources," explained Ñemboati Reta Assembly representative Marianela Baldelomar Davalos.[60] Free, prior, and informed consent was the first issue the Ñemboati Reta addressed, writing their own Framework Law of Consultation.[61]

Anthropologist Nancy Postero and political scientist Jason Tockman call the system in place in Charagua a "hybrid," arguing that local Guaraní leaders worked around the ambiguities in the 2009 constitution to advance their own goals of greater self-determination. "The Guaraní leaders who have guided this process have shown enormous patience and flexibility as they kept their long-term strategy and historical demands in view while acting tactically on every possible opening they saw," they write. They also acknowledge that a more complete type of autonomy will be extremely difficult to achieve, given that within it lies a challenge to national sovereignty.[62]

Beginning in 2009 the MAS government became more tentative about Indigenous autonomy, dispensing little assistance beyond the Ministry of Autonomy, which was downgraded to a vice ministry with a steep reduction in staff in January 2017. "Every year we receive less support from the state," said Baldelomar Davalos.[63]

Guaraní leaders are thinking beyond political autonomy. Vice Rector Chacay Guayupan argued: "We need to work on how to build an independent economy. It is not enough to have political autonomy; we need economic independence as well."[64]

Overall, full consent remains highly contested, even though Bolivia's process is among the most cutting edge in Latin America.[65] The experience in Charagua highlights how Indigenous autonomy has facilitated local Indigenous peoples governing themselves according to their own decision-making systems and values. "Finding our way is a very slow process," said Baldelomar Davalos, "but I think it is more important to work at a steady and thorough pace than to try and rush things through. We want to get it right, and not undermine processes of autonomy in other parts of the country."[66]

# UNRESOLVED CHALLENGES
## *EXTRACTIVISM: OLD HABITS DIE HARD*

Five hundred years of unremitting extraction of silver, tin, and more recently natural gas have left permanent scars on Bolivia's economic and political structure and natural landscape, as well as its collective imaginary. This pattern is widespread throughout Latin America, as the region has supplied Northern countries with natural resources for centuries.[67]

Extractivism has historically brought the local population few benefits, whether the country was run by Spanish or Bolivian elites or by the foreigners who controlled the export economy.

Bolivia repeatedly careened between boom-and-bust cycles that characterize mono-product economies with physical infrastructure such as roads and highways built to export primary materials.[68] Political scientists Luis Tapia and Marxa Chávez describe Bolivia's place in the world economy as a subordinate periphery.[69]

The MAS's goal of developing the country through expanded public infrastructure lured them down a well-trodden path that is in many aspects similar to one followed by their predecessors. Uruguayan social scientist Eduardo Gudynas calls this "neo-extractivism," a twenty-first-century model in which the state negotiates a larger share of the profits from mining, oil, and natural gas, which previously had almost entirely flowed to multinationals.[70]

Political scientist Steve Ellner rejects the tendency to equate neo-extractivism with neoliberalism, arguing that there are important differences between the Pink Tide governments' resource nationalism and that of the neoliberal and particularly the right-wing governments that preceded them.[71] He also takes issue with the idea that it is necessarily a bad strategy to use extractivism to fuel development and overcome extractivism itself. Rather, Ellner concurs with economists Alfredo Macías Vásquez and Jorge García-Arias, who contend that any effort to achieve structural change in Bolivia must confront the influence of global financial capital and its local counterparts, which Pink Tide governments have found themselves forced to negotiate with.[72]

It was an impossible task to break this five-hundred-year extractivist pattern in Bolivia's economy, politics, and society in just fourteen years, although many critics feel the MAS, like governments before them, were seduced by the relatively easy money extractivism brings rather than working diligently to create alternatives.[73] Bolivia is more dependent on extractive industries today than it was when Morales took office, and despite Evo's anti-imperialist rhetoric, foreign control over both hydrocarbons and mining multiplied during his time in office.[74] Unfortunately, critics on the left have rarely proposed alternatives that could come close to replacing the income from extractivism.[75]

The state-driven model, increasingly financed by Chinese capital, has had disastrous consequences for the physical environment and the lowland Indigenous peoples who depend on it.[76] In response to the critiques of the model, former vice president Álvaro García Linera wrote in 2012:

> It is our view ... that this criticism [of neo-extractivism] is best countered by meeting the urgent needs of the people, increasing the essential social benefits of the laboring classes and, on this basis, creating the cultural, educational and material conditions to democratize control of the common wealth ... and gradually overcoming extractivism. .... [This is] what we are doing as a government: generating wealth and redistributing it amongst the population; reducing poverty and extreme poverty; improving the educational status of the population. And parallel to all that, we are beginning industrialization.[77]

## MINING AND HYDROCARBONS: BONANZA AND CURSE

Beginning with the Conquest, the Spanish restructured Andean society to ensure labor for the mines at Potosí that supplied over half of Spanish silver and gold from the mid-sixteenth to mid-seventeenth centuries.[78] The Indigenous majority did not fare much better following independence in 1825, as mining and land-owning elites perpetuated the pattern, molding the country's politics and governments to suit their private interests. The tin and rubber booms in the late nineteenth and early twentieth century transformed both the country and its natural environment, causing enormous misery for workers in both industries.[79]

These experiences have contributed to the deep-seated public perception that the country has been exploited for the benefit of others, usually foreigners, condemning it to a preindustrial state where it is unable to compete against more developed economies.[80] Bolivians commonly refer to themselves as "beggars seated on a throne of gold."[81]

Even though mining has been a constant in Bolivia for over five hundred years, several estimates indicate that 90 percent of its total mineral wealth remain untouched. The current principal export in US dollar terms is gold, followed by zinc, lead, tin, silver, copper, tungsten, sulfur, potassium, borax, and semiprecious jewels. In 2017, 28 percent of Bolivia's exports came from mining.[82] While zinc, silver, tin, and lead dominate in the highlands, in the lowlands northeast of La Paz, artisanal gold mining in local rivers has become Bolivia's second most valuable export. Production is characterized by small-scale operations, largely outside government control, that produce highly toxic waste dumped into tributaries of the Amazon.[83]

Mining is split between the modern, capital-intensive multinational firms that run the largest operations, a shrunken state sector (whose tin mine at Huanuni is its largest), and hundreds of small cooperative mines. The multinational mines, which enjoy substantial returns on their investments, export the most but employ the least labor and contaminate less. They also provide safer working conditions than the cooperatives. The cooperatives, which now involve more miners than any other sector, often have working conditions similar to nineteenth-century mines in Northern countries, with high mortality and injury rates. Toxic dumping is widespread. However, their large numbers make them a political force to be reckoned with. In many respects, the cooperatives have taken the mining union militancy of the past and merged it with neoliberal capitalism in its most brutal form.

Cooperative miners repeatedly blocked passage of a mining law promised by the MAS since 2006 that sought to increase the state's share of royalties, and their taxes. A watered-down version finally passed in May 2014, which committed to providing these miners access to new mineral deposits, while stalling the controversial issue of raising their taxes and imposing penalties for environmental damage.

During the first Morales government, the cooperatives sometimes aligned with the MAS and at other times opposed them. After the contested October 2019 elections, they were among the first organizations not affiliated with the traditional elite to call on Evo to resign, even though some of the cooperative organizations later joined the resistance to the Áñez government.[84]

Since their discovery in the southeastern lowlands in the early twentieth century, first as oil and then decades later as natural gas, fossil fuels have shaped Bolivian politics. The country was the region's first to nationalize oil when it seized Standard Oil in 1937, followed by Mexico in 1938. Oil was nationalized again in 1969 during the left nationalist military government of Alfredo Ovando Candía.[85]

By the 1990s, natural gas was discovered to be more abundant than oil. Gas transformed the Chaco, the sleepy southeastern region where the major fields lie, primarily on ancestral lands of the Guaraní. While the bonanza delivered some financial benefits and jobs, it also brought environmental destruction, disruptive blasting and drilling near Guaraní communities, and large influxes of unattached male workers.[86]

The 2005 "nationalization" also injected new life into the much-reduced state hydrocarbons company, YPFB, turning it into a partner to multinational firms—especially those in Brazil and Argentina, where 80 percent of Bolivia's gas is currently exported.[87] Government revenues from natural gas exploded from approximately $500 million in 2006 to $6 billion by 2016.[88] This enabled the MAS government's public investment, but anthropologist Bret Gustafson cautions it also reinforced political and economic patterns that forestalled a more radical change.[89]

*Source: Eric H. Fox, Urban Design 4 Health*

Over the objections of environmentalists, in 2015, Bolivia passed a law that permits "the development of hydrocarbon exploration activities in the different zones and categories within protected areas" and specifies what companies should do if they want to exploit any "commercially viable discoveries" they encounter.[90] As a result, eleven of the country's twenty-two protected areas, which together encompass over twenty million hectares (almost fifty million acres), are now overlapped by oil and gas concessions. Much of this exploration is in the lowland Beni in the northeast, long considered by successive Bolivian governments to be "empty" despite the Indigenous peoples living there.[91] Then, in 2018, the Morales government announced it planned to explore introducing hydraulic fracturing projects.[92]

## INDUSTRIALIZATION

"Our economic recipe is to generate profits in natural resources, redistribute them, as well as develop a broader economic base through industrialization," explained Luis Arce in 2019, when he was finance minister.[93] The industrialization side of this equation has been a bumpy road, slowed by limited technical expertise, low worker productivity, insufficient transportation infrastructure, and Bolivia's lack of access to the sea. Often, the logic behind projects such as the construction of a paper plant in the intensely humid Chapare appeared driven by political rather than economic considerations. "All the machines rusted before they could get the plant operational," complained mechanic Carlos Ramos.[94]

Development of El Mutún, a huge iron ore deposit, was delayed repeatedly. Located in the Pantanal, the world's largest tropical wetlands that spills over from Brazil into eastern Santa Cruz, the Mutún project first appeared in the MAS government's 2007 National Development Plan and featured in every one since. That year, the MAS government negotiated a forty-year contract with India's Jindal Steel to exploit the site, but legal problems and inadequate infrastructure put the steel complex drastically behind schedule.[95] The project, even when fully operational, was designed to direct 90 percent of its production to relatively low-value-added pellet and sponge iron. In 2012, the deal fell apart among mutual accusations, and Jindal exited from the country, later winning a $22.5 million arbitration judgment against Bolivia.[96]

It took until January 2016 for a new contract to be negotiated with China's state-owned Sinosteel, including a loan to finance the plant's construction.[97] In April 2019, the first shipment of iron ore finally left for Argentina, while the rest of the facility is slated for completion by 2022, sixteen years after it began.[98]

In the Chapare, a fertilizer plant that cost almost $1 billion was constructed before markets and transportation infrastructure were secured.[99] Although it got off to a slow start, producing 6,372 tons for the national market in 2017, by 2018 this figure had soared to 265,258 tons, most of it destined for markets in neighboring countries. However, the plant stopped functioning when Morales was forced from office, and in 2020 Bolivia regressed to being a net importer of fertilizer rather than an exporter.[100] After the MAS won the elections in 2020, it took ten months and millions of dollars to get the plant operational again.[101]

Perhaps the biggest hopes for industrialization were pinned on lithium production—the alternative fuel for car batteries and consumer electronics. In 2008, the government broke ground on a pilot plant to refine lithium carbonate; ten years later, it struck a deal with a German company to build an integrated plant fabricating lithium compounds and battery components.[102] That agreement unraveled in early November 2019 over disputes about royalties, days before Morales fled the presidential palace.

Bolivia possesses an enormous supply of lithium, most of which lies in the spectacular Salar de Uyuni, the world's largest salt flat, now the country's major tourist attraction. But the lithium is isolated, hard to extract, and not as pure as that of its neighbors in the "lithium triangle," Argentina and Chile, which together are blessed with far greater expertise and infrastructure.[103] Many analysts doubt that Bolivia's effort will have much success.[104] There is also mounting evidence that lithium is not the magic bullet fuel that its promoters insist: environmental researchers worry about the enormous quantity of groundwater production requires and the chemical wastes generated during the refining process.[105] Meanwhile, lithium production is scaling up in countries that are Bolivia's potential customers.[106]

## FREE, PRIOR, AND INFORMED CONSENT

Bolivia's 2009 constitution and 2005 Hydrocarbon Law include some of the world's strongest language about the right to prior consultation for Indigenous peoples. These are reinforced in international human rights law, in particular the International Labour Organization's Convention 169 and the United Nations Declaration on the Rights of Indigenous Peoples. The concept that prior consultation involves consent, not merely consultation, appears six times in the UN declaration, and its prominence in other international documents and conferences makes it a centerpiece of global Indigenous rights norms.[107] Despite this, it is often unclear who is entitled to participate and how, as well as what participants can gain from the process.

As a policy, prior consultation under the MAS government has lacked clarity—about who is entitled to participate, how participation should be carried out, and its purposes. The result is that consultation has frequently been overlooked—most famously in the case of the road slated to run through the Indigenous territory TIPNIS[108]—or, in other situations, carried out unscrupulously and incompletely.[109] The uneven outcomes speak to the enormous economic pressures to get new extractive projects operational.[110]

Inclusive prior consultation has proven difficult to achieve for myriad reasons. Among them are differing interpretations of consultation and consent rights; large power asymmetries between the state, private corporations, and Indigenous communities; and Indigenous peoples' lack of technical knowledge and access to information.[111]

Consultation processes in Bolivia have mostly occurred in the southeastern gas lands. They have largely been initiated and controlled by the state, which determines when a consultation is required. "The Guaraní know that they have rights to a consultation, but even their leaders don't understand the process fully," explained José Luis Montero, a law student who interned with the Guaraní People's Assembly. "The government has failed to give them adequate training to participate," he asserted.[112] In general, those consulted "participate" in a process that excludes them from decision making, in which they answer questions about issues as defined by government professionals. As a consequence, Indigenous groups often express very little ownership of the process.[113]

Additional complications arise because the subject of consultations is collective, not individual. Because communities are not necessarily homogenous, internally democratic, or clearly bounded (either geographically or culturally), the consultation process itself can provoke or exacerbate existing social, cultural, and economic tensions. The principal division usually lies between community members who identify advantages to a growth in extraction and those who worry about the impact on their environment and culture.[114]

These rifts are often fostered by the multinational companies, on occasion with assistance from the Morales government, according to the indigenous organizations CONAMAQ and CIDOB.[115] Both governments and corporations have a pretty straightforward goal in prior consultations: to gain project approval as quickly as possible, in order to maximize tax revenues and profits. Indigenous communities' interests, however, are often more conflicted and complex, which can make them more vulnerable to outside manipulation.[116]

The process of prior consultation and hydrocarbon development are shaped by and also transform sociocultural patterns within Indigenous communities.[117] "Petroleum has changed the relationship of the Guaraní to money," said Montero. "Unfortunately, corruption is inevitable." Companies and the MAS government have often opted to pick and choose the leaders they work with, prioritizing those who are more open to their plans. Leaders with earlier consultation experience dominate decision making, often marginalizing monolingual Guaraní-speaking leaders.[118]

The Guaraní are cognizant of these pressures and have worked hard to counteract divisive practices and maintain unity in the context of both "their desire for inclusion in a hydrocarbon-based national development project and their experiences of dispossession," according to geographer Penelope Anthias.[119]

Despite these competing frameworks of what Anthias calls "hydrocarbon citizenship," the Guaraní are committed to trying to use the process to their advantage.[120] "One of our challenges is to supervise the process of prior consent, which hasn't been done well in the past," explains Assemblywoman Baldelomar Davalos. "For example, there has been no consultation on the big new road going through here. We want to make sure this doesn't happen in the future. We know that once the road comes through, the hydrocarbon companies won't be far behind."[121]

## THE RIFT BETWEEN ENVIRONMENTAL DISCOURSE AND PRACTICE

"Not only do human beings have rights, but Mother Earth should have them too," President Morales told the United Nations General Assembly on April 22, 2009. "The capitalist system has made the earth belong to human beings. Now it is time to recognize that we belong to the earth."[122] Three years later, the MAS government passed the Law of Mother Earth, which, for the first time in world history, granted rights to nature.

Words such as these played well for Morales on the international stage. But at home, the pressure to satisfy immediate economic needs through environmentally destructive extractive industries was huge. The long-standing demands of an impoverished population regularly trumped the small but insistent voices of the directly affected local Indigenous groups and a mostly middle- and upper-middle-class environmental movement. Perhaps unsurprisingly, by 2016, the Morales government had dropped most references to respect for Mother Earth.

The historical and present exploitation of Bolivia's considerable natural resources has been almost unparalleled: the Spanish colony's richest silver and gold mine for a century (Potosí); two of the world's largest silver mines (San Cristóbal and San Bartolomé); almost half the world's proven lithium reserves (Salar de Uyuni); and potentially the planet's largest iron ore mine (Mutún).

As a result, despite a relatively low population density, the principal environmental coalition, the Environmental Defense League (LIDEMA), argues that as much as half the country, is environmentally degraded.[123] Extractive agriculture—defined as farming that permanently impoverishes the land—in the form of agro-industrial soy production has roughly doubled since Morales took office. This has diminished the need for farm labor, a situation that geographers Ben McKay and Gonzalo Colque call "production exclusion."[124] There remains considerable potential for agricultural expansion, given that much of Santa Cruz's land is considered underutilized.

Bolivia, with the world's seventh-largest area of tropical forests, now suffers the highest rate of deforestation in South America.[125] Pesticide use has mushroomed, provoking destruction of fragile tropical soil structures, and eventual desertification. Morales's repeated international proclamations that his government would fulfill its international commitments for forest conservation drew outrage from Bolivia's environmentalists, who described such promises as at odds with actions on the ground.[126]

Brazilians and Mennonites are pushing large-scale soy farming northward.[127] "The most serious problem we face is not with small-scale colonizers from the highlands, but with large-scale farmers who use big machinery to clear-cut large swathes of land quickly. They destroy the forest at a rate we have never seen before," said Marcos Uzquiano, director of Madidi Park.[128]

Apolonia Rodríguez of the Sucre Association of Ecology (ASE) worries, "We are the tenth most biodiverse country in the world, but we are being devastated by uncontrolled forestry, mining, and hydrocarbon extraction, and ever-expanding soy cultivation." For her, "the MAS government has prioritized economic growth over everything else." Teresa Flores, formerly of the La Paz environmental organization Prodena, added, "We are deeply conflicted about these issues as a country."[129]

Uzquiano, who is from the Tacana Indigenous group, described how this conflict plays out in the context of the national parks:

Most lowland indigenous peoples understand the environmental crisis we are living—not just in Bolivia, but in the
whole world. But there is a large part of the population who
believe that the national parks are an imported idea—from
the gringos, from Europeans, and that the national parks are
there to safeguard resources for these foreigners in the future.
We have had people running for political office who say they
are going to fight against the national park because it leaves
us impoverished and doesn't allow us to develop. I come from
an Indigenous community, and I lived with this supposed poverty. But we have always lived fine; of course, we had needs,
but we never blamed the park or the preservation of the forest
for not having these fulfilled. But in the west—in the cities
and in the Altiplano—there is a different mentality. For those
who come here to log or mine, often with a lot of money, the
existence of a national park is a nuisance because they can't
exploit its resources.[130]

At the 2009 UN Climate Change Conference in Copenhagen,
Evo launched a passionate plea for climate change reparations for
low-income countries, arguing that Northern countries are disproportionately responsible for the impacts suffered by Southern
nations.[131] After Bolivia's proposal to make access to water a
universal right was approved by the UN, the General Assembly
named Morales "world hero of Mother Earth."[132]

Bolivia, like most countries in the Global South, is experiencing accelerating impacts from climate change. Since the 1970s,
glaciers in the Andes have melted at a rate unseen in the past
three hundred years, shrinking between 30 and 50 percent.
From Colombia to Chile, this melt affects tens of millions of
people who rely on glacial water for drinking, irrigation, and
electricity.[133]

Climate change is devastating rural communities as well as
threatening to destroy their livelihoods.[134] In 2016, the country's second-largest lake, Lake Poopó, dried up, a consequence
of drought, diversion of water for mining and agriculture, and
climate change. "We miss our lake very much," said an elderly
woman from one of the Andes' oldest Indigenous groups as she

gazed out at its salty and dusty remains. "We used to be able to live on the lake, on reed islands, not on the land like we do now."[135]

The chasm between the MAS discourse of protecting Indigenous peoples and its practice of favoring extraction-based economic development split wide open in 2011 when the government announced plans to build a road through a national park between the northeastern lowland Beni and the country's main highway. The road was to traverse an Indigenous territory, the TIPNIS, inhabited by Mosetén, Tsimané, and Yuracaré peoples, who were already threatened by expanding logging and coca cultivation. "Uncontrolled forestry is almost impossible to prevent," said Dr. Raúl Quispe, who worked in the region for ten years. "Loggers illegally chop down trees within Indigenous reserves and then float them downriver. They don't even use the entire tree."[136]

No prior consultation was carried out by the Bolivian government.[137] After the police attacked a march protesting the planned construction, repudiation of the project spread across the country, forcing the government to postpone the road indefinitely, although it repeatedly discussed reinitiating it. The TIPNIS dispute proved a turning point, fracturing the Indigenous Unity Pact as well as alienating many middle- and upper-middle-class supporters from the MAS. [138]

The country's dependence on resource extraction only intensified after the TIPNIS controversy. Large-scale hydroelectric projects in lowland areas were devised with the goal of converting Bolivia into a regional energy hub. Local Indigenous peoples and their allies organized blockades of planned dams at El Bala and El Chepete that will flood the Rio Beni, displace riverine communities, and alter the ecosystem of Madidi National Park, one of the most biologically diverse places on earth, as well as one of the world's largest protected areas.[139] After Morales was ousted, the plans were shelved.[140]

But it is unfair to say that the MAS government ignored all environmental concerns. For example, a fifty-megawatt solar power plant in Oruro is expected to account for half of the electricity consumption of the 265,000 people who live in the city. It began limited production in September 2019.[141]

As the middle-class population flourished, so did the number of cars choking city streets. In response, in 2011 the MAS-controlled legislature declared a yearly "Day of the Pedestrian and Cyclist in Defense of Mother Earth." On this day, unique in the world, all nonemergency vehicles are forbidden from circulating. The idea stemmed from a project that started in 1999 in Cochabamba, one of Latin America's most polluted cities.

"Pedestrian Day gives us a great opportunity to do environmental education about climate change and protecting the environment, as people enjoy it so very much," said Soledad Delgadillo of the municipal government. "Air pollution in Cochabamba drops by 60 to 70 percent, because 70 percent of our air contaminants come from vehicles."[142]

## CONCENTRATION OF POWER

"Renewing leadership is absolutely necessary," said Vice President García Linera in an interview just before the October 2019 election. "We made a big mistake in not training new leaders sooner."[143] Indeed, this error arguably cost the MAS the election, paved the way for a right-wing takeover that brought repression against working-class and Indigenous peoples, and discredited Morales among a significant section of the Bolivian population as well as internationally.

The leadership issues the party faced were widely recognized both inside and outside the MAS. "The MAS needs to find a new leaders as difficult as that is going to be," said political scientist Fernando Mayorga in late 2019.[144]

The question is, why was it so complicated?

While the tendency has been to cast blame on Evo the individual, as well as on the group surrounding him, in essence the difficulties mirror structural problems. In a presidential system, a division of powers is essential to provide the needed checks and balances. Bolivia has never had much of an independent, or even functional, judiciary, meaning these problems were not specific to the Morales government. With the MAS controlling two-thirds of Plurinational Legislative Assembly from 2009 to 2019, that body, while more diverse than in its entire history, was largely subject to the president's control and agenda.

Morales successfully embodied the MAS's two fundamental currents: he is a strong nationalist, and he draws on Indigenous roots. His background is Aymara and Quechua, and as a peasant trade unionist, but he is not owned by any of these movements. He is both charismatic and politically astute.

The political style ascribed to Morales is prevalent in Latin America both currently and historically, and it has been described as the region's first homegrown regime model.[145] While the approach is often derided pejoratively as nothing more than populism, political scientist Francisco Panizza argues that it is a mistake to posit a dichotomy between representative democracy and a more direct and participatory version. He argues instead that complementary forms of political representation, including populism, exist in every society.[146]

In the view of Juan Pablo Luna, also a political scientist, such leadership styles can be interpreted as a creative response to inequality and conservative dominance, particularly in settings where political parties are fragile and formal political representation low.[147] Nonetheless, according to some definitions of populists, Morales has displayed characteristics of one, particularly when he joined the ranks of leaders (on both the left and right) with poor track records of leaving power willingly.

Political scientist John Crabtree cautions about labeling Evo a classic populist, demonstrating that bottom-up social mobilization remains alive and well in today's Bolivia. As a result, he argues, the state, while larger and more intrusive than in the past, was unable to overlook or control social organizations to the extent that traditional populist leaders do.[148]

Morales's presidency perpetuated the tragedy of Bolivian history according to political scientist Manuel Suarez: every time a nationalist and popular project has advanced, it has been derailed by a domineering style of leadership. He characterizes Morales's governments as having one foot in the modern world and the other in *caudillismo*, a governing style that prioritizes a direct relationship between the leader and the people, and deftly deploys the image of a sovereign oppressed people with a shared identity.[149] Evo is, in a classic sense, a *caudillo*, pushing anyone he saw as a threat out of his way, beginning in his early days as a coca union leader in the Chapare.[150] Mayorga attributes a good part of his success to a skill in deploying radical rhetoric to satisfy his political bases, while taking moderate positions while governing.[151]

Over Morales's almost fourteen years in office, power was steadily concentrated in the executive branch and a small loyal group surrounding him. Suárez describes this group as closed, based on personal ties and selected by Evo, who retained decision-making power.[152] One ex-minister described how after the 2014 electoral win, cabinet meetings were torturous because the president would deliver a humiliating dressing-down to individual ministers in front of the group. As a result, criticism and suggestions were muffled, reinforcing top-down policy decisions.

Evo worked hard—usually sixteen-hour days—and expected everyone else to as well. A joke went around La Paz that no marriage could survive a job in the MAS government, and few did; the irony was that those working in a government oriented toward the needs of communities did not have time to take care of their own community. According to one anonymous MAS employee, "Evo was up working at 5 a.m. and would often finish at 1 a.m. Whatever you think about him, he genuinely cared about the country, which was reflected in how hard he worked. But it was exhausting trying to keep up. None of us had lives."[153]

Sociologist Jaime Zambrana described concentrated decision making throughout the MAS: "The Chapare union leaders follow the party line and grant personal favors to ensure loyalty. This problem goes to the heart of what we are struggling with—this verticalism and caudillismo has undermined the 'process of change.' You simply can't create a true government of social movements if they are controlled through a *caudillista* system."[154]

Former vice president García Linera insisted early in the MAS government that this concentration of power was inconsequential. Governing "from below," he argued, requires "an elevated concentration of power in the president but with broad participation of social movements."[155] Not only has the MAS proven incapable of consolidating itself as other parties born in social movements have, such as the Workers' Party (PT) in Brazil, but it inherited a fragmented and personalized state apparatus. These factors compound its internal difficulties in establishing decentralized decision making, which have been further aggravated by a lack of organization and coordination.[156]

These hurdles meant that innovation never became so deeply institutionalized within government structures that they could not be easily reversed. What is remarkable is that with such flimsy internal democracy, the MAS nonetheless successfully integrated sectors of society that had never before had a voice.[157]

Morales's expulsion left a vacuum that empowered the grass roots to reclaim much of their agency, and for the first time, a faction within the party operated relatively independently of Evo. Nevertheless, he still headed the MAS 2020 election campaign. The final decision on who would be the MAS candidates for the 2020 election—Luis Arce for president and David Choquehuanca, ex–minister of foreign relations, for vice president—was made by Evo and his circle exiled in Buenos Aires. This provoked tensions with the MAS's grassroots because they wanted Choquehuanca as the presidential candidate, accompanied by young coca leader Andrónico Rodríguez. But despite their initial disapproval, they grudgingly approved the Arce-Choquehuanca ticket in the interests of unity.

The absence of strong political parties compounds these problems. Bolivian political parties tend to ebb and flow with their leaders' rise and fall from power. The last time a leadership transition occurred within a major political party was in 1956 when Víctor Paz Estenssoro passed the baton on to Hernán Siles Suazo. The challenge persists of how to construct a political process where, as LGBT activist David Aruquipa describes, "the ego of the leader to maintain power doesn't become more important than the political project of social and economic justice."[158]

Climate activist Pablo Solón, who served as Bolivia's UN representative, observed in 2016:

> We continued with a hierarchical state structure from the past.... The concept of "The Leader" or "the big boss" was an extremely serious error from the beginning ... at first committed under the pressure of circumstance.... Added to [this] was the conspiracy and sabotage of the Right and imperialism, which forced us to close ranks many times in an acritical way. ... Obsequiousness was prioritized and criticism was treated like the plague, [and] ... strengthened the delusion that the process of change involving millions of people depended on a pair of individuals.[159]

Morales, along with a small entourage, achieved cohesion through a combination of power and patronage, assigning the MAS party and the legislative branch, now run largely by women, a minor role in decision making. The tendency toward marginalization of social movements was both a cause and result of this process.

## CONCLUSIONS

The economic and political metamorphosis promised by MAS has been curtailed by the inherent constraints facing a small landlocked country whose economy has been driven by extractivism in service of foreigners for five hundred years. The situation in which Bolivia finds itself is profoundly contradictory: in its current struggle against underdevelopment and poverty, sustainability and environmental protection have been pushed to the back burner.

As dependence on foreign capital has escalated, local Indigenous rights and environments have come under increased threat. Bolivia renegotiated the terms of extraction in its favor, using the arguments of resource nationalism. But extractivism for the social good is, as it always has been, a slippery slope too often used to justify the destruction of lands and peoples. However, as valid as many of the criticisms of the extractivist model perpetuated by the MAS are, alternative macroeconomic solutions are scarce, while the structural, path-dependent obstacles remain enormous.

Gregoria Siles cries over the coffin of her son, who was killed in Sacaba.
Copyright 2019, Thomas Becker

Tending the memorial to those killed in Sacaba. Copyright 2019, Marcelo Pérez del Carpio

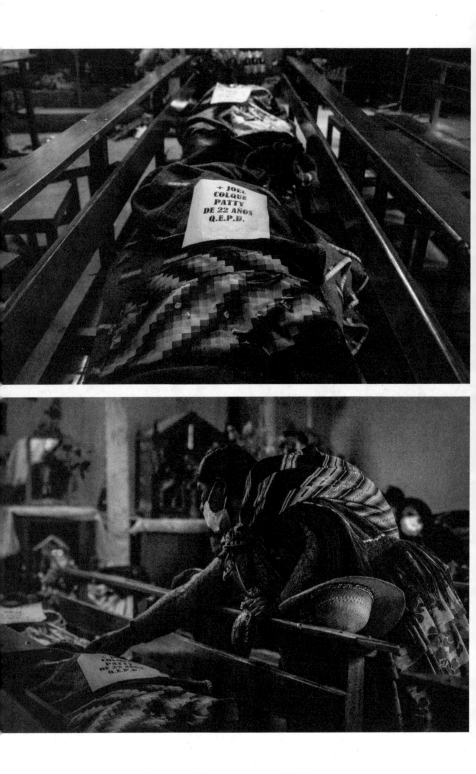

Bodies line the San Francisco de Asís Parish following the Senkata massacre. Copyright 2019, Marcelo Pérez del Carpio

A woman mourns over a coffin at the San Francisco de Asís Parish in Senkata. Copyright 2019, Marcelo Pérez del Carpio

Women seated at the Huallyani bridge, site of the Sacaba massacre. The graffiti reads: "Death is always for the people. Justice is only for the rich" and "It wasn't a confrontation, it was a massacre." Copyright 2020, Thomas Becker

Woman makes an offering for those killed in the Senkata massacre. Copyright 2020, Thomas Becker

Families of those killed in Senkata hold photos of the victims outside the San Francisco de Asís Parish. Copyright 2020, Thomas Becker

"Our struggle is without bullets," reads a mural outside of San Francisco de Asís Parish.
Copyright 2020, Thomas Becker

Families create a mesa for those killed in the Senkata Zone on All Saints Day.
Copyright 2020, Thomas Becker

Armored vehicles block a funeral procession for those killed in Senkata.
Copyright 2019, Marcelo Pérez del Carpio

Sketch of a mural in Leonel Jurado Pajsi's notebook that led police to arrest him for "seditious"
activity. Copyright 2019, Thomas Becker

The arrest of Mauricio Jara, charged with sedition for calling Interim President Áñez a "coup leader."
Copyright 2020, Guider Arancibia Guillén

# PART III: THE AFTERMATH

## CHAPTER 5

# "BLACK NOVEMBER"

Jeanine Áñez stood before a sea of cameras in Plaza Murillo, in front of the presidential palace, brandishing a Bible slightly larger than her torso.[1] "The Bible has returned to the government palace," she declared in her first proclamation as interim president.[2] Áñez was flanked by her political allies—light-skinned elites who more closely resembled the Spanish who conquered the country with Bible in hand centuries before than the country's Indigenous and *mestizo* majority. "Glory to God!" they shouted as cameras flashed.[3]

Police restrained the Indigenous protestors who crowded into the plaza. Many were Morales supporters. Others joined them to express their concern about the affront to democracy unfolding in real time as an unelected official with a racist past seized power. Demonstrators shouted, "Coup plotter!" and "We want democracy!" But their calls were drowned out by the chants of Áñez's defenders. "Fuck Pachamama!" her supporters yelled.[4]

Like US president Donald Trump's infamous Bible photo op in front of St. John's Church during the 2020 Black Lives Matter protests, Áñez's performance was anything but subtle. She was signaling to her evangelical base that Indigenous rule had come to an end. Morales had previously banned the Bible from government ceremonies and had removed certain colonial and Christian imagery from the palace, installing Indigenous artwork in their place. "The opposition is using God to justify the mistreatment of people,

141

of violence, of racism," said MAS deputy Brígida Quiroga, who was one of dozens who went into hiding after Áñez took power.[5]

The fifty-two-year-old ultraconservative Christian described her new role as "something God put in my path."[6] She had branded Indigenous religious rites "satanic," referred to Evo Morales as a "savage,"[7] and suggested that genuine Indigenous people would not wear jeans or tennis shoes.[8] Áñez had worked as a media personality, attorney, and eventually senator from the Amazonian cattle-ranching region of the Beni. Her husband, Héctor Hernando Hincapié Carvajal, is a right-wing politician from Colombia allied with former president Álvaro Uribe.[9]

Áñez is part of the conservative Democratic Social Movement (MDS) party, which garnered just 4 percent of the national vote in 2019, with Áñez winning her party's only Senate seat. Most Bolivians had no idea who she was when she was named president. Her swearing-in ceremony unfolded in a nearly empty Senate as the MAS senators, who controlled two-thirds of the seats, were absent—in no small part because they feared for their safety—and, thus, failed to provide the necessary quorum.

## THE CHANGING OF THE GUARD

The day after Áñez assumed power, she designated a new cabinet comprised almost exclusively of business elites from the eastern part of the country. They too took their oath of office in front of a large Bible as Áñez made speeches accompanied by an aide carrying a cross.[10]

All but one of her new ministers were critics of Evo Morales. Despite stating that she sought to be a "democratic tool of inclusion and unity," initially Áñez did not appoint a single Indigenous person to her new government.[11] After a widespread uproar, Áñez named a Pentecostal Indigenous woman, Martha Yujra Apaza, as minister of cultures and tourism the following day. Her new job did not last long, as the Áñez government subsequently dissolved her ministry to the dismay of artists of all kinds.

Perhaps the most consequential appointment was the minister of the interior, fifty-seven-year-old Arturo Murillo. Often referred to as Áñez's henchman, Murillo was a business owner and senator from Cochabamba known for his hot temper and far-right views. In 2015, a criminal court sentenced him to prison for two years for falsifying records that he utilized in his run for political office.[12] He never served time.

As senator, Murillo was constantly on the attack. Leftists, the MAS party, coca farmers, and women were favorite targets. When discussing the issue of abortion before Legislative Assembly, he told women, "Kill yourselves . . . commit suicide, do whatever you want . . . but not to a life that doesn't belong to you."[13]

During Murillo's first televised speech as minister, he promised to "hunt" former officials, describing a former minister as an "animal." He said foreigners, particularly those from countries like Cuba and Venezuela, should "start running because we are going to catch them."[14]

Notably absent from Áñez's cabinet was a key player in the coup, Luis Fernando Camacho. The right wing's shooting star, Camacho had disappeared from the center of the political landscape as fast as he had appeared. But his ideology and allies nonetheless found a home in the new government when Áñez designated Camacho's "communications advisor," Luis Fernando López Julio, as minister of defense. López was an important player in the forced removal of Morales, serving as the liaison between Camacho's father and the military.[15] Camacho later signaled that the appointment was López's reward for the role he had played.[16]

Áñez also appointed Camacho's lawyer, Jerjes Justiniano, to the post of minister of presidential affairs. Justiniano was part of the secret meetings that selected Áñez as president, but his tenure as minister lasted only a few weeks. He was driven to step down over alleged abuse of his new political position to curry favors for clients, including one who stood accused in the rape of a minor.[17]

## THE TINDERBOX IGNITES

Jeanine Áñez's appointment to the presidency set off a cascade of marches throughout the country. On one side were *pititas*, some of whom took to the streets to support Áñez, others to oppose Evo's return. While many marched peacefully, denouncing alleged abuses during Morales's presidency and his disrespect for the constitution and 2016 referendum, a number burned the *wiphala* (the Indigenous flag), yelled racist slogans, and committed acts of violence, especially against Indigenous people.

In Cochabamba, *motoqueros* (motorcyclists), vigilante youth resembling the neofascist Proud Boys in the United States and allied with the Áñez government, patrolled the streets and attacked pro-Morales supporters and Indigenous people, especially *señoras de pollera*—Quechua and Aymara women who are easily recognizable by their traditional dress.[18] A market vendor in a town outside Cochabamba said that after the coup, "motorbikes drive by and hit us. They call us *indios*. They want to finish us off and get rid of us."[19]

The majority of the protests following Áñez's installment, however, were organized by those opposed to her unelected regime. Thousands of Indigenous demonstrators marched from the mountainous highlands and jungle lowlands into the main cities, with between fifty and one hundred thousand descending into La Paz alone during Áñez's first days in office.[20] The Bolivian Workers Central (COB) and the Unified Confederation of Bolivian Peasants' Unions (CSUTCB) called for nationwide strikes, while neighborhood councils mounted vigils and initiated the traditional tactic of road blockades in El Alto.[21] Garbage piled up in city streets because of shortages of gasoline.

Demonstrators shut down central La Paz and blockaded roads into the capital, chanting, "There was no fraud, just a coup d'état." A middle-class, middle-aged woman who said she had no political affiliation prepared food for the marchers streaming in from the countryside. "We feel like we've gone back forty or fifty years in a week," she said.[22]

As the protests spread, tanks and lines of police officers built a barrier several blocks deep around the presidential palace and government buildings. They shot tear gas and rubber bullets, scattering demonstrators. Arrested protestors were accused of being Cuban or Venezuelan terrorists, drug traffickers, or, even worse for many of the state forces, MAS supporters.

Police arrested Paola Paniagua, a young teacher from La Paz who demonstrated after witnessing attacks on Indigenous women. Once they had her and other protestors in custody, they tortured them and called them racist names. Paniagua was placed in a cell alone, where a lieutenant threatened her. "I can rape you," he said. "You have no one here. There's no one to see." She felt momentary relief when another high-level official arrived, but he too terrorized her: "I know your face. I'll see you in the street and you know what's going to happen. Outside, we are in groups and we're going to shoot you. We'll find you and kill you, *sediciosa* [seditious person]."[23]

On November 13, Senate president Adriana Salvatierra endeavored to open a parliamentary session on the crisis but was intercepted by police and attacked by pro-Áñez protestors.[24] Salvatierra held a press conference shortly after, hoping to find a constitutional solution in the increasingly violent climate. "After the attack, I have no guarantee that I can fulfill our legislative responsibilities," she said.[25]

That same day, in La Paz, tens of thousands of protestors organized a *cabildo*, a large outdoor meeting, in Plaza San Francisco to discuss how to resist the new regime.[26] Some called for a nationwide strike. Others wanted to march to the palace to demand Áñez's resignation. Still others highlighted the need to protect themselves from the wave of racism that was inundating the country.[27]

In El Alto, police, who days earlier had been filmed ripping the wiphala off their uniforms, patrolled the streets, using force to disperse meetings and blockades. "We were gathered around in a circle when police came up to us on their motorbikes," said Aymara high school student Mariela. "After throwing gas, a police officer grabbed the hair of a señora de pollera and started dragging her while driving the bike. . . . The neighbors grabbed their babies and ran because they were choking on gas."

Mariela was marching against the growing racist violence, not necessarily to support the return of Morales. "We are not *masistas*," she said of her group. "We are not even demanding Evo return. People cried when Evo left because they were frightened about our future and how we would be treated."[28] Mariela's fears materialized only days later when she and other Indigenous women were detained and abused by state forces.

Indigenous rights activist Iván Apaza also took issue with the opposition's attempts to label protestors as MAS supporters:

> It's not the masista who blocks the roads. It's not the masista who is furious about the racist offense of burning of the wiphala, for the indifference, the hypocrisy, for the paternalism. No, a thousand times no. Understand. It's not the masista who is in the streets. It's an entire society of migrants from Aymara territory who are mobilizing. In this Aymara city, it is the veterans of 2003 (the Gas War). It's the orphans who lost their parents because of government bullets by those who now propose "democracy." It's not the masista, it's *el alteño* who is fighting. It's the Aymara.[29]

Over the next week, protests exploded all over the country, with demonstrators barricading at least sixteen highways at ninety blockade points.[30] Áñez ignored calls for negotiations; instead, she deployed the military to suppress the marchers. The result was bloodshed.

## SACABA: "THE PEOPLE DIDN'T HAVE WEAPONS; THEY HAD BABIES"[31]

On Friday, November 15, thousands of *campesinos* from the Chapare set out on a several-day march to La Paz to oppose the appointment of Áñez. The protest was organized by the Six Federations of the Tropics of Cochabamba, the country's largest aggregation of coca growers, which is fiercely loyal to Evo

Morales, who has headed the organization for decades. The march was slated to join protestors in the city of Cochabamba who had already begun mobilizing to travel to La Paz.

Though many participated to demand Morales's reinstatement, the stated goal was to advocate for Indigenous rights. "They treat us like animals. They insult us and hit us because of our [traditional] clothes," stated Margarita Solís, a Quechua-speaking woman from a small village in the Chapare. "I'm from the countryside. They want us to stay there. I don't have the right to enter the city. That's why I joined the march."[32]

Coca growers are regularly denigrated in the Bolivian press and conservative public opinion as violent drug traffickers, when in reality the majority are peasant farmers who grow the leaf, with some involved in the lowest rungs of the drug trade. Coca grower leadership agreed before the march that participants must remain nonviolent.[33] Protestors primarily carried *aguayos* (Indigenous carrying cloths) packed with food, coca, and clothing, as well as the multicolored wiphala flag on sticks.[34] *Petardos* (firecrackers), traditionally used in Bolivian protests, were to be limited.[35]

Just after lunchtime, the protestors passed through Sacaba, a town east of the city of Cochabamba. At the Huayllani bridge, a cordon of masked police officers and military vehicles, including tanks and camouflaged soldiers armed with high-powered weapons, blocked their progress. A military plane flew back and forth overhead, while a helicopter with armed soldiers in the door swooped low, circling the demonstrators. "It looked like a war zone," said one protester.[36]

The officers at the front informed the marchers that they could proceeded in thirty minutes if they stripped off their gas masks and deposited them, along with their wiphalas, on the ground.[37] The protestors complied. The police then announced through a megaphone that women should come to the front.[38]

Sheila Pérez, a Sacaba resident working at a nearby store, was dubious about the police invitation. "I heard police tell the people 'Be patient, you will go through.' The people even clapped for the police," she recounted.[39] At the same time, the police and military began moving in additional weapons and personnel reinforcements.[40]

Suddenly and without warning, police fired off tear gas. "It was horrible. There were women with babies and grandmothers there," recalled Pérez. Without their gas masks, demonstrators were unprepared.[41] People fell to the ground, choking, while others raced to find refuge. "There was nowhere to escape," remembered Abraham Cuiza. "People were vomiting. The women in front were collapsing. I saw moms with babies on their back on the ground choking.... This scared me."[42]

When the barrage of gas finally died down nearly an hour later, demonstrators believed the attacks were over. Again, without warning, soldiers started firing, this time with live bullets. "It was like a war movie when they started shooting," stated Julia Vallejas, a local vendor.[43]

Eyewitnesses reported that those who attempted to reach the injured were targeted. "I had the hand of a person I was helping and [a soldier] shot my eye. And now here I am," stated Dionisio Gamarra from his hospital bed the day after the shootings.[44]

Soldiers chased protestors who fled. Rodolfo Larico Quispe sought shelter in a nearby home after being shot in the neck. State forces broke into the house, assaulting the people inside, including elderly people hiding there. "I heard them beat my friends, saying, 'Fucking dogs, Indians. Why were you coming to the city?' . . . The police dragged the others away. I didn't know where they went," Rodolfo recounted through tears.[45]

Soldiers pursued 56-year-old Gregoria Siles, who dashed into a house when the shooting began. In the commotion, she lost sight of her son Omar. Soldiers found Gregoria hiding under a table. They dragged her out of the house and brutally beat her, crushing her arm before stealing her money. Gregoria managed to escape and staggered to a nearby hospital, which was overflowing with wounded people.

While she was receiving treatment, she saw something on television that she relives daily: soldiers had shot and killed Omar, her only son. Sobbing, Gregoria fled the hospital, no longer concerned about her broken arm. Nurses gave her slippers because she had lost her shoes when the soldiers attacked her.

Over the next few hours, state forces continued to assault the protestors. The desperate and frightened marchers tried to pick up the injured, but the few taxis and ambulances that could get near the site of the massacre were overwhelmed by the deluge of casualties.

Abel Colque recalled that state forces shot the four people next to him before he was hit in the foot with a bullet. Demonstrators quickly carried him to a nearby ambulance. Because the back was full of bodies, the demonstrators crammed him and others in the front. Abel remembers, "A third injured person was stacked on top of us. He was shot in the chest three times. He bled all over us." Despite the gruesome scene, all Abel could think about was the children and elderly he saw dodging bullets, hoping that they were not among those heaped up in the back of the vehicle.[46]

"Military tanks arrived and sprayed water to remove the blood," stated Marco Paz Fernández, a bystander who witnessed the massacre. "I saw soldiers looking for bullets on the ground and picking them up. . . . The police tried to clean up the evidence."[47]

By the end of the day, Áñez's fourth in office, state forces had killed at least 10 and injured over 120 protestors and bystanders.[48] All casualties were Indigenous; not a single police officer or soldier was harmed.[49] In what became a standard response to criticisms of human rights violations, Interior Minister Arturo Murillo blamed the MAS party and protestors for the deaths, accusing the victims of shooting themselves.[50]

Almost immediately, the government was condemned internationally, accused of planning an attack using lethal force. The day before the Sacaba massacre, the Áñez administration had proclaimed Supreme Decree 4708, which granted immunity from criminal responsibility to soldiers.[51] After former and current special rapporteurs from the United Nations and the Inter-American Commission on Human Rights (IACHR) published a

letter questioning the decree's legality, the interim government
was forced to repeal it.[52] Nonetheless, Áñez sought to cement her
relationship with the armed forces a week later by channeling
them US$5 million for "equipment."[53]

## SENKATA: "THE SOLDIERS SHOT US LIKE DOGS AND THEN THEY BLAMED US"[54]

Following the Sacaba killings, the protests against the Áñez government skyrocketed, particularly in Bolivia's "rebel city," El Alto.
According to resident Iveth Saravia, "We originally protested to
demand respect for the wiphala and *cholitas*.[55] After the Sacaba
killings, this grew to calling for a trial of responsibilities and
Áñez's resignation."[56]

Demonstrators piled up rocks, tires, and tin roof panels at
intersections on the major arteries connecting El Alto with La
Paz. The Council of Peasant Federations of the Yungas of La Paz
(COFECAY) and other unions marched through the Ceja,[57] El
Alto's central business district, demanding Áñez's resignation,
while students from the Public University of El Alto (UPEA) organized *cabildos*.[58]

A main location for vigils was in front of the Senkata natural
gas plant in the city's southern district. The plant had served as
a key site of protest for decades because of its strategic position
on a major highway and as the main supplier of fuel and cooking
gas to La Paz. Paola Febrero, a human rights activist based in El
Alto, explained that "poor and humble people use the plant as a
way of negotiating with the government."[59]

During the 2003 Gas War, demonstrators blocked cisterns
from exiting the plant to spotlight then-president Sánchez de
Lozada's violent attacks on protestors. During the Morales administration, demonstrators assembled in front to press for expansion of water and sewage services. Now, protestors were
utilizing the plant to highlight abuses carried out by Áñez's transitional government.

Residents from the Senkata neighborhood launched vigils from the start of Áñez's presidency, but the number of participants multiplied dramatically after the attacks in Sacaba. As the demonstrations intensified and cooking gas became scarce, people in the neighborhood worried about government retaliation. At cabildos, neighbors expressed fears that a massacre like the one in Sacaba was imminent.

On Saturday, November 16, police gassed demonstrators near the plant.[60] Two days later, the government sent a caravan of tanks and other military vehicles to install soldiers inside the plant itself, where they were stationed for the night. The following day, only four days after the Sacaba slaughter, the soldiers carried out Áñez's second massacre in her first week in office.

Between 9 a.m. and 11 a.m. on November 19, soldiers began firing at the hundreds of protestors. Like in Sacaba, the military started with gas, creating an atmosphere of total confusion. Erika Mamani, a local bystander, raced from her house with a first aid kit to help the injured. "I had never seen anything like that. There was so much gas. Everyone was suffocating," she recalled.[61]

Soldiers shot gas into people's homes. "Grandmothers and children were fleeing from their houses. . . . It was horrible," recounted David Laura, who was on his way to the local bank.[62] Residents broke their own windows and poured out into the streets to avoid the gas. Witnesses reported that soldiers burst into the empty homes and climbed onto roofs to shoot at civilians.[63]

The soldiers then started shooting live bullets. Like the military forces four days earlier, they gave no warning. As protestors and bystanders ran "like crazy" from the bullets,[64] a helicopter fired at them from overhead.[65]

As in Sacaba, soldiers attacked people helping the injured. Soldiers shot 24-year-old Yosimar Choque Flores, who had run into the line of fire and moved four injured people, but as he was dragging a fifth woman to a side street, a soldier shot him in the arm, striking an artery. "People had no guns, no dynamite, nothing. Just sticks," he later said. "I didn't even see them throw rocks at the military."[66]

Antonio Ronald Quispe Ticona was also assisting people when the military shot him. As the helicopter sprayed bullets, Antonio jumped on top of two people to shield them, and was killed. Antonio's sister Gloria said her brother's death devastated her family. "My mother is suffering most, her heart is broken," she stated. "She spends all her time in his room looking at his clothes, waiting for Antonio to come home from work."[67]

Many of those executed and injured in Senkata were not actively participating in the protests. Milton Zenteno and Joel Colque were returning to their houses, Milton from canceled classes and Joel from work, when they were killed. Joel's family still questions why soldiers would kill a "kind" Christian boy who "played saxophone and keyboard in the church band" and did not engage in politics.[68]

Several locals heard soldiers yell racist comments at the protestors and bystanders like they had in Sacaba. Soldiers surrounded Mariela Mamani, who works at a local foundation for children, and other Indigenous women, beating them and forcing them to beg for forgiveness for demonstrating. "The soldiers kept calling us racist names like 'Indians' and shouting things like 'We will bloody you up' from their tanks," she recalled.[69]

Eyewitnesses saw soldiers cart people who had been shot into the plant, sparking fears that the government would disappear their bodies as it had during the dictatorships. One anonymous detainee in the plant said soldiers hauled in several injured people, including "one person not moving who was bleeding."[70] The fear that the soldiers would make the dead disappear motivated demonstrators outside to push down parts of the plant's wall to collect the bodies, but they quickly fled when the soldiers inside opened fire on them.

As the casualties mounted, locals raced the wounded to nearby hospitals and clinics. Soon, police appeared at the medical centers to harass the injured protestors and their families. One anonymous hospital worker reported that plainclothes police officers abducted injured people from the hospital, accusing them of being terrorists or Cubans.[71]

Many of the wounded did not seek medical attention. As one father who lost his son stated, "Many injured people went to their houses to recuperate because [they were] frightened they would be seized from the hospital."[72] This resulted in people not obtaining necessary medical attention and an underreporting of injured protestors and bystanders.

Soldiers killed eleven people and injured dozens of others outside the Senkata plant that day.[73] And just as in Sacaba, not one soldier or police officer was shot.[74] Áñez's de facto government denied responsibility, again blaming the killings on the demonstrators and the MAS party. The Minister of Defense Fernando López Julio, stated that the military "did not shoot a single bullet," despite videos that showed otherwise. He claimed that the protestors, who he called "delinquents, vandals, and terrorists," were paid by the MAS party and were "receiving orders, money, alcohol, and coca to cause vandalism, terror, and panic."[75]

The families, frightened that their relatives' corpses would disappear from the morgue or hospitals, brought their dead to a local church, Francisco de Asís. Father Gechi Revelin, who oversaw the parish that day, recalled: "The Church was converted into a morgue, a hospital for the injured, a place to stay for the persecuted.... I want to tell you categorically that terrible human rights violations were committed."[76] There, they held a wake, and doctors and investigators conducted autopsies, confirming that all the dead had died of gunshot wounds.

Two days later, the families organized a funeral procession from El Alto to La Paz to demand justice for the victims. Tens of thousands were in attendance.[77] When they reached downtown La Paz, the police, backed by the military, attacked the procession, gassing the marchers, and the families were compelled to drop the caskets of their loved ones into the street as they fled.[78]

On November 22, the IACHR sent a delegation led by then–executive secretary Paulo Abrão to Bolivia to investigate the abuses that had unfolded over the previous weeks.[79] The San Francisco de Asís church once again served as a base for the Senkata victims, hosting a meeting with the IACHR delegation and the survivors of the massacre and family members of those killed. Handwritten signs covered the bare brick walls of the church, demanding Áñez's resignation and the repeal of Law 4078, which granted the military immunity.

Women draped in black from head to toe cried at the human rights delegates: "Please, please, help us. More people can't die." Almost all the dead were young men who left behind small children, and in some cases, pregnant wives. "What do I tell my son who asks every day where his father is?" sobbed one young widow.[80]

An older woman at the meeting described how she was walking down the main avenue when she saw tanks coming toward her. "The military and police immediately started firing," she told the commission. "Don't they usually start with a warning before attacking? I saw more than twenty-five people shot. Then the military/police picked up all the bullets. I've been in hiding ever since because I'm a witness. It was a massacre."[81]

Executive Secretary Abrão reassured the emotionally charged room that their testimony would be recorded, their identities protected, and that action would be taken. Weeks later, the IACHR issued a report condemning the massacres in Senkata as well as Sacaba.

Four days after the IACHR left the country, the government offered the victims' families monetary compensation amounting to about US$7,200 per person, with the stipulation that the victims relinquish their right to file international legal complaints about the killings.[82] For most victims, the figure was symbolic—insufficient in economic terms and entirely lacking in accountability. Gregoria Siles said, "My son doesn't cost fifty thousand bolivianos; he doesn't have a price. He was young with the chance to study. I want justice."[83] The wounded also expressed frustration that the sum did not adequately cover medical costs.[84] Bruno Santana, who was shot in the foot, said, "I cannot walk or work. There is no justice for humble people like us."[85]

In addition to the killings in Sacaba and Senkata, security forces resorted to excessive force to disperse protests in other parts of the country in November, including La Paz's Southern Zone, where they killed six and injured dozens of civilian onlookers.[86]

At least thirty-five people were killed, the vast majority Indigenous and working-class opponents of the Áñez takeover.[87] November 2019—known as "Black November"—was the second-deadliest month in terms of state killings in the nearly forty years since Bolivia regained democracy.

The next week the de facto government reached agreements with MAS leaders in Plurinational Legislative Assembly and the principal social organizations in the streets to dismantle the blockades in exchange for new elections without the participation of Evo Morales or Álvaro García Linera, and the withdrawal of the army and police. Áñez pulled out the troops and began to release arrested protesters. But the organizations lost in their demands for Interior Minister Murillo to resign, as well as in the effort to secure guarantees that protest leaders would not face prosecution.[88] During the entire Áñez's presidency, no significant government investigation into these deaths and injuries occurred. In fact, November would prove to be just the beginning of nearly a year of widespread persecution.

# CHAPTER 6

# "DICTA-SUAVE"

## A SOFT DICTATORSHIP

It seems nothing short of a miracle that Bolivia's fragile democracy has withstood the repeated waves of political instability it suffered over the past thirty-nine years. When Evo Morales was elected in 2005, he became the tenth president since Bolivians reclaimed democracy in 1982. While his nearly fourteen-year rule marked Bolivia's most settled period, Jeanine Áñez's takeover signaled a step backward to the volatile rule so common in the country.

Áñez was not Bolivia's only interim president in recent years. In June 2005, then-president of the Supreme Court Eduardo Rodríguez Veltzé assumed power following the resignation of Gonzalo Sanchez de Lozada's vice president turned president, Carlos Mesa. Rodríguez Veltzé made it abundantly clear that he had nothing more on his agenda than overseeing the election of a new president within 150 days. He postponed every possible decision until the new elected administration assumed office, vowing that his presidency would not be swayed by "any political, partisan, or personal purpose."[1]

Rodríguez Veltzé stuck to his word, acting as a political placeholder until elections were held. During those six months, the interim government registered no major violent clashes with protestors. When Morales won in December 2005, presidential power was transferred without incident.

In stark contrast, when Áñez took power, she systematically persecuted her critics and political rivals. Her government targeted politicians and MAS government officials, as well as journalists and human rights activists, rounding up and arresting critics for "sedition" and "terrorism."

Áñez reversed policies of the Morales administration and chipped away at democratic safeguards. "This government has been acting as if they have a legal mandate rather than the backing of a small far-right minority," tweeted Kathryn Ledebur of the Andean Information Network.[2]

On her Twitter account, Áñez described herself as "president"—not "interim" or "acting" president. After repeatedly insisting she had no intention of running for the presidency, she did a U-turn in January 2020 and threw her hat into the ring. "This government is tainted by its own electoral interests," ex–interim president Rodríguez Veltzé said, "rather than advancing a more plural and independent period in the country."[3]

When the COVID-19 pandemic hit weeks later, Áñez, like repressive government leaders throughout the world, seized on the virus as cover to attack her political enemies. Her government's repeated postponement of elections—from the original date of May 3 to September 6 to October 18—was motivated less by public health concerns than the consolidation of her authority. In its first few months, her autocratic rule had set into motion one of the most tumultuous periods in decades.

## PERSECUTING POLITICAL OPPONENTS

According to David Inca, lawyer for some of the 2019 Senkata victims, Áñez pursued anyone with ties to the MAS through a "politics of vengeance."[4] Interior Minister Arturo Murillo accumulated MAS arrests "like trophies," according to his predecessor in the ministry.[5] During his first week, Murillo formed a special task force mandated with the detention of officials affiliated with the MAS. "There are senators, legislators . . . whose names I am going to start publishing who are subversive," he informed the press. "We will start detaining them with prosecution orders."[6]

He demanded that the attorney general "purge" the prosecutor's office of anyone associated with the former government and announced that he would personally "pursue those judges or prosecutors who are seeking to harm Bolivian citizens by freeing criminals."[7] The "criminals" he was referring to were members of the MAS party.

By early 2020, the Áñez government had detained or pressed charges against more than one hundred MAS politicians, and almost six hundred former officials and their families were under investigation for "sedition," "terrorism," or belonging to a criminal "association," including "all relatives" of Evo Morales.[8] Human rights observers reported that prosecutors filed sedition charges against twenty-two people from mid-February to mid-March alone.[9]

Police arrested former interior minister Carlos Romero while he was hospitalized for hypertension and dehydration after being trapped in his home for days by *grupos de choque* ("shock groups"). Then, the government arrested MAS legislator Gustavo Torrico and charged him with sedition, terrorism, and financing terrorism. "If they detain me for being a *masista*, they will have to give me a life sentence because I will never stop being one," he retorted.[10]

Like Torrico, the government charged Evo Morales with terrorism for calling for blockades and strikes, as well as for characterizing the Áñez government as a "dictatorship." Human Rights Watch declared the accusations to be "so broad that they can be used to criminalize behavior protected by freedoms of expression and association, and disproportionately punish actions that fall far short of what most reasonable observers would consider a terrorist act."[11]

In August 2020, the de facto government escalated its legal attacks on Morales by bringing genocide charges and filing a complaint before the International Criminal Court for alleged crimes against humanity.[12] Both processes were launched in response to Evo's support for blockades urging elections after Áñez repeatedly postponed them. In late August, the Ministry of Justice launched an investigation of Morales for statutory rape and human trafficking.[13]

Several persecuted MAS officials fled the country. "I felt fear like I never had before," said one former government functionary who asked to remain anonymous. "I was terrified that the only way to stay out of jail was to get out, even though it meant I had to leave my small children behind."[14]

Her boss was one of nine former MAS top officials who fled to the Mexican embassy in La Paz in early December 2019. Seven of the nine were forced to remain there throughout Áñez's presidency, even though Mexico protested vociferously that Bolivia was violating international law by refusing to permit their departure. Vigilante groups and large numbers of police, as well as the embassy's location up against an uninhabited hillside, made any rescue operation or escape almost impossible. The diplomatic kerfuffle resulted in the Áñez government's expulsion, at the end of December, of the Mexican ambassador and two Spanish embassy officials.[15]

Former president of the Justice Commission and ex-congress-woman Valeria Silva Guzmán escaped from the country with her family after the government raided their home. She described the frightening encounter:

> They arrived just before dawn. There were more than a dozen armed policemen, prosecutors, and other unidentified people. They broke into all the rooms, the kitchen, and even the bathrooms. . . . In the search they took with them books, films and documentaries, paintings and music records. If someone asked why, the answer was they were "seditious." . . . That day other valuables also disappeared. . . . Anyone would think you were reading an account of Hitler's time in Nazi Germany; or perhaps

one of the dictatorships of Videla or Pinochet. And despite all
the effort in building collective memory that made us think
it would never happen again, it happened in Bolivia after the
2019 coup d'état. That . . . raid at my parents' house sought to
take prisoners with no more reason than hatred and revenge.[16]

High-level officials were not the only ones in the Áñez government's sights. Police jailed Edith Chávez Arauco, the babysit-
ter of former interior minister Juan Ramón Quintana, while he
was trapped in the Mexican Embassy.[17] They also arrested Luis
Hernán Soliz, Evo's personal and family assistant, as well as his
lawyer, Patricia Hermosa. Their crime? Having telephone conversations with Morales.[18] Hermosa, who was pregnant, was provided no medical attention, even though she suffered ten days
of intense bleeding in jail. As a consequence, she lost her baby.[19]

Bolivian Canadian Juan Tellez, who was mayor until May
2021 of the southern Bolivia town of Betanzos, was charged
with sedition, terrorism, and crimes against public health at the
end of August. Along with a dozen others from the MAS, he
was accused of organizing protests demanding a free and fair
election.[20]

Perhaps the most egregious case was that of Mayor Patricia
Arce of Vinto, a dusty valley town outside of Cochabamba that is a
MAS party stronghold. Days before Morales's resignation, violent
protestors, many of whom later formed a vigilante group supporting Áñez's presidency, burned the Vinto City Hall and kidnapped
her. The mob physically assaulted and groped her, cutting off her
hair and part of her scalp. They doused her with red paint and gasoline and forced her to walk barefoot down a street full of broken
glass.[21] The vigilantes then paraded her before television cameras
and demanded she renounce the MAS party, which she refused
to do. Police on the scene did not arrest members of the mob, but
they extricated Arce and escorted her to the hospital. "This was a
clear message to all women: we should not be public servants," she
stated after she had gone into hiding.[22]

A few weeks later, the Inter-American Commission on Human
Rights (IACHR) granted Arce and her children precautionary

measures, obligating the transitional government to protect their rights to life and personal integrity.[23] Arce emerged from hiding and resumed her role as mayor, but the threats persisted. The government declined to investigate or prosecute any of the perpetrators. After vigilante groups poisoned and killed her four dogs, she dispatched her family into hiding again.

Arce's persecution was not only at the hands of paramilitary groups. The government, for its part, informed her that if she denounced the state's noncompliance with IACHR stipulations, she "would pay."[24] After she reported this to the IACHR, she was charged with sedition and orchestrating her own attack.[25] In late April, she was arrested along with her children for allegedly breaking COVID-19 quarantine rules. "They will clearly do what they can to prevent me from running for office," said Arce, who denied the charges.[26] Pressure from the human rights community led to her release.

"We are living in times like those fifty years ago, during the dictatorships," Arce said. "I never wanted to be a symbol of the violence we are experiencing, but just as the paramilitary groups allied with the [Áñez] government dragged me through the street, this government is dragging human rights through the street. Since November [2019], my country, Bolivia, has spiraled into authoritarianism."[27]

## "SEDITIOUS" JOURNALISM

At 1 a.m. on New Year's Eve, Orestes Sotomayor Vásquez was startled by a loud knock at the door. "Who on earth would be coming by so late?" he asked himself. The six men dressed in civilian clothes outside identified themselves as police officers. They wanted him to come to the police station to talk about a "cybercrime."

The police officers admitted that they did not have an arrest order but encouraged him to come along. Otherwise, they would wait at his house until they got a warrant. "Just give a declaration as a witness and you will have no problem," they told him. Orestes felt nervous. He remembers noticing just how bitterly cold the Altiplano air felt at that moment.

Orestes had never been arrested before. "I'm a graphic designer, not a criminal," he thought as he convinced himself to cooperate. He climbed into one of the two police trucks and was transported to the Special Force to Fight against Crime (FELCC) offices. Officials interrogated him for several hours, then arrested him. His crime: owning the domain of a website critical of the Áñez government.

Meanwhile, officers took Alejandra Salinas into custody. She was Orestes's colleague, a master's degree student who had written Facebook posts that condemned Áñez government violence and called what had happened in Sacaba and Senkata "massacres." Orestes and Alejandra were both charged with sedition.[28]

These prisoners were two of what became hundreds of people associated with the press who were targeted by the interim government from its earliest days in office. On November 14, Minister of Communications Roxana Lizárraga boasted that the government had identified national and international journalists engaged in sedition and that Minister Murillo would intercede against them.[29] Only after a public outcry spearheaded by the national press did she retract her threat. But in general, most media outlets fell into line behind the anti-Morales forces in November 2019.[30] More than once, we were out in the street interviewing pro-MAS working-class and Indigenous protestors and the local press was nowhere to be seen. But when we went to anti-Morales events, they were tripping over each other.

Áñez's minister of defense, Fernando López Julio, added fuel to Lizárraga's fire by linking journalism to terrorism. "Terrorism is attacking us on all fronts. . . . [T]errorism is digital . . . and communicational," he declared.[31] Minister of Foreign Relations Karen Longaric also bullied the media, claiming that the government had pinpointed problematic international journalists.[32] The government then shut down the broadcast of the international news channels RT Spanish and Telesur.[33]

It also closed community radio stations, many broadcasting in Indigenous languages, that were critical of Áñez or perceived as sympathetic to the MAS. In all, some fifty-three community radio stations went off the air, cutting off the primary or sole news source for many Indigenous and *campesino* communities.[34] Other stations were charged fines and taxes that had never previously existed. Some had their signal intermittently shut off or experienced raids by government forces who confiscated their equipment.[35]

The government then targeted noncompliant commercial stations. A press chief from a large television station who asked to remain anonymous feared that his channel would be shuttered for "having a different opinion and for criticizing the government."[36] After the de facto government seized power, journalists at his station were repeatedly assaulted by pro-Áñez vigilante groups—often in front of police or military—and were regularly barred from covering events. Those from blacklisted stations like his had to borrow press credentials from "sympathetic" outlets aligned with the government to get past police barricades to cover events or access information.

Police and vigilante groups associated with the government physically attacked members of the press, including Al Jazeera reporter Teresa Bo, and independent journalist Andrea Tapia, who was forced into hiding when a Molotov cocktail was thrown at her home after she posted articles criticizing government violence.[37]

The most tragic attack was the one that killed Argentinian journalist Sebastián Moro. The day before Evo resigned, Moro wrote an article for Argentina's *Página/12* titled "A Coup D'état Is Underway in Bolivia."[38] That same day, anti-MAS vigilante groups kidnapped his boss, José Aramayo, tied him to a tree, and assaulted him. They then broke into Sebastian's home, where they beat him to death. For months, his family sought justice in Bolivia, but after the government refused to open a serious investigation into his killing, his family brought the case before the IACHR.[39]

The de facto government also pursued people who used so-cial media to condemn the Áñez administration. Mauricio Jara was jailed in late April, charged with sedition for forming seven WhatsApp groups critical of the government.[40] Forty-eight prom-inent Bolivian journalists on both the left and right denounced his arrest. "Beyond whether we agree or not with Jara's opinions, we want to make it clear that his detention is illegal," read their public statement.[41]

Many of the signatories had actively participated in the movement opposing Morales. "I believe in freedom of expres-sion and opinion," said Juan Cristóbal Soruco, former editor of the Cochabamba daily *Los Tiempos*, who signed the petition. He had vociferously denounced Morales for seeking a fourth term in office.[42]

These actions created a climate of fear that pervaded the press. A veteran reporter at a large television station in La Paz said anonymously, "I lived through two past dictatorships. This is even worse. I am scared."[43]

## A CARETAKER WITH AUTHORITARIAN AMBITIONS

Immediately after assuming office, Jeanine Áñez fired 80 per-cent of Bolivia's ambassadors abroad, branding them as "political operators, spokesmen for Evo Morales and the policies of the MAS."[44] One anonymous foreign service official said that he was subject to threats that persuaded him to not return to Bolivia be-cause, he said, "I am worried that if I go back, I will be harassed or worse."[45]

Others felt they were being driven out of government either directly or indirectly. The minister of foreign affairs implemented a new dress code requiring Western-style clothing: dark suits for men, and suits, dresses, or pants for women. The policy was withdrawn following public outcry, but the message stuck that Indigenous people, whose clothing did not conform to the new rule, were unwelcome in the new government.[46]

Promptly after seizing power, Áñez cut relations with leftist governments, especially those that had been close to Morales. On her third day in office, she expelled 725 Cubans,[47] many of whom were doctors or staff with the Cuban medical brigade that had brought medical services to poor rural communities. Áñez's government then arrested Carlos de la Rocha, the brigade's Bolivian medical supervisor, charging him with engaging in "anti-economic activity."[48]

Venezuelans were high on the government's hit list. Diplomats associated with President Nicolás Maduro were forced to leave, replaced by representatives of Juan Guiadó's self-declared government.[49] Bolivian authorities subsequently arrested nine allegedly armed Venezuelans and charged them with sedition for their supposed coordination and funding of protests.[50]

After the diplomatic catastrophe at the Mexican embassy, Áñez's delegate to the international community, former Bolivian president Tuto Quiroga, publicly called Mexican president Andrés Manuel López Obrador "cowardly," "servile," and a "scoundrel."[51] Days after expelling the diplomats, Interior Minister Murillo and Defense Minister López slighted the Spanish government by meeting with members of Spain's extreme-right Vox party, who accused the asylum seekers of having links with Spain's ruling leftist party and drug traffickers.[52]

Áñez renewed diplomatic ties with Israel, which Morales had broken off following its three-week siege on Gaza in early 2009.[53] Minister Murillo asked Israel for assistance to fight "leftist terrorism" in Bolivia,[54] and the interim government eliminated the $160 tourist visa fees for Israelis.[55]

Áñez also courted the United States, Republican leaders in particular. The US government immediately recognized Áñez as the new president, with congratulatory statements from Secretary of State Mike Pompeo[56] and President Donald Trump, who tweeted, "We support [Jeanine Áñez] in Bolivia as she works to ensure a peaceful democratic transition through free elections."[57] As it had done with Israel, the de facto government abolished the tourist-visa fee for US citizens and named an ambassador to the United States, which Bolivia had lacked since 2008.[58] Six weeks later, the US government published a presidential determination proclaiming that it was "vital to the national interests of the United States" to deliver aid to the Áñez government.[59]

Áñez rewarded an emboldened military for their role in facilitating her rise to power, immediately increasing the military budget.[60] She later promoted generals loyal to her regime, circumventing the requisite approval of the Plurinational Legislative Assembly.[61] As a further rebuke of MAS policy, Áñez renamed the military's Anti-Imperialist Command School, created by Morales, to the Heroes of Ñancahuazú School, in honor of the soldiers who killed Che Guevara.[62] On June 5, in the midst of the COVID-19 pandemic, the government awarded the military another sizable budget increase.[63]

The de facto government immediately pulled Bolivia out of the Bolivarian Alliance for the Peoples of Our America (ALBA), the trade pact between left-wing countries in Latin America and the Caribbean. In a revival of neoliberal policies, the government also announced its intention to privatize state industries. "The government should be reduced and give a more leading role to private companies," declared the Minister of Development, Wilfredo Rojo.[64]

That led to an attempt to privatize the state electrical system, ELFEC. When officials in Áñez's government—including Minister of Economy Óscar Ortiz and Attorney General José María Cabrera—disputed the move, calling it illegal, the government fired them.[65] Officials also publicly discussed intentions to sell off the state airline and the country's largest airport.[66]

Though the government did not privatize the state-run channel, Bolivia TV, it rebranded the station's logo with the *pitita*, the symbol of the anti-Evo protest movement and the name of Áñez's dog. It immediately ran ads accusing Morales of inciting confrontations that would starve Bolivians.[67] The state telecommunications company, Entel, unveiled a promotion called "Mega Pitita" to honor the protestors who had removed Morales from power.[68]

## COVID-19 AND CORRUPTION

Áñez's early and forceful actions against COVID-19, including a complete quarantine across the country in late March, initially won her praise.[69] A survey in early May found that her popularity had soared,[70] despite government restrictions allowing people to leave their homes only one morning a week to go food shopping—a daunting constraint in the world's largest informal economy.[71] Her support waned quickly, however.

Bolivia's challenges in confronting the virus were enormous. Despite substantial investments in healthcare infrastructure under the MAS, the county was ill-equipped to cope, possessing approximately one-third of the intensive care beds public health officials estimated necessary.[72] In poor areas such as the city of El Alto, only eight beds were available for a population of about a million.

The quarantine fell hardest on the poorest and most vulnerable.[73] Potable water, needed for handwashing, is inaccessible to about a quarter of the population. While some middle-class Bolivians organized food drives, in one of South America's poorest countries, this was a drop in the bucket.[74] A third of the population surveyed by the firm Ciesmori in mid-April said that they did not have enough food for the following seven days.[75] At the same time, the government regularly referred to those who broke quarantine rules as "terrorists" and "subversives."[76]

Just like everywhere in the world, violence against women spiked during the pandemic. The country already had the region's second-highest rate of femicide.[77] "We are considerably alarmed that a high level of resources is directed toward prosecuting those who are protesting government action on COVID-19, and there are almost no resources to address the increasing violence against women," Nadia Cruz of the publicly funded Ombudsman's Office (Defensoría del Pueblo) told *La Razón* newspaper.[78]

Many residents in working-class neighborhoods feared the quarantine was an excuse to unleash more repression, undermining its effectiveness. Protestors in Cochabamba told the press,

"We aren't afraid of COVID-19; it's an invention of the right wing . . . they want us to die of hunger."[79]

Few could stick to three months of one of the strictest lockdowns in the world, given the limited and tardy public assistance on offer. This accelerated the spread of the virus and, combined with inadequate medical resources, catapulted Bolivia to the world's third-highest per capita death rate by October 2020.[80] Across the country, students struggled as the government declared an early end to the school year, slated to end in November, slashing the number of low-income youth able to pursue higher education.[81]

As the Áñez government's missteps multiplied, many of the impoverished people who had risen into the middle class during the MAS government once again found themselves struggling financially. Whatever public confidence remained dissipated in late May when Áñez's health minister was arrested for fraud involving a multi-million-dollar ventilator purchase. He had authorized the purchase of more than a hundred Spanish respirators not designed for use in intensive care wards at a price four times higher than they were listed.[82]

The handling of the pandemic was not the only area plagued by corruption and mismanagement. The de facto government steamrollered decisions that benefited its friends and supporters in agribusiness.[83] Meanwhile, 2020 marked the second year of disastrous fires in the southeast, most of them deliberately set to clear land by large-scale soy and cattle producers.[84] Export of beef to China had increased threefold over the previous year, which meant that deforestation largely continued unabated, despite the Áñez administration's prohibition on slash-and-burn agriculture.[85] The respected Bolivian research organization Fundación Tierra reported that in September 2020, properties were illegally granted to opposition leader Branko Marinković, then the newly appointed economy minister who years earlier had been charged with terrorism for involvement in an alleged plot to overthrow Morales.[86]

Áñez's popularity took a further dive when the economy contracted into a profound recession. Even though much of the responsibility lay with the virus, many Bolivians, remembering the economic good times under the MAS, blamed the Áñez government for the downturn. Her government was also incompetent: all told, thirty-four different ministers occupied seventeen positions over the course of the year.[87]

In response to Áñez's mismanagement of the pandemic, sporadic protests erupted in low-income neighborhoods across the country.[88] They demanded the easing of total lockdown and called for immediate elections. Hunger drove the poor into the streets. "Here, 80 percent of us live day to day, and if we don't work, we don't eat. That's why we're protesting," an anonymous blockader in Cochabamba told the local newspaper, *Los Tiempos*.[89]

One of the most contentious demonstrations was in K'ara K'ara, on the southern outskirts of Cochabamba.[90] Protestors prevented access to the municipal dump located in the neighborhood, and garbage piled up around the city. The right-wing motorcycle gang Cochala Youth Resistance threatened to break up the roadblocks by force.[91] The gang backed down, and the blockade ended on May 22 after a commitment by the city government to supply free drinking water to the area and forward the demand to ease the quarantine to national health authorities. However, the conflict surged again in July when the Áñez government arrested community leaders who were active in the May protests which provoked further confrontations with the police.[92]

The government viewed these demonstrations as instigated by the MAS party, with Interior Vice Minister Javier Issa claiming that "[t]here is a subversive plan inside these protests."[93] "The MAS wants to destabilize the country," echoed Interior Minister Murillo at a press conference. "We believe in pacifying the country. . . . They want us to send in the police so they can do what they did last year: kill one of their own and blame it on us."[94]

## COCA GROWERS UNDER ATTACK

Like many policies under Áñez, the caretaker government's approach to coca and coca growers was calamitous. After ten coca growers from Evo Morales's home base of the Chapare died at the hands of the military and police on November 15, 2019, growers immediately expelled the police. Banks refused to operate in the Chapare after the police left, which meant that when COVID-19 exploded, residents were unable to collect one of three government emergency subsidies and loans.[95]

The government quickly reverted to pre-Morales attitudes toward coca farmers. Leading the charge was Interior Minister Murillo, whose luxury hotel in the Chapare had been burned following Evo's resignation. From then on, Murillo threatened to isolate and cut off the region, declaring that "the majority of Chapare residents are prisoners of coca grower union leaders and drug traffickers" and suggesting that MAS presidential candidate Luis Arce was substituting for Morales as "the godfather of drug traffickers."[96] This fed into a well-established discourse among opponents of Morales: the narrative that coca production had soared during his government and that most coca growers are closely linked to traffickers. Neither of these accusations is borne out by the available evidence.[97]

In mid-April 2020, the government cut off the Chapare's gasoline supply, insisting that the move was essential to curb trafficking because gasoline is a critical ingredient in cocaine paste production.[98] Growers denounced the action, stating that the shortage of gas hamstrung fishponds, which were constructed during the Morales administration as an alternative to growing coca leaf and are run by local farmers. Without gasoline to drive aeration pumps, millions of fish died.[99]

The fuel shortages also meant that the growers' unions lacked gasoline needed to distribute food to impoverished people, both in their region and in the cities of Santa Cruz and Cochabamba. "Solidarity has become criminalized," tweeted Andrónico Rodríguez,[100] vice president of the Chapare's six federations.

In mid-April, the government dispatched eighty-four police personnel into the Chapare unannounced.[101] Coca growers and local town residents reacted with a spontaneous protest insisting that the police should be quarantined. "For the police to enter the Chapare . . . without following sanitary protocols and without coordinating with local authorities puts the health of my brothers and sisters at risk," tweeted Evo from Buenos Aires.[102]

On April 22, an agreement was reached that allowed the police to return, on the condition that banks reopened and gasoline was supplied, although it was subsequently rationed at a level insufficient to adequately operate the fish farms.[103] No gasoline shortages were reported elsewhere in the country. "The measures are a way of undermining our opposition and of unleashing repression against us, particularly those of us in leadership positions," said Leonardo Loza, former vice president of the six federations of coca growers.[104]

Even though coca leaf production jumped 10 percent countrywide in 2019, with the greatest expansion in northern La Paz, by early 2020 coca leaf prices slumped to one-third or less of their previous levels as drug trafficking routes dwindled because of COVID-19.[105] Leaf shortages were registered as far away as northern Argentina.[106]

In the Yungas, "[a]ll the markets are closed, but there is corruption and people selling under the table," said Magdalena Condori, former executive director of the Regional Federation of Women in Inquisivi. "For a bushel (30 pounds), we used to get US$144, but now people are not even bothering to sell it because it is around $36."[107]

"We're concerned about feeding our families because the price of coca continues to drop," explained coca union leader Alvino Pinto. "We face restrictions in moving coca and other goods to the central market. This is blocking both local consumption and export, but our production continues at the same level."[108] Integrated development projects in both the Yungas and the Chapare ground to a halt in 2020, creating even greater economic hardships for families.

Despite the US government's affinity to Áñez, in September 2021 it repeated its long-standing annual ritual of "decertifying" Bolivia for failing to sufficiently limit drug production, complaining that production exceeded legal limits.[109] Part of the explanation lies with the interim government's decision to avoid often controversial coca eradication offensives, although it maintained anti-drug operations at a pace similar to that in 2019. By October 2020, legal coca markets had reopened, and the price rebounded. The UN later reported that coca cultivation surged 15 percent overall during 2020.[110]

In February, Áñez introduced a drug-control strategy drafted with assistance from European Union experts and consultants. EU participation reflected an abrupt about-face from previous policy. As recently as mid-2018, the EU commissioner for development in Bolivia, Neven Mimica, tweeted, "The fight against drugs trafficking in #Bolivia is progressing thanks to #EU cooperation centred on alternative development and law enforcement."[111] Now, the Áñez government derided the type of strategy previously favored by the EU as "permissive and impractical" and "merely a political discourse."[112] Among coca growers, the response was dismay. "Before, we worked closely with the European Union so as to stay within the legal limits," explained a leader who didn't want his name used because of fear of government retaliation. "We want to keep this going, but everything has broken down with this government. They don't communicate or coordinate with us at all."[113]

The accumulated lessons from the experiment with social control of coca were quickly disappearing. "It would be a disaster to lose all the progress Bolivia made on coca control," lamented a local drug policy expert who asked not to be identified. "The technical focus has gone down the drain. All this transitional government cares about is having political weapons they can use against the party of the former government."[114]

## SILENCE FROM ABOVE, RESISTANCE FROM BELOW

Despite widespread condemnation by the international community, including the IACHR, the Office of the High Commissioner for Human Rights of the United Nations, Human Rights Watch, and Amnesty International, the response in Bolivia to Áñez's human rights and political abuses was mixed. The right-wing base felt emboldened, with sectors of business elites and conservative politicians praising her actions as necessary steps to restoring democracy, while membership in vigilante groups sympathetic to the government mushroomed.[115]

Moderate groups who opposed Morales in the 2019 elections, particularly those in the middle and upper classes, were more ambivalent, though most remained silent when the Áñez government strayed from its caretaker role and committed human rights violations. Some were so caught up in what Molina calls "anti-MAS hysteria," that they simply ignored the de facto government's behavior.[116] Others overlooked Áñez's repression because to acknowledge it would amount to recognition of their own errors in collaborating with the anti-democratic and racist groups that thrust her to power.[117]

Some simply did not comprehend what was happening in the complex post-election climate, due to the scale of the misinformation campaign. The Áñez administration was initially successful at painting itself as a democratic government committed to purging corruption and drugs. As La Paz–based journalist William Wroblewski observed, "By repressing criticisms, the Áñez administration was able to limit access to information for many people, particularly those who were isolated in the bubbles of wealthier neighborhoods."[118]

In mid-December 2019, the Áñez government hired CLS Strategies, a Washington-based public relations firm, to refashion the government's image on human rights, the "strengthening" of democracy, and elections. CLS Strategies is notorious for assisting the Honduran government after the 2009 coup, and members of the CLS team were incorporated into Gonzalo Sánchez de

Lozada's 2002 presidential campaign to manufacture a "crisis" to help him get elected.[119] Following Áñez's takeover, CLS created sham accounts on social media to vilify critics of her government and share "fake news." In September 2020, CLS became the first US-based communications company to be chastised by Facebook for activating fake accounts "to secretly manipulate politics in another country, in violation of Facebook's prohibition on foreign interference."[120]

While the middle and upper classes remained generally silent about Áñez's abuses, the social movements resisted. Their response, however, was often tentative, in part due to their decline during Morales's tenure in government, but also because of the widespread climate of fear that permeated Bolivia under Áñez. As one of the witnesses to the Sacaba massacres stated: "I am scared to speak. We are all scared to speak out."[121]

"The government is criminalizing social leaders—all of them are under serious investigation," explained journalist Fernando Molina.[122] According to veteran union leader Rolando Borda Padilla, from Santa Cruz, "The repression we suffered was worse than under the dictatorships that I lived through as a student because they threatened to harm our families and burn our houses down."[123]

For months, police and soldiers routinely stopped people in primarily Indigenous villages and neighborhoods all over the country. Porfirio Ramírez, a worker in Sacaba, explained how security forces "went through everything on our phones. They asked me for my passcode. They looked at my photos, WhatsApp, Facebook."[124] Abel, a protestor from the Chapare, had a similar experience with the militarized police. "I erased the footage I had on my phone because [state forces] were taking people's photos of marches from their cameras, so I was frightened police would go after my friends, torture them or arrest them for terrorism," he stated.[125]

Security forces visited high schools to identify and harass teenagers who may have been involved in demonstrations. An anonymous student in El Alto complained: "The police look up at the students and then back down at their phones, swiping through pictures. . . . I am frightened they will come after us."[126]

When groups threatened to hold protests against the repression, as well as Áñez's failure to call elections, on January 22, Day of the Plurinational State, the interim government deployed seventy thousand soldiers and police to conduct joint operations "to guarantee the mandate of the constitutional presidency of Jeanine Áñez."[127] The demonstrations were canceled because of generalized fears that marching would almost certainly result in a slaughter.

In March 2020, police attacked locals in Senkata as they protested politicians associated with the Áñez government, who were in El Alto to celebrate its thirty-fifth anniversary. "It was like reliving that day [in November]," said one of the victims who lost her brother in the November 2019 attacks.[128] Police injured dozens, including young students at a nearby elementary school. After footage of the bleeding children went public, Áñez reiterated her commitment to quashing protestors, stating, "We have real enemies and I believe, absolutely, that they must be identified, persecuted, contained, and, above all, they must be defeated."[129] The following week, police arrested and tortured journalist René Huarachi, who had filmed and shared footage of the injured schoolchildren.[130]

The COVID-19 pandemic brought additional obstacles to resistance. In late March, Áñez passed Supreme Decree 4200, stating that those who "misinform or cause uncertainty to the population will be subject to criminal charges for crimes against public health."[131] A few days later, Public Works Minister Iván Arias threatened to "catch" those who publish "false information" on social media and jail them for ten years.[132] The reasoning behind the new decree, tweeted Education Vice Minister Christian Tejada, was "to protect state stability, because we are victims of narco-guerrilla, communist attacks that seek to destabilize the government by misinforming the public."[133]

Within the decree's first month, the Áñez government had charged at least sixty-seven people for violations, swiftly convicting thirty-seven of them.[134] The government passed a second decree the first week of May that criminalized the dissemination of information "written, printed, and/or artistic that generates uncertainty in the population."[135] The law sparked domestic and international outrage, including a declaration by the IACHR that the decree's use of criminal sanctions was incompatible with human rights. "Disinformation must be fought by access to public information," tweeted the special rapporteur for freedom of expression.[136] The backlash forced the Áñez administration to retract the decree, but the message nonetheless was clear: dissent would lead to arrest.

## THE REBIRTH OF RESISTANCE

While the urgency of the MAS's call to set up new elections was undiminished throughout May and June, Bolivia remained in the grip of COVID-19, with the number of cases still trending upward. This placed the party in a quandary: since the country lacked the capacity for mail-in voting, holding elections too soon could cause infections to explode, while it would be next to impossible to ensure the participation of international observers. But the longer elections were delayed, the more Áñez and the circle around her could shore up power and hound their enemies.

Throughout Áñez's presidency, the MAS remained the most popular political force. In a mid-March poll,[137] Luis Arce led, marshalling just over 33 percent of voters' support, followed by the former president Carlos Mesa with 18 percent, and Áñez with 16 percent.

The first sign of reactivation of the MAS as a legislative force surfaced at the end of April with the approval of a law that required elections by August 2.[138] With majority control of the Legislative Assembly in MAS hands, Senate president Eva Copa insisted that if Áñez did not announce a new election date in ten days, she would exercise her constitutional right to call them.

The MAS won this standoff when Áñez capitulated, although she pushed the elections back a month, to September 6.

On July 23, however, the government suspended elections for a third time, this time completely circumventing the required support of the Legislative Assembly. The government scheduled them for October 18, almost one year to the day after the controversial 2019 elections. While the pandemic certainly created safety issues for voting, a critical mass of disenfranchised Bolivians did not trust the transitional government's motives. Months of repression, political obfuscation, and pandemic mismanagement came to a head, and social movements mobilized quickly in response to what they perceived as a further affront to democracy.

The Bolivian Workers Central (COB), alongside the newly revived Indigenous Unity Pact (which had decided to disband the MAS government-dominated CONALCAM) and others, organized protests.[139] After negotiations with the Supreme Electoral Court (TSE) collapsed, these groups embarked on a nationwide strike.[140] With this coordinated action, the grassroots groups that make up the MAS reasserted a degree of independence, which political scientist Fernando Mayorga argues was a revitalization of the party's origins as the "political instrument" of the country's urban and rural unions.[141]

On August 3, protestors erected blockades on over one hundred of Bolivia's highways and principal roads.[142] A week later, the number hit 170.[143] One hundred fifty thousand protestors marched as groups scattered rocks and dug trenches on the roads, some setting off dynamite to destroy highway pedestrian overpasses.[144] In some cases, confrontations were violent, such as the clash in the small town of Samaipata, in the foothills of the Andes west of Santa Cruz, where MAS supporters took hostages. In response, right-wing Cruceños launched a counterattack, and on the other side of the country, the COB headquarters in La Paz was bombed.

Heidi Motiño, an accountancy student in El Alto who participated in the demonstrations, told a National Public Radio reporter: "We have a government that is illegitimate because we haven't elected it. Many of us know the risk [voting] entails because of the pandemic, but we want to hold elections.... We can't stand it anymore."[145]

The government alleged that the demonstrators were blocking the transportation of oxygen and medical supplies, causing dozens of deaths. Protest leaders insisted that they were allowing ambulances and trucks carrying medical supplies through the blockades.[146]

Following its usual playbook, the Áñez government leveled charges of terrorism against protest and MAS leaders. MAS party officials, however, had not been in charge of the August mobilizations. In fact, the social movements criticized MAS leaders for negotiating with the TSE without consulting them.[147]

## A TOUGH YEAR DRAWS TO A CLOSE

The August 2020 protests were a success on two levels. First, they prompted an agreement that the October 18 election date could not be postponed. After a year of widespread persecution, rampant corruption, and repeated election delays, Áñez had to carry out her mandate. Bolivians would finally be able to vote for a leader.

Second, the demonstrations signaled the return of large-scale grassroots mobilizations that operated independently of MAS leadership. This mass movement had sufficient strength to prevent the full consolidation of the Áñez regime and to force new elections. As in the 2003 Gas War and the 2000 Water War, the demonstrators represented diverse groups, and decision making was for the most part bottom-up, rendering the government's strategy of zeroing in on leaders ineffective. As Bolivia advanced toward elections, grassroots organizations and their supporters seemed reinvigorated. But fear of further repression still loomed, as well as skepticism over whether the elections would be fair. Philosopher Rafael Bautista captured these worries when he wrote in August, "We don't live under the rule of law . . . [but] rather by the rule of the strongest that has converted Bolivia into a land without rights."[148]

Above: Vinto Mayor Patricia Arce speaks to reporters after anti-MAS protestors kidnapped her.
Copyright 2019, Jorge Abrego

Below: Luis Arce announces his electoral win in the MAS headquarters in Sopocachi.
Copyright 2020, Thomas Becker

People celebrate Luis Arce's electoral win outside MAS headquarters. Copyright 2020, Thomas Becker

Thousands line the highway awaiting the return of Evo. Copyright 2020, Thomas Becker

People walked for miles to witness the return of Evo Morales. Copyright 2020, Thomas Becker

An Aymara vendor feeds Evo Morales his favorite lunch on his return to Bolivia. Copyright 2020, Thomas Becker

Communities from all over the country celebrated the electoral win of Luis Arce and David Choquehuanca in El Alto. Copyright 2020, Thomas Becker

Indigenous women sell fruit next to graffiti referring to the MAS party as "Indians of shit." Copyright 2021, Thomas Becker

# PART IV:
# "LA LUCHA SIGUE":
# THE STRUGGLE CONTINUES

## CHAPTER 7

# THE "PROCESS OF CHANGE" REVIVED?

"I can't believe it. It hardly seems real," said Patricia Arce over the phone, her voice barely penetrating the clamor that had just taken over the MAS headquarters in La Paz's Sopocachi neighborhood.

Earlier that day, millions of Bolivians across the country had cast their ballots. Despite COVID-19, the turnout on Sunday, October 18, 2020, was the second highest in the country's history, surprising observers who believed that the tens of thousands of troops and police that President Jeanine Áñez had dispatched into the streets the night before might scare people away from the polling stations.[1]

The atmosphere at the MAS headquarters, mirroring the rest of the country, was tense. Anti-MAS protestors had assembled outside. Some wondered if the marchers would try to attack them, as they had MAS representatives the previous month, but this time the shouting protestors quickly moved on.

Dozens of armed police were stationed along Calle Ecuador, where the headquarters is located. Any other night, the quiet Sopocachi street would have been deserted at this hour. To add to the anxious atmosphere, fake election results had already circulated and then been retracted. The uncertainty was fed further by the last-minute decision of the Supreme Electoral Court (TSE) to cancel the reconfigured quick-count system over fears about its reliability.[2] This was precisely the system that had played such a critical role in propelling the idea of fraud in the voting fiasco a year earlier.

Around midnight, the headquarters erupted. With a stunning 55.1 percent of the votes, in the first election since 2002 without Evo Morales at the helm of the MAS, longtime finance minister Luis "Lucho" Arce and his vice presidential running mate, former foreign minister David Choquehuanca, swept the MAS back into power. They defeated their nearest rival, Carlos Mesa, by more than 25 percent and won more votes than Morales had in the contested elections a year earlier. The victory made it clear that the electorate did not reject the MAS social democratic project; rather, it indicated, at least in part, how weary they had become of Morales. But the triumph also stemmed from voters' resounding rejection of the racism and violence associated with the Áñez government. The victory reinforced democracy not only in Bolivia but throughout the region.

Patricia—who only a year before had been dragged through the streets, tortured, thrown in jail, charged with sedition, and ultimately forced into hiding—would be joining Lucho. She had just been elected senator of Cochabamba.

Patricia tried to hold it together on the phone. Her voice was lighter than in many of our previous conversations, not so much because she had just been elected to office, but rather because she realized that she and her family might finally be safe. "At last, I can breathe," she said before she hung up.[3]

Meanwhile, people in the headquarters took turns hugging each other. "The dictatorship is over," cried a middle-aged woman as she embraced another teary-eyed official. Though the atmosphere was certainly celebratory, it was relief that flooded the room.

As he gave his acceptance speech, Lucho stood next to his soon-to-be vice president, Choquehuanca, and social movement leaders. As cameras flashed, he declared, "We have recovered democracy and hope."[4]

Outside, hundreds of MAS supporters gathered, chanting, "Somos MAS" ("We are the MAS," which also means "We are more"). They waved their party's blue-and-white flags and jumped up and down, beaming with joy. A woman in a red *pollera* and matching COVID mask yelled, "The *wiphala* will be respected, damn it!" People cheered.

Over the next few days, the festivities around La Paz were sporadic and curiously low-key. The day after the elections, a man near the Plaza Murillo explained the state of mind: "After such a horrible year, it feels strange to throw a party. I'm still numb from everything we experienced."[5] He was not alone in worrying that it was premature to celebrate, considering Áñez's tight grip on power and an emboldened and violent right wing.

Six days after the elections, the MAS held a "Grand Cultural Festival for the Recuperation of Democracy" in El Alto. For ten hours, miners from the south, Indigenous women's groups from the Altiplano, and *campesinos* from Santa Cruz, Luis Fernando Camacho's stronghold, marched through the streets yelling slogans about democracy and justice. When Patricia Arce walked out on stage, the crowd chanted, "Patricia, Patricia!" Her life, and the lives of most of the people in the crowd, had changed dramatically from the year before.

The victory came at a high price. As Ollie Vargas, a journalist who had reported from the Chapare since the November 2019 coup, tweeted: "The return of democracy in Bolivia didn't come for free. So many young people gave their lives in the fight. . . . These are the heroes of Sacaba. In Senkata, Yapacaní and Pedregal too, so many paid the ultimate price for their country."[6]

Despite how hostile and racist Áñez's anti-MAS rhetoric had been during her year in office, her interim government recognized the 2020 election results almost immediately. As did Carlos Mesa. The international community, including the United States, also quickly acknowledged the MAS win. On October 19, Bernie Sanders, who had traveled to Bolivia as part of a congressional delegation in 2014, tweeted: "The Bolivian people made their voices heard in yesterday's election after a difficult, year-long fight to restore democracy. As minister of economy, Mr. Arce helped slash poverty and inequality. I congratulate him on his victory and wish him well."[7] President Jair Bolsonaro of South America's powerhouse, Brazil, was the last in the region to recognize the MAS victory.

Though Arce repeatedly polled as the frontrunner, the impressive margin of victory came as a surprise, given widespread doubts about the whether elections would be free and fair. "How do you run a campaign when the party's leadership has been systematically criminalized, and its base fears retribution from Áñez and Murillo?" questioned a MAS supporter in Cochabamba on the first anniversary of the Sacaba killings.[8] In the weeks leading up to the election, Áñez had repeatedly characterized the former MAS government as a "dictatorship" and Morales as a "tyrant."[9]

Fears of rigged elections had spiked when government officials harassed international observers invited to monitor the voting process and anti-MAS groups doxed them, sharing their photos and referring to them as "terrorists" on social media.[10] Police illegally picked up Argentinian left-wing national deputy Federico Fagioli, who was to serve as an electoral observer, prompting Argentinian president Alberto Fernández to denounce the mistreatment.[11] Fagioli was quickly released.

Election monitors associated with the MAS expressed fears of retribution. Observer Doug Hertzler of Academics for Democracy in Latin America and the Caribbean (ADLAC) reported from Santa Cruz that "in some pro–Luis Camacho neighborhoods, the MAS could not get people to volunteer as polling delegates because they were afraid of attack, but the party still pulled in 30 percent of the vote."[12] ADLAC also reported that some MAS delegates informed them that they were afraid to observe the elections in La Paz.

Camacho came in third with 14 percent of the votes, registering first in the department (state or province) of Santa Cruz. His racist diatribes had polarized the local population to such an extent that once again he pushed Carlos Mesa right off the stage, allowing the Arce-Choquehuanca ticket to log a solid second place in Bolivia's most populous region.[13]

Despite at least forty-one reported incidences of political violence, voting was remarkably peaceful.[14] The election itself was a credit to the TSE under Salvador Romero, who was appointed by Áñez but only after a negotiation between the major parties. Romero and his team had vowed to work hard to make the electoral system transparent and carry out a fair election.

By all reports, they did exactly that.[15] The robust process affirmed the viability of the electoral system and signaled that Bolivians prefer a democratically elected government as well as a rotation of leadership. "Diffusing the tense standoff in Bolivia through the ballot box is a remarkable feat, not just for Bolivia but for the region," reported journalist Pablo Stefanoni.[16]

Despite unanimous statements by election observers and candidates from differing parties that the elections were not fraudulent, far-right groups vehemently rejected the results. For several weeks, protestors gathered in front of the TSE in La Paz, jumping up and down and chanting phrases such as, "If you don't jump, you're a faggot MAS supporter." One of the demonstrators explained, "Mesa, Áñez, and Arce conspired with [TSE president] Romero to steal the vote. There was fraud because the MAS won. That's the proof."[17] Her friend added, "Indians aren't that smart. They shouldn't vote anyway because they are easily tricked."[18]

Meanwhile, demonstrators set up small blockades and vigils in Santa Cruz, Cochabamba, Beni, and Tarija. Protestors in Santa Cruz called for a civic strike and denounced "*Indios*" (Indians), while in Cochabamba the right-wing Cochala Youth Resistance attacked candidates belonging to Mesa's Civic Community party as traitors and prayed in front of a police station, demanding the security forces carry out a coup.[19] As journalists Laurence Blair and Ryan Grim subsequently discovered, a second coup to prevent Arce from taking power had been plotted—although eventually abandoned—by Áñez's Minister of Defense, Fernando López Julio.[20]

While some saw the overwhelming MAS win as an inherent indication of fraud, others viewed it as further proof that no voting irregularities had taken place in the previous year's elections. Both Luis Arce and Evo Morales called on Luis Almagro, who political scientist Gabriel Hetland has referred to as "the Trumpian head" of the Organization of American States, to resign over the charges of fraud the organization had brought. "What happened in Bolivia is an extension of the OAS's decades-long bad history," Hetland said. "It was technically incompetent and politically biased."[21]

Analysis comparing the 2019 and 2020 elections by Jake Johnston of the Washington, DC–based Center for Economic and Policy Research cast further doubt on the OAS fraud accusations. He analyzed the 2020 results from the eighty-six voting centers that the OAS had identified as suspicious in 2019 based, in part, on the high MAS share of votes in these locations and found that in all but nine of the centers, support for the MAS increased in 2020.[22] Mexican government spokesman Maximiliano Reyes accused Almagro of decrying an electoral fraud "that never existed."[23]

Although Arce and Choquehuanca scored a decisive victory, this did not guarantee a solid base of support going forward. The MAS still held a majority in the Legislative Assembly, though it lost the two-thirds supermajority it had enjoyed since 2011. According to sociologist Julio Córdova Villazón, after eight years of almost complete hegemony, the MAS needs to relearn how to negotiate with the opposition, which will inevitably require more compromises.[24]

A positive result of the elections was the diverse composition of the new Plurinational Legislative Assembly. For the first time, women outnumber men, with a total of 51.9 percent overall. Women now dominate the Senate twenty to sixteen.[25] This consolidation of women's legislative participation began during the Áñez government's time in office, when the heads of the executive, judicial, and legislative branches were all women. The Senate was run by Eva Copa, the 33-year female MAS senator from El Alto. In spite of accusations by radical MAS members that she was too compromising, Eva Copa had played an important role in rebuilding the party both in Plurinational Legislative Assembly and in the streets.[26]

Just as the new Assembly was set to take over, a political controversy arose: the MAS, which still held two-thirds of the votes, passed a law that permitted approval of eleven categories of parliamentary decisions by simple majority. This meant that the MAS could control certain elements of the parliamentary agenda and process, as well as the appointment of high-ranking military officials and ambassadors.

This move made those who had rallied against Morales's drift toward permanent rule nervous. The head of the opposition, Carlos Mesa, was furious. "They are continuing authoritarianism and abuse," he told the Cochabamba newspaper *Opinión*.[27]

The MAS denied Mesa's accusations. "It is ridiculous that they are saying that we are breaking the law," stated then–Senate president Eva Copa.[28] The MAS's goal was to address illicit acts carried out by Áñez, such as the illegal appointment of military officials without the support of the Senate. The opposition had colluded with Áñez by rubber-stamping them. The proposed change was intentionally limited to internal administrative procedures, leaving the previous prerequisites in place for many laws.[29]

## BEHIND THE VICTORY

On November 1, All Saints' Day, the victims of Senkata gathered outside the gas plant where soldiers had killed their family and friends nearly a year before. Under a pair of tents erected to block the blazing Altiplano sun, they prepared an ornate *mesa* (altar) adorned with flowers, coca leaves, favorite foods of their loved ones, and elaborate *t'antawawas* (Andean "bread babies"). Despite the colorful spread, it was the photos of those killed in the massacre that stood out.

Though the offering was located next to a bustling market along the La Paz–Oruro highway, the honking horns and shouting market vendors were almost unnoticeable once the somber ceremony began. A spiritual leader chanted in Aymara as he lit the prepared offering. Each of the relatives circled the fire, dousing it with drops of alcohol, which created small crackling bursts of flames. On this day, the *ajayus* (souls) of the dead return to the world of the living.

Shortly after the ceremony began, soon-to-be president Lucho arrived unannounced. The families immediately surrounded him and hugged him. Gloria Quisbert, the leader of the Senkata victims' association, cried to Lucho about her 21-year-old brother Antonio and the other victims: "They took their youth. They left their children orphaned.... Then [the government] called us terrorists."[30]

Senator Eva Copa, who was also there, sidestepped the cameras to console a mother who had lost her son. As they spoke, a young woman sitting near them commented: "The MAS were the only ones who said what happened here was a massacre. It should be no surprise they won. When your choice is between the MAS, who stood up for the humble, or the fascists—or at best people who aligned with fascists by staying silent—the choice is obvious."[31] A week later, before Lucho gave his inauguration speech, he asked "for a moment of silence for those killed in Senkata, El Alto; Sacaba, Cochabamba; Montero, Santa Cruz; Betanzos, Potosí; Ovejuyo, Zona Sur La Paz; Pedregal, La Paz."[32]

Many people all over the country who had supported Morales's ouster had become increasingly uncomfortable with the open hunting down of the MAS and its supporters. Interior Minister Arturo Murillo seemed out of control, continuously threatening imprisonment for social and labor movement leaders. Carlos Mesa's strategy of courting the right and his complicity in the abuses carried out by Áñez undermined whatever trust voters placed in him. For these reasons, many who had grown weary of the MAS returned to the party's fold.[33] "People may have been too scared to speak out against the Áñez government's repression and corruption," said Kathryn Ledebur of the Andean Information Network, "but this result shows they voted with their conscience."[34]

"The 2020 election was not a choice between political platforms, but between fears and socio-cultural identifications," writes climate change activist and former UN ambassador Pablo Solón.[35] Indeed, the bigotry expressed by the far-right opposition convinced many of those with Indigenous roots that they were safer with the MAS. "There has been a huge exacerbation of racism," said Wilmer Machaca of the Indigenist media group Jichha. "It wasn't so much a vote for the MAS as a vote against Áñez and what she stood for."[36]

Many voters were also enraged by the Áñez government's general incompetence as well as its incapacity to effectively manage COVID-19, with corruption and nepotism cases going public during the height of the pandemic. As the economy went into freefall in the midst of talk of privatizing key sectors, the electorate soundly rejected the attempt to revive the neoliberal economic policies that had served Bolivia so poorly in the past.

Few could stick to the initially strict COVID-19 lockdown imposed by Áñez when they were receiving so little in the way of public assistance.[37] As a result, the virus had spread like wildfire. If the election had been held the previous January as originally proposed, when the MAS was still reeling from the coup, it is doubtful the party could have scored such a resounding win. Indeed, it had taken the Áñez government's subsequent missteps to ensure that.

The reinvigoration of popular Indigenous, peasant, and union movements also cemented the party's massive win. Their growing independence became clear when they differed with Morales and his circle on candidates for the elections originally scheduled for May 2020.[38] Arce and Choquehuanca were the compromise choice.

Similar to when the COB compelled the return to democracy in 1982, the massive blockade across the country in August 2020 was the catalyst that forced the October elections. But those protests also signaled the strength of the MAS as the only party with an established structure, ongoing national membership, and a loyal voter base.[39]

Another significant factor was the candidates themselves. As the architect of Bolivia's economic success during the commodity boom, many believed that putting Arce in power would guarantee a return to previous prosperity. "My family lived better than they ever had thanks to Luis Arce," said Juan Rivero, who works at a hotel in Santa Cruz. "We need him to come and fix things so we can live like that again."[40]

During the presidential race, Arce and Choquehuanca astutely emphasized the economic stability the MAS had fostered in comparison to the meltdown over the previous year. In contrast, the opposition candidates focused their campaigns on defeating the MAS at all costs, with little in the way of concrete proposals for addressing COVID-19 or the accompanying economic free-fall; moreover, they paid almost no attention to working-class or Indigenous areas. According to journalist Fernando Molina, the country's elites failed to recognize the MAS as "a genuine expression of the least privileged and most Indigenous sectors of the country."[41]

## THE PATH AHEAD

As the newest standard-bearers for progressive politics in Latin America, Luis Arce and David Choquehuanca faced formidable obstacles. First, though the massive margin of their victory gave the MAS electoral capital in a still-polarized context, they lost their two-thirds legislative majority. Under such conditions, the MAS cannot underestimate the right wing. The firebrand and third-place finisher Luis Fernando Camacho remains a powerful force. After he refused to recognize the October 2020 election results for five days, tweeting that they were fraudulent, protests erupted in at least three cities. Though little violence was reported, a week after the inauguration, part of the house of MAS ex-deputy Muriel Cruz was set on fire, allegedly by Camacho supporters.[42]

A goal high on the MAS agenda is to persuade the military and police, who played a critical role in the ouster of Morales and whose privileges expanded under Áñez, to fully commit to civilian rule. Arce had promised just before the election that there would be no vengeance against soldiers and low-ranking police officers for the 2019 coup and its bloody aftermath.[43] Nonetheless, police reform remains crucial for the new government. Previous MAS efforts ended in a mutiny that propelled a government retreat on the issue, so it will not be easy.

In November 2020, the head of the Cochabamba army garrison, General Alfredo Cuéllar, was arrested for the 2019 Sacaba massacre. The military high command immediately appeared on television announcing they were "disconcerted" that the general was to be tried in civilian rather than military court, reminding listeners that Jeanine Áñez had signed an agreement that protected them from all civil investigations.[44]

Attempts to identify and possibly try other military officials have been obstructed: both military and police leadership have repeatedly refused to release key information about the operations in Sacaba and Senkata,[45] and, according to the minister of defense, the military high command has destroyed pertinent evidence.[46] Despite these obstacles and Arce's efforts to keep peace with the security forces, in January 2021, the vice minister of decolonization accused twenty-six police officials of grave disciplinary breaches, and on March 17, the former head of the army, Jorge Pastor Mendieta, was jailed on terrorism, sedition, and conspiracy. By August 2021, fifteen military officials had been charged.

In March 2021, police arrested ex–interim president Áñez for her role in the coup. The government charged her and other high-level officials with sedition, terrorism, and conspiracy, sparking cries of political prosecution from the opposition. Protestors marched in several cities in support of Áñez, or at least in opposition to her arrest. In Santa Cruz, Camacho spoke to a crowd of thousands at the foot of the Christ the Redeemer statue, proclaiming, "The only time we return to La Paz will be to defeat a tyrant government."[47]

OAS Secretary General Almagro also condemned the detention, suggesting that a legal process instead be initiated against

Evo Morales. Almagro's statement sparked outrage from the international community, including the Mexican government, which told the secretary general to "conduct himself according to his powers" and stay out of Bolivia's internal affairs.[48] Almagro's statement prompted Arce's government to announce a legal process against Almagro for breaching his duties.[49] The reaction by Áñez supporters and the diplomatic posturing highlight the obstacles in bringing trials against those who carried out the coup and committed human rights abuses.

Another immediate challenge is COVID-19. A *New York Times* review of June and July 2020 mortality figures concluded that Bolivia had suffered one of the world's worst epidemics.[50] At least 140 doctors and nurses have died of the disease. However, given the size of the informal economy, the Arce administration wanted to avoid a return to the rigid lockdown of 2020 at all cost.

With Bolivia at the tail end of the vaccination line, Arce shrewdly allotted $80 million to accelerate obtaining vaccines as soon as he was inaugurated. By the end of January, 15.8 million vaccines had been delivered to the country, and 180,000 healthcare personnel were given top priority for the shots.[51] Arce also managed to purchase 1.6 million COVID-19 tests in record time to be deployed in a nationwide free campaign.[52] By September 2021, just over 30 percent of Bolivians were fully vaccinated, comparable to Peru and Paraguay although lagging vaccination rates in Ecuador.

Bolivia became a leading voice calling for the removal of vaccine patents and for assistance from Global North countries to combat the pandemic. "Rich countries that bought more vaccines than they require for their populations should redistribute them to the countries that need them. Only when we are all vaccinated will we be safe," tweeted Foreign Relations Minister Rogelio Mayta.[53] In May 2021, the government ramped up its lobbying efforts by organizing an international forum on the proposed suspension of COVID-19 vaccine patents.[54]

A Health Emergency Law passed in February 2021 makes COVID-19 vaccines free, requires fourteen days of quarantine for international arrivals, and caps charges in private clinics and for drugs. But the most controversial provisions allow the Ministry of Health to hire new medical personnel and prohibit health, phone, and internet services from being disrupted during health emergencies. Even though the draft bill was reviewed twice by doctors' representatives with many of their suggestions incorporated, doctors and health workers went on strike for a month. They contend that the law curtails their right to protest and fear that foreign doctors (particularly Cubans) will take their jobs. The strike, which began just before regional elections, echoed prior doctors' strike actions that were timed to discredit the MAS before elections.[55]

To tackle many of the hurdles ahead, Arce quickly appointed a younger, better-educated administration than that in place during Morales's tenure. In Lucho's words, his new government represented "a technocracy of the left," mirroring the staff makeup of the Ministry of the Economy and Public Finance during the twelve years he was in charge. While several new ministers were of Indigenous origin, only three of sixteen cabinet members were women.

The new team set about tackling issues as divergent as land titling, the reform of the notoriously corrupt judicial system, and the expansion of household natural gas installation. But while younger and more technocratic, his administration resembled more a continuation of the Morales years than any definitive break with the past.

That continuity was very much in evidence in late December 2020, when Arce was visibly buoyed by the discovery of a major new national gas field in the Chaco. "Our Pachamama [Indigenous Mother Earth] is giving Bolivians a lovely Christmas present," he said, beaming. The first significant discovery since 2006, the find boosts proven natural gas reserves that in 2018 were calculated to last only another fifteen years.[56]

The gas find was all the more welcome because of how badly the economy tanked in 2020, the worst tumble in decades. Gas revenues took a 28 percent dive, although in January 2021 demand from Argentina jumped by 58 percent. Gross domestic product fell 8 percent, and open unemployment soared to 11 percent, more than double the 2019 rate.[57] Financial reserves plunged from $3.77 to $2.14 billion dollars. Ninety percent of Bolivian companies could not afford to pay the annual Christmas bonus in 2020, and certain industries, such as tourism, were almost completely gutted.[58]

In the face of this gloomy outlook, Arce drew on the policies that had proven so effective when he was minister of the economy: stimulation of internal demand through public investment, accompanied by efforts to accelerate import substitution. "We've increased savings, government spending, redistributed wealth from natural resource profits, and constructed a broader economic base," he said in an October 2019 interview.[59]

Immediately upon assuming office, Arce announced a subsidy to four million people without formal employment or a pension, and he suspended loan repayments, free of extra interest, for a further six months. These measures were intended to offset some of the setbacks to the gains made by Bolivia's poor and Indigenous majority during the Morales government that have arisen because of COVID-19.

At the other end of the economic spectrum, Arce levied an annual tax on personal fortunes above US$4.3 million, which will impact about 1 percent of the population. In a country with no effective income tax, it was a bold move and one immediately derided by the opposition.

Returning to the previous MAS playbook, and its emphasis on industrialization, Lucho proposed growing biodiesel production and the industrialization of Bolivia's vast lithium reserves. However, both these options raise the same kinds of environmental and climatic concerns that plagued the Morales government, particularly in its later years. While biodiesel is nontoxic and biodegradable and uses waste products derived from agriculture, its production may worsen the deforestation that has already reached alarming levels in Bolivia.

Lithium also faces hitches: it is too remote, impure, and difficult to extract for it to compete effectively with Bolivia's regional rivals, Argentina and Chile, anytime in the foreseeable future. But sociologist Juan Carlos Pinto Quintanilla, employed in the vice presidency for five years under Morales, was convinced that this time the MAS discourse in favor of the environment will merge into greater harmony with actual policies. "We really want to advance in developing alternatives," he said.[60] How those alternatives will affect the pact with agro-industry that the Morales administration forged after 2011 remains to be seen.[61]

A significant question is whether the new MAS government will be successful in prosecuting Jeanine Áñez, Arturo Murillo (the architect of much of the repression), and other officials for the violence they unleashed. As historian Craig Johnson points out, "This victory is only the beginning of another struggle: that of returning to democratic rule after a coup, a long and complex process under the best of conditions."[62]

The day after Arce was sworn in, Murillo and Defense Minister Fernando López Julio flew to Brazil in a military plane; Murillo traveled to Panama days later before heading to the United States.[63] In mid-May 2021, Murillo, his chief of staff, Sergio Rodrigo Méndez, along with three businessmen with dual US-Bolivian citizenship were charged with corruption and money laundering by the US Justice Department. Murillo was accused of taking bribes from the US company that brokered multimillion-dollar contracts to furnish tear gas and nonlethal police equipment to the Bolivian government. If convicted, Murillo and his associates face up to 20 years in a US prison. Even though the opposition joined the Arce government's calls for Murillo's extradition to Bolivia to face related charges, Jeanine Áñez had approved the purchase, which made the "tear gas case" a significant blow to those who had supported the Áñez government.[64]

In mid-November 2020, the Inter-American Commission on Human Rights sent a five-person Interdisciplinary Group of

Independent Experts (GIEI) to investigate abuses during 2019, including the burning of electoral commissions and houses, as well as confrontations between protestors and the massacres in Sacaba and Senkata. Though the group's work had been slated to begin in early 2020, the Áñez government had repeatedly blocked attempts to launch its inquiry.

The Arce administration installed the GIEI immediately. At the inauguration, Foreign Relations Minister Rogelio Mayta, who represented the victims of the 2003 Black October massacres, told a packed room of journalists and foreign diplomats, "'Reconciliation' is not just a phrase.... We cannot have reconciliation if there is no justice."[65]

On August 17, 2021, the GIEI published the results of their investigation. The 470-page report presented a blistering account of the abuses committed by the Áñez government, as well as crimes committed by pro- and anti-MAS groups.[66] Allies quickly distanced themselves from Áñez until four days later when she tried to commit suicide in jail, revitalizing sympathy for the disgraced leader.

The continued support for Áñez and her collaborators raises concerns about reparations for the victims. Despite the conviction of ex-dictator García Meza in 1993, it took until 2017 for the Morales government to replace the ineffective truth commission established in the early 1980s, despite sustained pressure from families of the disappeared, some of whom camped out in front of the Justice Ministry for eight years. Anthropologists Francisco García Jerez and Julianne Müller argue that this foot dragging stems, at least in part, from the MAS government's entente with the military.[67] Like in much of Latin America, where leaders are eager to maintain the peace with the military and police, the need to placate the security forces could compel Arce to also adopt a process that is more rhetoric than substance.

## THE EVO FACTOR

A year after Evo fled the country, vendors in Chimoré, a steamy town in the Chapare, sold T-shirts that read, "Evo—I returned as millions." It was a spinoff on the supposed final words of revered Indigenous leader Tupac Katari, who is reputed to have proclaimed, "I will return as millions" moments before the Spanish quartered and decapitated him. As it turned out, the shirt turned out to be relatively accurate.

Morales's triumphant return came on November 9, one day after Luis Arce was sworn in as president, to the cheers of an estimated five hundred thousand supporters.[68] He and other political exiles crossed the border at the town of Villazón, then embarked on a three-day caravan to the Chapare, home to Morales's most ardent base. Along the way, Indigenous people lined the roads to cheer for him and shower him with flowers. Some traveled for days to get the chance to see, and perhaps even meet, the former president.

In a small village on the Potosí–Oruro border, an Aymara vendor wearing a straw hat and carrying a maroon *aguayo* waited patiently for Morales to arrive. "I made him his favorite meal," she said shyly. "I hope I get to meet him to thank him for everything he's done for us. He made us proud to be Indigenous. He built roads to our community. We wouldn't be who we are without Evo."[69] Moments later, Morales's cavalcade stopped, and he emerged, hugging each person in the crowd. He approached the eager vendor and tried the plate she had prepared: *chuño* (freeze-dried potatoes) and *charque* (dehydrated meat). "How delicious!" he told her. She burst into tears.

The next day Morales swept into Chimoré. Hundreds of thousands congregated on the runway of the airport, where he was scheduled to speak. A barricade of security guards held them back, but when Evo's truck pulled up, thousands of screaming supporters broke through and rushed him. "I've never seen anything like this. Rock stars don't get this kind of attention," commented a journalist covering the event.[70]

The crowd escorted him to the stage, where he delivered one of his signature fiery speeches: he denounced the United States for its imperialism, criticized the Áñez government for its abuses of Bolivia's people, and lionized the social movements for their resistance against both. There could be no doubt: Evo was back.

Arce and Choquehuanca were notable by their absence. "That was a real surprise," said a person who worked closely with Morales for years. "I see it as a sign that Evo won't be part of this government, and that may ruffle some feathers with his supporters."[71] Many saw Arce's inauguration speech, which did not mention Morales, as a further indication of his commitment to govern without the former president and his entourage.[72] Choquehuanca had told local media on the campaign trail, "The people are telling us in meetings that those who surrounded [Evo] shouldn't come back. . . . We have to give new people a chance."[73] Juan Carlos Pinto Quintanilla concurred: "We must strengthen mid-level leadership in the MAS to succeed. We need many Evos, not just one."[74]

Before the elections, Arce had no political trajectory independent of Morales. Both he and Choquehuanca worked under him for over a decade in a government whose internal culture rotated around Evo. Lucho's low-key style contrasts with Evo's often flamboyant, in-your-face approach, which may help to ease tensions after the turmoil of 2019 and 2020.

Choquehuanca, the social movements' first-choice presidential candidate, enjoys strong grassroots support, particularly in Aymara highland communities, and describes himself as part of those movements rather than the MAS party per se. For years he was considered the third wheel in the MAS after Evo and Alvaro, the head of the moderate "cultural" Indigenist wing that stuck with the MAS after more radical factions abandoned the party. He has never been afraid to disagree with Morales, who eventually forced him out during a 2017 cabinet reshuffle that favored those aligned with the Vice President Alvaro García Linera.[75]

Arce seemed determined not to succumb to the addiction to holding office that had consumed Evo. He told the *New York Times*, "I have no interest in power. I want to move the country forward, leave it in the hands of young people, and then I'll go."[76] Arce promised to "govern for all Bolivians" and "build a government of national unity."

Over the course of 2020, the MAS saw a surge in youth leadership, from Adriana Salvatierra to Andrónico Rodríguez to Eva Copa.[77] Whatever role Morales plays in Bolivia's future, a newer generation of the MAS is coming of age. "A lot of our new candidates are young," said 38-year-old doctor and MAS militant Angelica Johan of Santa Cruz. "It is time for young people to bring a new vision of governance."[78]

## REGIONAL ELECTIONS

A work division was installed early on between Arce and Morales, with Lucho running the government and Evo acting as head of the party and campaign manager for the regional elections scheduled for March 7, 2021. For twenty years, Morales had been perceived as essential to MAS electoral success, acquiring almost mythical status. However, this tunnel vision underestimated the political process, both within and between the MAS party bases, and convinced the opposition to mistakenly assume that without him, the MAS could be easily defeated.[79]

Indications that Evo's influence may be on the wane were evident during the *dedazo* (appointment) of municipal and departmental candidates. In the southern city of Potosí, Evo fled a meeting because of outrage over his choice of candidates; soon after he had a plastic chair hurled at him in the Chapare, again over one of his picks.

But the most serious split erupted in El Alto, the only city the MAS had swept in the previous municipal elections, when Morales opposed Eva Copa for mayoral candidate. His decision prompted Copa to run independently. She was immediately expelled from the MAS but went on to win 66 percent of the vote, the highest percentage in the country. Some speculate that her move, bolstered by wins by other ex-MAS candidates in Pando, Beni, and Chuquisaca, could constitute the nucleus of a left-wing alternative to the MAS.[80]

On election day, far-right-wing Luis Fernando Camacho, who had played such a pivotal role in the 2019 ouster of Morales, easily won the governorship of Santa Cruz with 55.6 percent of the vote, proving just how strong the right remains regionally. His erstwhile ally, ex–interim president Áñez, ran for governor in her home department of the Beni in the northeast, where she came in third. And Morales and Arce's principal rival in the national elections, the party built around former president Carlos Mesa, obtained so few votes that it was rendered irrelevant.[81]

The MAS assumed governorships in three departments and went to a second round in four more, losing all of them. The MAS lost in the four major cities, but won in 240 of the country's 336 municipalities, 13 more than in 2015.[82]

Several issues stood out in the races. One is that only 16 percent of candidates to key posts were women, showing that gender parity at top levels is still a long way off. Second is that the MAS remains *the* national political force, or at least the only one capable of fielding candidates across the county, even though the party's percentage of the urban vote shrunk compared to 2015.[83] Other political configurations comprised a potpourri of local parties built around a particular candidate, another sign of the opposition's inability to forge a united front. Many of these candidates represented the lurch to the right that Bolivia has experienced: the victorious opposition candidates in Santa Cruz and Cochabamba were far more conservative than Carlos Mesa and effectively weakened the historic center-right even further. Finally, the diversity of political platforms, parties, and outcomes in the regional contests confirms that electoral democracy remains very much alive.

## LESSONS LEARNED

The MAS's national win will hopefully allow the recent period of self-criticism, particularly among the young generation of *masistas*, to flourish.[84] For the first time in many years, leaders of the union movement and MAS militants, such as the head of the COB in Santa Cruz, Rolando Borda Padilla, began articulating "the errors we made. We had people who took advantage of the process for personal ends," he explained. "We must engage in criticism and self-criticism."[85]

President Arce has publicly admitted that the previous MAS government made miscalculations that need addressing, without specifying what those errors were. "We are going to restart our process of change . . . by recognizing and overcoming the mistakes we have made in the past," he said on election night.[86] Without such introspection—something hard to incorporate when needs are so pressing and the right wing is such a constant threat—it will be difficult for the MAS to reinvigorate the "process of change."

In the words of Aymara communitarian feminist Julieta Paredes, "It is very important to reflect, evaluate and embark on self-criticism on the fourteen years of the 'process of change.' The errors made belong to all of us. . . . Now is the moment to speak out about what we think was wrong. Enough with staying quiet because we fear that the fascists will take advantage of any public critiques."[87] Along similar lines, Juan Carlos Pinto Quintanilla observed, "If we are going to make this process of change sustainable over the long term, we must engage in self-criticism and re-politicizing the population."[88]

## COUPS COME IN ALL SHAPES AND SIZES

What Bolivia illustrates is that, sadly, coups in Latin America are not a thing of the past. They have simply evolved. Indeed, the combination of older military leaders still gun-shy from the negative consequences of earlier dictatorships, the internet, and stronger regional institutions make it harder to get away with the traditional

military coups that afflicted Latin America's last century.[89] As
*Axios*'s David Lawler writes, "The days of opportunistic military
officers making a play for power seem to have come to an end."[90]

The new coups are often called "neo-coups" or "lite coups."
While explicit military intervention has taken place in countries
like Honduras, Ecuador, Haiti, and Venezuela during this century, coups in places such as Brazil and Paraguay have drawn
on parliamentary, judicial, or civilian interventions to legitimize
the removal of democratically elected leaders. Though the military and police have played roles in these coups, as they did in
Bolivia, state forces were never their public face.

Sociologists Octavio Humberto Moreno Velador and Carlos
Figueroa Ibarra discuss how branding is used to give the twenty-first-century coups a veneer of legitimacy. Many of these illegal
transitions, the authors assert, "have tried to pass off the coup as
an alternative to solve problems of ungovernability, government
inefficiency, political impasse, or even strong confrontations between groups of politicians."[91] Bolivia has been no exception. The
coup was labeled a return to democracy, and the protest movements
that ousted Morales were lauded as organic, nonviolent crusaders
who foiled a dictatorship and advanced human rights. "The new
legalistic, human rights frame provides a powerful and distinctive
platform for rightists," argues anthropologist Nicole Fabricant.[92]

Although the new coups, veiled as they are in human rights
and democratic discourse, may be savvier and more refined than
those in the previous century, they are just as insidious. As one
former Latin American president stated before the 2020 elections, "Bolivia has become the litmus test to see what the right
can get away with. If they win, it will legitimize all the frightening undemocratic behavior of the last year and open the door for
more coups in the region."[93]

## AUTHORITARIANS MAKE FOR STRANGE BEDFELLOWS

In the lead-up to the 2019 elections, legitimate criticisms of Evo
Morales drove people to the streets. Unfortunately, however,

many of these protestors were willing to ally with far-right groups. Because these were frequently unambiguously racist and authoritarian, affiliation with them undermined the moderates' critiques of the MAS and opened a space for the right wing to usurp power. As Lorena Pérez, who works with the victims of the 2003 Black October massacres in the lawsuit against Sánchez de Lozada, put it, "It is absurd to think you can jump into bed with anti-democratic groups—particularly in a struggle characterized as a 'fight for democracy'—and it won't come back to bite you."[94]

Some anti-Morales protesters lament that their struggle was co-opted by the Bolivian right. "We were completely disheartened when the transitional government co-opted a civic movement that had very legitimate grievances for the political and economic gain of the Santa Cruz Civic Committee, Rubén Costas's political party (Creemos), and members of economic power groups in Santa Cruz," said one organizer of anti-Morales protests.[95]

But it is hard claim surprise as the extremist nature of the far-right forces was always on display. Groups in the anti-MAS coalition openly made racist comments, assaulted leftists and Indigenous people, and distributed videos that showed members of the Santa Cruz Youth Union, an organization that had largely gone dormant in the previous ten years, giving Nazi salutes.[96] The US embassy in La Paz characterized the group as "racist" for attacking Indigenous people and MAS supporters.[97]

Journalist and historian Benjamin Dangl describes the Santa Cruz Youth Union as the "brass knuckles" of the racist right, and the Pro–Santa Cruz Civic Committee, a leading player in Morales's downfall, as its mouthpiece.[98] The International Federation for Human Rights, which represents 192 human rights organizations in 117 countries, has documented their hate crimes and other racist behavior, denouncing the Pro–Santa Cruz Civic Committee as an "actor and promoter of violence and racism in Bolivia."[99] Nonetheless, prominent leaders in the National Committee for the Defense of Democracy (CONADE) and other groups protesting Morales repeatedly participated in marches, public talks, and strategy meetings with their representatives.

One critic of Morales who openly denounced the fascist elements of the opposition was feminist activist María Galindo. At the final *cabildo* in La Paz before the 2019 elections (attended by Camacho, representatives from CONADE, and other Morales critics), Galindo publicly condemned the reactionary groups speaking that day. Her speech was cut short, and people in the crowd booed her.[100] Other moderates and progressives present remained silent.

Though criticisms such as Galindo's were few and far between, after Áñez was named president, some who had protested Morales immediately realized their strategic error. An Aymara student from the Higher University of San Andrés (UMSA) who marched with campesinos through the center of La Paz explained:

> I was part of the 21F protests against Evo. A bunch of my classmates were. CONADE leader Waldo [Albarracín] was the chancellor of the university, so we all kind of got involved without thinking about it. . . . We were so focused on Evo that we completely ignored those who were even worse. I'm out here protesting Áñez and the attacks on my people, but I'm afraid it's too late. We messed up.[101]

The 2019 coup serves as a powerful lesson in how, by working with racists, sexists, and homophobes, the anti-Morales struggle gave legitimacy to illegitimate groups and enabled extremists to hijack the political narrative. It also set the stage for a leader to seize power under the veil of "restoring democracy" and served to whitewash nearly a year of widespread abuses.

## SOCIAL MOVEMENTS ARE THE DRIVERS OF CHANGE

Social movements' loss of strength can impede progressive social change in any country.[102] But in Bolivia, where political culture is still based largely in the streets, such a loss of momentum is devastating. The key to rearticulating Bolivia's "process of change" lies in continued efforts to rebuild autonomy in social movement organizations. By bolstering their capacity to propose alternate agendas, movements can diminish the chance of slipping toward co-optation as they did under Morales—which was, ironically, a principal factor in his 2019 downfall.[103] Anthropologist Nicole Fabricant sums this up: "The task will be to return to the roots of MAS as a political party of social movements, advancing future policies and politics by building sustainable power alongside Indigenous peoples, trade unionists, leaders of federations, and neighborhood associations."[104]

In the past, backroom deals negotiated by a tiny elite were often trumped by the sheer volume of angry and articulate working-class and Indigenous people, as well as their middle-class allies, who all took to the streets. But to sustain a high level of mobilization is taxing—at times, nearly impossible. People eventually need to attend to the concerns of their everyday lives, which means protests tend to come in cycles or waves, a reality that organizers must accommodate as much as possible.[105] In part, what facilitated the MAS's failure to push a more radical agenda in 2009, when it controlled the legislature, was the winding down of the protest cycle that had lasted from 2000 to 2005. With those voices ebbing, there was a growing tendency to turn the change process over to officials and the state bureaucracy.

Clientelism proved the easiest path to keep social movements quiet while responding to the long-standing assumptions of both movements and militants that they could count on party and state patronage.[106] The MAS never found an effective way to contest or reduce these deeply entrenched expectations, preferring a pragmatic emphasis on outcomes and immediate needs over any serious debate within the party about ideology and practice.

Because of the strength and breadth of Bolivia's social movements, both the MAS government and the movements that created it were, more than any other left-leaning government in Latin America, in a position to create a more participatory, bottom-up process. While it was inevitable that movements and government would drift apart to some extent—since governing entails obligations that movements do not need to respond to—there was an incapacity to change or at least modify how politics is conducted from the local union to the highest reaches of government.[107]

Nonetheless, both within and outside of government, the collective agency and strategic decision making of leaders and activists were impressive. Bolivia's activists are reorienting in the face of electoral victories, moving from "protests to proposals," in the words of one Cochabamba activist, and seeking ways to sustain independent oversight and pressure on the newly elected government.[108]

## POLITICAL EDUCATION

To solidify social change, a population must maintain a robust political consciousness. However, the MAS neglected to prioritize Bolivians' ongoing political engagement. "While the material conditions of the population have improved, this has not been accompanied by a process of political education, of consciousness and self-criticism," contends communitarian feminist América Maceda Llanque.[109] MAS officials have echoed Llanque's critique. "We did not engage in an adequate political education process, either within the party or in the population at large," said a former minister in 2018. "The successful reduction of poverty was not accompanied by an ideological project."[110]

To capture public space and build consciousness, a political party has no option but to adapt to generational changes and implement sophisticated strategies that reflect diverse demographics, including a growing urban population. For political scientist Lorenza Fontana, the MAS under Morales relied on "old patterns of collective action and mobilization instead of implementing innovative mechanisms and spaces of dialogue between the state and civil society."[111] In the lead-up to the 2019 elections, the MAS failed to engage large sectors of the population in the savvy manner that the right wing did—particularly when it came to social media—a failing which proved catastrophic for the party.

Educating Bolivians also means training public servants. While public administration is often given short shrift because it is not as exciting as organizing in the streets, success for progressive and leftist governments can hinge on its management.

Without concerted effort to transform how governing is exercised, entrenched unjust structures and relationships persist.

## LEADING BY OBEYING: ADDRESSING CAUDILLISMO AND CONCENTRATIONS OF POWER

Progressive and radical movements cannot rely on a political party or its leadership as the only mechanism for social change. But, beyond valid criticisms of how representative democracy almost always serves dominant classes, is the issue of how the left has too often failed to control the charismatic leadership needed to win elections, especially in countries without strong institutional buffers against corruption and abuses of power. Bolivia, like many Pink Tide countries, rode the wave of a populist leader, but drowned out much of the vibrancy of its social movements in the process.

A chronic challenge faced by the left is how to marshal charismatic people to lead and win elections (within all the inherent limitations of "democracy") while ensuring that their party, social movements, and government structures limit their desires to hold onto power. The left's shortsighted, though pragmatic, focus on the enormous challenges of winning often overshadows the paramount task of holding their leaders to account. Without that accountability at the forefront, the left will never be able to ensure that progressive and radical political projects remain more critical than keeping an individual (and the sycophants around him or her) in power.

"Evo has brought us things we never had before—schools, roads, productive projects. We want him to stay," said a woman from a small community near Lake Titicaca in 2018. When pressed about whether his decision to stay in power for more than two terms violated the constitution, she insisted that "he must stay because he has made things so much better for us."[112] Unfortunately, as time went on, such adulation invited Morales and his cohort to concentrate power even further. One anonymous government employee highlighted the pressure within the party before 2019 to conform to this assumption: "Even though there are people in the MAS party who think Evo should go after this term, they won't say a word. The party has become so top down it's turned them into sheep." Former MAS government official Tom Kruse said in 2018, "In a radical movement, it's not about the individual, but individuals radically matter. This human side of it was not something that any of us understood."[113]

To ensure a healthy exercise of power, political and personal maturity as well as strong institutions are crucial. According to Kruse, "On the left we tend to talk about structures, but I came away from my work in the MAS government understanding how Evo filled in the space of the state. When institutions don't or can't function, the space is filled in by leadership." Fernando Molina argues that the left's dependence on "a very strong charismatic leadership . . . [has] facilitated the articulation of [progressive] forces . . . [but] created problems because this has not allowed the institutionalization of political movements."[114]

Although the path has been rocky and costly in terms of lives lost, on October 18, 2020, the public exercised the sort of control that the MAS could not—or would not—when it gave more votes to a new leader than it had to the one who tried to remain in power. "It was time for Evo to go," said Miriam Chávez, a 24-year-old taxi dispatcher in Sucre, "He played an important role, but we need new leaders and new perspectives."[115]

The Arce government is now tasked with reining in the patronage politics that plagued the prior MAS government,[116] just as they have all administrations in Bolivia, Áñez's included. That challenge will be far from easy, as evidenced by reports of MAS supporters and ex–government officials entering ministries days after Arce's inauguration and demanding that staff, many of them long-standing professionals, turn their jobs over to MAS loyalists because they had remained at their posts under Áñez.[117] Though there is no evidence this behavior was directed by MAS leadership—in fact, they denounced it—the conflicts and resentments inherent in the competition for access to a limited number of political and administrative posts consistently serve to dilute the MAS's ideological orientation.[118]

## CONFRONTING STRUCTURAL CHALLENGES

The blatant intervention of Bolivia's conservative neighbors abetted by the United States under Donald Trump speaks to a disturbing return to extrajudicial forms of resolving internal conflict in the country and the rest of the region. The specter of Operation Condor, also backed by the United States, hangs even more heavily over South America after Bolivia's coup. Key to minimizing this intervention as much as possible is international solidarity from letters to the editor to civil society organizations' statements.

The economic and political metamorphosis promised by the MAS has been thwarted by Bolivia's underlying conditions: it remains a small, landlocked country, among the poorest in South America, saddled with an economy that has been driven by extractivism for five hundred years. While a new class of (often Indigenous) truckers, merchants, contraband traders, and small mine owners have become wealthy, and the traditional elites have mostly lost direct political power, the economic clout of the latter has remained largely untouched.

In Bolivia's struggle against underdevelopment and poverty, efforts to promote a culture of sustainability and of serious environmental protection often went by the wayside, driven off course by the frequent collusion of state and private sector interests. But with the end of the commodity boom, that deal began to fray.

The MAS did its best to skirt the thorny dilemma of raising living standards without destroying the natural environment. This reflects the structural constraints progressive movements face in low-income countries but elsewhere as well. Extractivism for the social good remains a slippery slope that is used to justify the destruction of lands and peoples; as such, it is urgent that the Arce government move to tighten its criteria and controls. New projects must incorporate systems for robust prior consultation, feasible and marketable value-added components to reduce the export of raw materials, and clear environmental protection and remediation plans. These can be backed by initiatives in Northern countries, such the 2020 Swiss effort to hold multinationals headquartered in its territory accountable for their human rights and environmental actions abroad.[119] Although the Swiss proposal won a majority of public support, it failed to get enough cantons (states) on board. Nonetheless, it signals a path forward for building people- and environment-centered development.

In order to reduce the influence of extractivism, it is also crucial that Bolivia devise alternative ways to fund the government. Though a daunting task politically, it may prove key over the long term to diversify the tax base by strengthening personal income tax. Aside from tax avoidance by the wealthy, distrust of taxes is particularly strong among the rural poor, who historically carried the country's largest tax burden.[120]

## CONCLUSIONS

By any measure, and certainly compared with its predecessors, what the MAS administration achieved under Evo Morales was remarkable. With all its shortfalls and challenges, the government made tremendous strides in economic development, national sovereignty, and women's and Indigenous rights, while raising living standards, education levels, and healthcare coverage. Nonetheless, the global position of Bolivia and countries like it, along with concessions the Morales government felt obliged to make to the eastern elites, fundamentally constrained its options.

Of course, Bolivia is not the only country in the Western Hemisphere to have suffered an affront on democratic norms and institutions in recent years. Indeed, there are unsettling parallels between events in the United States and in Bolivia's 2019 coup. Serious threats to democracy have permeated both countries, from Trump's and Áñez's uses of the Bible (and religious faith) as a political prop, to police attacks on one group of protestors while limiting the use of force against others, to government intimidation through the deployment of tanks and soldiers in the streets and planes and helicopters overhead.

In 2006, the MAS was thrust into power unexpectedly and unprepared. In the ensuing almost fourteen years, it struggled to prioritize a process that could examine, critique, and transform the way power is utilized. Moving forward, this poses a significant hurdle. "One of the biggest problems the Arce-Choquehuanca government will have is with Evo," said Jichha's Wilmer Machaca. "There is still not a strong political project outside the MAS. Many have an unerring loyalty and are not critical [of it]. The social organizations supported the MAS in the 2020 election in a mechanistic way." But he also expressed optimism that grassroots organizations are broadening their vision. "In the last year, they have become politicized again because of the Áñez government. Hopefully, this will continue and not be co-opted by the MAS."[121]

It is striking that this little country in the Andes has catapulted such a beacon of hope for the left worldwide. As Nicole Fabricant writes, the victory of Luis Arce and David Choquehuanca "represents a radical vision of hope at a time when we need it most." She continues: "Given MAS's roots and political commitments, there's enormous potential for a more participatory form of democracy that decenters presidential power and expands decision-making to local bodies of government, that provides spaces where social movement activists can debate and reach agreements, if not consensus. Bolivia is poised to teach us; we should watch and envision how we might bring some of their lessons home."[122]

Nonetheless, Bolivia raises many questions about the limits on radical projects that need to be wrestled with by progressives everywhere. What can be achieved in a dependent, peripheral country? And where is the best place for progressive and left forces to focus their efforts? How can international backers of progressive political change support a process that is uneven and often contradictory?

Despite the complexity these questions raise, one thing is certain: the Bolivian people will continue to fight for a more just and equal country. Julieta Paredes captures this sentiment well, writing, "We did it! What a marvelous effort by Bolivian women and men; we have recuperated the possibility of choosing and deciding our future. . . . Bolivia is an example for the world."[123] Once again, it is social movements that have thrust the MAS back into the driver's seat. As the party faces another opportunity to transform the country, creativity on the ground, constructive criticism, and international support can all serve to keep Bolivia at the forefront of struggles around the globe to make another world possible.

# ACKNOWLEDGMENTS

From our earliest uninformed questions until now, Bolivians have been generous with their time and perspectives in helping us untangle the complex web of their country. Our thanks go to the hundreds of Bolivians who helped us reach those moments of comprehension and flashes of insight. Some of them are quoted here.

We would like to especially thank Ben Dangl who started this journey with us, and helped us enormously in formulating the proposal and finding a publisher. Time and circumstances dictated that he did not become a co-author but his insights and support were invaluable.

Alix Shand did an excellent first copy edit that helped us identify inconsistencies and holes, and the people we worked with at Haymarket–Nisha Bolsey, Ashley Smith, Sam Smith, and particularly Rachel Cohen–were committed, charitable with their time, and instrumental in helping us move the book to production. Thanks also go to Eric Fox who so generously and patiently created the maps. Pedro Albornoz encouraged us to translate the book into Spanish and publish it in Bolivia and went a long way to making that possible. Enormous appreciation also goes out to Marcelo Pérez del Carpio who excellent photos grace these pages.

Linda would like to especially thank Reina Ayala, Félix Muruchi Poma, Amaru Villanueva Rance, Susanna Rance, the students of the Ben Kohl scholarship fund, Clarita Caceres Ayala, Bryanha Garcia Caceres, Alberto Borda, Freddy Condo, Lilia Camacho, Kath Ledebur, José de la Fuente, Juan Tellez, Sharoll Fernandez Siñani, Javier Arevelica Vasquez, Khantuta Muruchi

Escobar, Oscar "Oki" Vega, Boris Miranda, Rene Nuñez, Charo León, Anne Catherine Bajard, Juan Carlos Pinto Quintanilla, Julieta Paredes, José Luis "Pepe" Pereira, Christina Tellez, Manuel de la Fuente, David Aruquipa, Richard Fidler, Jaime Vilela, Guido Montaño, Sara Shields, Tom Grisaffi, Hugo Salvatierra, Ricardo Rocha, Monica Guzmán, Jose Martínez Montaño, Alejandra Anzaldo Garcia, Nancy Romer, Lew Friedman, Eli Peredo, Saul Arias, David Maradiegue Revollo, Wilmer Machaca, Eve Schnitzer, Estella Machaca, Juanita Roca, Marisabel Villagomez, Jose Pereira, Jose Antonio Quiroga, Pati Parra, Rocio Jimenez, Pablo Solón, Angus McNelly, Kirsten Francescone, Vladi Díaz Cuellar, Jean Elliott Manning, Aiko Ikemura, Bill Wrobeloski, Karina Guzmán, Chris Krueger, Claudia Peña Claros and Jill Benton who in different ways all enabled this book – many by sharing their considerable insights with her, informing the result even in the cases where they disagreed politically and others in ways far more practical.

This book could never have been written without Maureen Feely and George Kohl, Linda's sister- and brother-in-law who generously gave her shelter when COVID hit. Their house in Takoma Park, MD became her home for eight months and was where the bulk of this book was written.

Thomas would like to thank his family, whose support has always been unconditional even in the most challenging times. His mom maintains that he is responsible for every gray hair on her head, so each threat or attack he endured in 2019 and 2020 surely added countless more.

He would also like to thank his colleagues and students at University Network for Human Rights, Harvard Law School's International Human Rights Clinic, and Yale Law School, including Fabiola Alvelais, Lindsay Bailey, Camila Bustos, Gemma Canham, Hannah Carrese, James Cavallaro, Laura Clark, Luke Connell, Mohammed Elshafie, Matthew Farrell, Susan Farbstein, Belén García Martínez, Tyler Giannini, Kelsey Jost-Creegan, Rund Khayyat, Celeste Kmiotek, Luis Martinez, Ruhan Nagra, Gerald Neuman, Josh Petersen, Mahmoud Serewel, Jasmine Shin,

Sabrina Singh, Delany Sisiruca, Claret Vargas, Nicolas Walker, Dana Walters, and Julia Wenck. They helped people he cares about stay alive, and he will forever be grateful.

Thank you to Travis Matteson, Rod Roddenberry, Bill Wroblewski, Adri Zegarra, and Wood Iron for providing Thomas a home to write this book.

Finally, Thomas would like to thank all the people in Bolivia who took risks to share their stories, advocate for the marginalized, and resist during the most oppressive period he has experienced in the country. There are too many to name, but here's a start: Paulo Abrão, Soraya Aguilar, Patricia Arce, ASOFAC-DG, Vanesa Besaga, Amy Booth, Marcelo Bracamonte, Angelica Calle, Frida Conde, Nelson Cox, Nadia Cruz, Pamela Delgadillo, Noah Friedman-Rudovsky, Jaime Fuentes, Maria Galindo and Mujeres Creando, Alan Garcia, Caro Gálvez, Nadeshda Guevara, David Inca, Ruth Llanos, Kathryn Ledebur, Camila Maia, Rogelio Mayta, Lorena Pérez, Gerardo Puma, Gloria Quisbert, Marisol Rodriguez, and Iveth Saravia. You have changed the world, and Thomas feels so fortunate to get to tag along for the ride.

# NOTES

## Preface

1. Unless otherwise specified, all translations are by Linda Farthing and Thomas Becker.

## Introduction: Unpacking Bolivia

1. "What Are Biodiversity Hotspots?," Conservation International, https://www.conservation.org/priorities/biodiversity-hotspots.

2. "Mapped: The 6 Cradles of Civilization," *Mapscaping*, May 30, 2018, https://mapscaping.com/blogs/geo-candy/mapped-the-6-cradles-of-civilization.

3. Michael W. Binford et al., "Climate Variation and the Rise and Fall of an Andean Civilization," *Quaternary Research* 47 (1997): 235–48.

4. John Wayne Janusek, *Ancient Tiwanaku* (Cambridge, UK: Cambridge University Press, 2008).

5. José de Mesa, Teresa Gisbert, and Carlos Mesa, *Manual de historia boliviana* (La Paz: Editorial Gisbert, 1999).

6. Bret Gustafson, "Bolivia 9/11: Bodies and Power on a Feudal Frontier," *Caterwaul Quarterly* 3 (Summer/Spring 2009): 20–24.

7. Philipp Horn, "Indigenous Peoples, the City and Inclusive Urban Development Policies in Latin America: Lessons from Bolivia and Ecuador," *Development Policy Review* 36 (July 2018): 483–501.

8. Leandro Medina and Friedrich Schneider, "Shadow Economies around the World: What Did We Learn over the Last 20 Years?," International Monetary Fund, January 25, 2018, https://www.imf.org/en/Publications/WP/Issues/2018/01/25/Shadow-Economies-Around-the-World-What-Did-We-Learn-Over-the-Last-20-Years-45583.

9. "Indigenous Peoples in Bolivia," International Work Group for Indigenous Affairs, https://www.iwgia.org/en/bolivia.html.

10. "7 de cada 10 Bolivianos se sienten parte de un pueblo indígena, pero se declaran mestizos," *Opinión Bolivia*, October 14, 2012, https://www.opinion.com.bo/articulo/el-pais/7-cada-10-bolivianos-sienten-parte-pueblo-indigena-declaran-mestizos/20121014094200434864.amp.html.

11    Fernando Molina, *Modos del privilegio: Alta burguesía y alta gerencia en la Bolivia contemporánea* (La Paz: Centro de Investigaciones Sociales, 2019).

12    Nico Tassi et al., *"Hacer plata sin plata." El desborde de los comerciantes populares en Bolivia* (La Paz: Programa de Investigación Estratégica en Bolivia, 2013).

13    Carlos D. Mesa Gisbert, José de Mesa, and Teresa Gisbert, *Historia de Bolivia* (La Paz: Editorial Gisbert, 1997).

14    "World Countries," *Washington Post,* 2007, https://www.washingtonpost.com/wp-srv/world/countries/bolivia.html?nav=el.

15    Eduardo Galeano, *Open Veins of Latin America: Five Centuries of the Pillage of a Continent,* Cedric Belfrage, trans. (New York: Monthly Review Press, 1973); James Michael Malloy, *Bolivia: The Uncompleted Revolution* (Pittsburgh: University of Pittsburgh Press, 1970).

16    Kevin A. Young, *Blood of the Earth: Resource Nationalism, Revolution, and Empire in Bolivia* (Austin: University of Texas Press, 2017); Benjamin Kohl and Linda Farthing, "Material Constraints to Popular Imaginaries: The Extractive Economy and Resource Nationalism in Bolivia," *Political Geography* 31 (2012): 225–35.

17    Luis Tapia and Marxa Chávez, *Producción y reproducción de desigualdades: Organización social y poder político* (La Paz: CEDLA, 2020), 78–79.

18    Galeano, *Open Veins of Latin America.*

19    Ben Dangl, *The Price of Fire* (Oakland, CA: AK Press, 2007), 15.

20    Silvia Rivera Cusicanqui, *Oppressed but Not Defeated: Peasant Struggles among the Aymara and Qhechwa in Bolivia, 1900–1980* (Geneva: UN Research Institute for Social Development, 1987); Laura Gotkowitz, *A Revolution for Our Rights: Indigenous Struggles for Land and Justice in Bolivia, 1880–1952* (Durham, NC: Duke University Press, 2007).

21    Rivera Cusicanqui, *Oppressed but Not Defeated.*

22    US Department of State, *Bolivia,* vol. 2005 (Washington, DC: Library of Congress, 2004).

23    *Campesino:* literally, a person who lives in the country; in the Bolivian context, the term refers to Indigenous small-scale farmers. It was introduced after the 1952 revolution as an alternative to *indio* (Indian), which was widely viewed as derogatory. Renaming Indigenous peoples "campesino" reflects the modernist aspirations of the 1952 revolutionary project, which largely saw Indigenous people as backward.

24    S. Sándor John, *Bolivia's Radical Tradition: Permanent Revolution in the Andes* (Tucson: University of Arizona Press, 2009).

25    Angus McNelly, "The Incorporation of Social Organizations under the MAS in Bolivia," *Latin American Perspectives* 47, no. 4 (2020): 76–95.

26    Robert Jackson Alexander and Eldon M. Parker, *A History of Organized Labor in Bolivia* (Westport, CT: Praeger Publishers, 2005).

27    Domitila Chungara de Barrios and Moema Viezzer, *Let Me Speak* (New York: Monthly Review Press, 1978).

28    John Crabtree, Gavan Duffy, and Jenny Pearce, *The Great Tin Crash: Bolivia and the World Tin Market* (London: Latin American Bureau, 1987).

29    Jorge León Trujillo and Susan Spronk, "Socialism without Workers? Trade Unions and the New Left in Bolivia and Ecuador," in *Reshaping the Political Arena in Latin America: From Resisting Neoliberalism to the Second Incorporation*, Eduardo Silva and Federico Rossi, eds. (Pittsburgh: University of Pittsburgh Press, 2018), 129–56.

30    Nicole Fabricant and Bret Gustafson, "The Fall of Evo Morales," *Catalyst* 4, no. 1 (Spring 2020).

31    Urban population (% of total population) - Bolivia, *World Bank*, https://data.worldbank.org/indicator/SP.URB.TOTL.IN.ZS?locations=BO.

32    Thomas Grisaffi, *Coca Yes, Cocaine No: How Bolivia's Coca Growers Re-shaped Democracy* (Durham: Duke University Press, 2019).

33    "Bolivia—GINI Index," World Bank, https://data.worldbank.org/indicator/SI.POV.GINI?locations=BO.

34    Willem Assies, "David versus Goliath in Cochabamba," *Latin American Perspectives* 30, no. 3 (2003): 14–36.

35    Steve Ellner, ed., *Latin America's Pink Tide: Breakthroughs and Shortcomings* (Lanham, MD: Rowman & Littlefield, 2020).

36    Omar G. Encarnación, "The Rise and Fall of the Latin American Left," *The Nation*, May 9, 2018.

37    Elisabeth Jay Friedman and Constanza Tabbush, "Introduction: Contesting the Pink Tide," in *Seeking Rights from the Left: Gender, Sexuality, and the Latin American Pink Tide*, Elizabeth Jay Friedman, ed. (Durham: Duke University Press, 2018).

38    Santiago Levy, "Poverty in Latin America: Where Do We Come from, Where Are We Going?," *Brookings*, May 10, 2016, https://www.brookings.edu/opinions/poverty-in-latin-america-where-do-we-come-from-where-are-we-going/.

39    For examples, see Kurt Weyland, Raúl L. Madrid, and Wendy Hunter, *Leftist Governments in Latin America: Successes and Shortcomings* (Cambridge, UK: Cambridge University Press, 2010); and Jorge Casteñada, "Latin America's Left Turn: There Is More Than One Pink Tide," *Foreign Affairs*, May–June 2006.

40    Steven Levitsky, *The Resurgence of the Latin American Left* (Baltimore: Johns Hopkins University Press, 2011).

41    "Bolivia to Extend Morales Era: Correction," *Argus*, October 28, 2020, https://www.argusmedia.com/en/news/2003037-bolivia-to-extend-morales-era-correction.

42    "Another world is possible" is a popular slogan of globally oriented social movements. Its origins are often attributed to the phrase "to divine another possible world," in Eduardo Galeano, *Upside Down: A Primer for the Looking-Glass World* (London: Picador, 2001). The slogan quickly became the rallying cry of the World Social Forum, which originated in Porto Alegre, Brazil.

43   Evan Romero-Castillo, "Cumbre climática de Cochabamba. 'Intereses contrarios al medio ambiente,'" *DW*, April 19, 2010, https://www.dw.com/es/cumbre-clim%C3%A1tica-de-cochabamba-intereses-contrarios-al-medio-ambiente/a-5483813.

44   Linda Farthing and Benjamin Kohl, "Mobilizing Memory: Bolivia's Enduring Social Movements," *Social Movement Studies* 12, no. 4 (2013): 1–15; Benjamin Dangl, *The Five Hundred Year Rebellion: Indigenous Movements and the Decolonization of History in Bolivia* (Chico, CA: AK Press, 2019).

45   Forrest Hylton and Sinclair Thomson, *Revolutionary Horizons: Past and Present in Bolivian Politics* (London and New York: Verso, 2007).

46   Bartolina Sisa was an Aymara woman who in 1781, along with her husband, Túpac Katari, led the country's most celebrated Indigenous rebellion, putting La Paz under siege. The Bartolinas organization depended heavily on their male counterparts for over two decades as a federation within the CSTUCB, furnishing grassroots women with vital support and education. By time of Morales's election, they had become independent of the CSTUCB and were the largest women's organization in the country with 1.7 million members. See Fernando García Yapur, Marizol Soliz Romero, Alberto García Orellana, Rodrigo Rosales Rocha, Mariana Zeballos Ibáñez, *"No Somos del MAS, el MAS es nuestro": Historias de vida y conversaciones con campesinos indigenas de Bolivia* (La Paz: Centro de Investigaciones Sociales, 2015).

47   Angus McNelly, "Social Organizations under the MAS in Bolivia."

48   CONAMAQ critiques the CSUTCB's campesino union structure as alien to Indigenous culture. See Radosław Powęska, *Indigenous Movements and Building the Plurinational State in Bolivia: Organisation and Identity in the Trajectory of the CSUTCB and CONAMAQ* (Warsaw: CESLA, 2013).

49   "Historia. El voto femenino llegó de la mano de mujeres de clases altas," *PIEB*, October 23, 2012, https://www.pieb.com.bo/sipieb_nota.php?idn=7505.

50   Benjamin H. Kohl, Félix Muruchi Poma, and Linda Farthing, *From the Mines to the Streets: A Bolivian Activist's Life* (Austin: University of Texas Press, 2012).

51   Kate Maclean, "Chachawarmi: Rhetorics and Lived Realities," *Bulletin of Latin American Research* 33, no. 1 (2014): 76–90.

52   Morales grew up in an Aymara community southwest of Oruro. At twenty-one, he joined his family after they moved to the coca-growing Chapare region, which was dominated by Quechua speakers.

53   Benjamin Kohl, "Democratizing Decentralization in Bolivia," *Journal of Planning Education and Research* 23, no. 2 (2003): 153–64.

54   A critical ideologue in the creation of the MAS was ex–mining union leader and later legislative deputy Filemón Escobar, who combined Marxist analysis with Indigenous struggle. See Filemón Escóbar, *De la revolución al pachakuti. El aprendizaje del respeto recíproco entre blancos e indianos* (La Paz: Garza Azul, 2008).

55    Vladimir Diez Cuellar, "Requiem for the Process of Change in Bolivia," *Toward Freedom*, December 19, 2019, https://towardfreedom.org/story/requiem-for-the-process-of-change-in-bolivia/.

56    Moira Zuazo, "¿Los movimientos sociales en el poder? El gobierno del MAS en Bolivia," *Nueva Sociedad* 227 (2010): 120–35.

57    Much of the highland resistance was led by Aymara leader Felipe Quispe Huanca, known as El Mallku (a high-ranking political authority). A founder of guerilla organizations and political parties, including the Pachakuti Indigenous Movement (MIP), he served as both head of the CSUTCB and a legislative deputy, later running unsuccessfully for both governor of La Paz and president on a pro–Indigenous rights platform. He died at the age of 78 in January 2021.

58    Benjamin H. Kohl and Linda C. Farthing, *Impasse in Bolivia: Neoliberal Hegemony and Popular Resistance* (London: Zed Books, 2006).

59    Mesa later challenged Morales in the 2019 election.

60    Dangl, *Five Hundred Year Rebellion*.

61    Zuazo, "¿Los movimientos sociales en el poder?"

62    Fernando Garcés, *El pacto de unidad y el proceso de construcción de una propuesta de constitución política del estado. Sistematización de la experiencia* (La Paz: Programa NINA, 2010), 94.

63    Fernando Mayorga, interview, Cochabamba, October 10, 2019.

64    Hervé Do Alto and Pablo Stefanoni, "El MAS: Las ambivalencias de la democracia corporativa," in *Mutaciones del campo político en Bolivia*, Alberto García and Fernando García, eds. (La Paz: PNUD-Bolivia, 2010), 305–34.

65    Manuel Suárez, "Evo Morales ante la historia," in *Crisis y cambio político en Bolivia. Octubre y noviembre de 2019: La democracia en una encrucijada*, Fernando Mayorga, ed. (La Paz: CESU/Oxfam, 2020), 215–36.

66    Rafael Archondo, "La ruta de Evo Morales," *Nueva Sociedad* 209 (2007): 82–99.

67    Lorenza Fontana, "On the Perils and Potentialities of Revolution: Conflict and Collective Action in Contemporary Bolivia," *Latin American Perspectives* 40, no. 3 (2013): 26–42.

68    Do Alto and Stefanoni, "El MAS."

69    The incapacity of elites to evolve to match current conditions is what one of Bolivia's most influential sociologists and philosophers, René Zavaleta Mercado, calls the "lordship contradiction." See René Zavaleta Mercado, *Lo nacional-popular en Bolivia* (La Paz: Plural Editores, 2008).

70    Andreas Tsolakis, "Transnational Elite Forces, Restructuring, and Resistance in Bolivia," *Law, Social Justice and Global Development* (2009).

71    Molina, *Modos del privilegio*.

72    A war in 1899 between tin mining elites (centered in La Paz) and the centuries-old silver oligarchy (located in Sucre) ended with the government seat moving to La Paz, although the judiciary remained in Sucre.

73 The Media Luna incorporates the four lowland departments of Pando, Beni, Santa Cruz, and Tarija.

74 Clementine Winkler and David Seale, "Santa Cruz Bolivia's Booming Business Capital," *Forbes*, December 2015, 72–73.

75 Pablo Ortiz, Fernando Molina, Verónica Rocha Fuentes, and Julio Córdova Villazón, "¿Por qué volvió a ganar el MAS? Lecturas de las elecciones bolivianas," *Nueva Sociedad*, October 2020, https://nuso.org/articulo/Bolivia-Luis-Arce-Evo-Morales/.

76 Jake Johnston and Stephan Lefebvre, "Bolivia's Economy under Evo in 10 Graphs," *Center for Policy Research*, 2014, https://www.cepr.net/bolivias-economy-under-evo-in-10-graphs/.

77 Hernán Pruden, "Las luchas 'cívicas' y las no tan cívicas. Santa Cruz de la Sierra (1957–59)," *Ciencia y Cultura* 29 (December 2012): 127–60.

78 Ximena Soruco, "De la goma a la soya. El proyecto histórico de la élite cruceña," in *Los barones del Oriente: El poder en Santa Cruz ayer y hoy*, Wilfredo Plata and Gustavo Medeiros, eds. (Santa Cruz: Fundación Tierra, 2008), 1–100.

79 Claudia Peña Claros, "Un pueblo eminente: Autonomist Populism in Santa Cruz," *Latin American Perspectives* 37 (2010): 125–39.

80 "Soja de Sudamérica. Reporte de actualización a mitad de año 2020," Cargill, June 30, 2020, https://www.cargill.com/doc/1432166467470/soy-progress-mid-year-report-2020-es.pdf.

81 Jonas Wolff, "Business Power and the Politics of Postneoliberalism: Relations between Governments and Economic Elites in Bolivia and Ecuador," *Latin American Politics and Society* 58 (2016): 124–47.

82 Molina, *Modos del privilegio*.

83 Kent Eaton, "Recentralization and the Left Turn in Latin America: Diverging Outcomes in Bolivia, Ecuador, and Venezuela," *Comparative Political Studies* 48, no. 8 (2014): 1130–57.

84 Paula Peña Hasbún, "Identidades regionales. El caso de Santa Cruz," *ReVista: Harvard Review of Latin America* (Fall 2011).

85 Nicole Fabricant, "The Roots of the Right-Wing Coup in Bolivia," *Dissent*, December 23, 2019, https://www.dissentmagazine.org/online_articles/roots-coup-bolivia-morales-anez-camacho.

86 Neil Burron, "Unpacking U.S. Democracy Promotion in Bolivia: From Soft Tactics to Regime Change," *Latin American Perspectives* 39, no. 1 (2012): 115–32.

87 In Brazil, Marinković became an ardent supporter of Brazil's far-right leader, Jair Bolsonaro. He returned to Bolivia in January 2020, serving in the Áñez government as minister of planning and then as finance minister.

88 Anatoly Kurmanaev and Monica Machicao, "As Amazon Burns, Fires in Next-Door Bolivia Also Wreak Havoc," *New York Times*, August 26, 2019, https://www.nytimes.com/2019/08/25/world/americas/bolivia-fires-amazon.html.

89    Monica Machicao and Daniel Ramos, "As Bolivian Forests Burn, Evo's Bet on Big Farming Comes under Fire," *Reuters*, September 9, 2019, https://www.reuters.com/article/us-bolivia-wildfires-politics-feature-idUSKCN1VU08T; "Bolivia triplica la exportación de carne bovina, China es su principal mercado de destino," *Correo del Sur*, November 11, 2020, https://correodelsur.com/economia/20201111_bolivia-triplica-la-exportacion-de-carne-bovina-china-es-su-principal-mercado-de-destino.html.

90    Ortiz et al., "¿Por qué volvió a ganar el MAS?"

91    "Religious Commitment and Practice," in *Religion in Latin America*, Pew Research Center, 2014, https://www.pewforum.org/2014/11/13/chapter-2-religious-commitment-and-practice/.

## Chapter 1: The "Process of Change" Cut Short

1    "'Nunca más volverá la Pachamama al palacio de gobierno,' sentencia aliado del líder cívico Camacho," *La Jornada*, November 11, 2019, https://www.jornada.com.mx/2019/11/11/politica/008n2pol.

2    2005 was the first time a candidate had gained an absolute majority since the end of eighteen years of dictatorship in 1982.

3    Pablo Stefanoni, "Las lecciones que nos deja Bolivia," *Nueva Sociedad*, March 2020, https://nuso.org/articulo/Bolivia-Evo-Morales-elecciones/.

4    Interviews, La Paz, October 22–28, 2019.

5    "Camacho abre una fisura en la oposición boliviana y se desvincula de Mesa," *Notimérica*, November 8, 2019, https://www.notimerica.com/politica/noticia-bolivia-camacho-abre-fisura-oposicion-boliviana-desvincula-mesa-20191108191039.html.

6    Rubén Atahuichi, "Nueve momentos: Carlos Mesa fue el factor clave de la sucesión de Jeanine Áñez," *La Razón*, June 14, 2021, www.la-razon.com/nacional/2021/06/14/nueve-momentos-carlos-mesa-fue-el-factor-clave-de-la-sucesion-de-jeanine-anez; Melvy Ruiz, "Evo: Confesión de Áñez confirma que Carlos Mesa es el principal golpista que hoy bloquea juicios al régimen," *eju.tv*, June 12, 2021, http://eju.tv/2021/06/evo-confesion-de-anez-confirma-que-carlos-mesa-es-el-golpista-principal-que-hoy-bloquea-juicios-el-regimen.

7    "Camacho emocionado agradece a la Policía 'por estar con su pueblo,'" *Opinión*, November 8, 2019, https://www.opinion.com.bo/articulo/pais/camacho-emocionado-agradece-policia-estar-pueblo/20191108220134736113.html.

8    In Bolivia's presidential system, "Plurinational Legislative Assembly" refers to both the Senate and the Chamber of Deputies.

9    Telephone interview, November 12, 2019.

10    Personal communication, La Paz, November 9, 2019.

11    Luis Ramos, interview, La Paz, November 10, 2019.

12    Marcelo Arequipa, "El Antimasismo como identidad consolidada," in *Crisis y cambio político en Bolivia. Octubre y noviembre de 2019: La democracia*

*en una encrucijada*, Fernando Mayorga, ed. (La Paz: CESU/Oxfam, 2020), 193–214.

13   Pablo Mamani Ramírez, "Wiphalas, luchas y la nueva nación. Relatos, análisis y memorias de octubre-noviembre de 2019 desde El Alto, Cochabamba y Santa Cruz," *Revista Willka* (October 2020): 84.

14   Armando Ortuño Yáñez, "Movilizados, Satisfechos e indiferentes: Maneras de vivir la crisis," in Mayorga, *Crisis y cambio político en Bolivia*, 61–78.

15   Damian López, interview, Potosí, February 22, 2019.

16   Fernando Mayorga, "Derrota política del MAS y proyecto de restauración oligárquico-señorial," in Mayorga, *Crisis y cambio político en Bolivia*, 1–28.

17   Roberto Mamani Soliz, personal communication, Tahua, January 10, 2015.

18   Félix Muruchi Poma, personal communication, La Paz, February 22, 2017.

19   Ortuño Yáñez, *Movilizados, satisfechos e indiferentes*, 72.

20   Manuel Suárez, "Evo Morales ante la historia," in Mayorga, *Crisis y cambio político en Bolivia*, 215.

21   Álvaro García Linera, interview, La Paz, October 16, 2019.

22   Ortuño Yáñez, *Movilizados, satisfechos e indiferentes*, 72.

23   Pablo Stefanoni, "Bolivia: Biblias, balas y votos," *Letras Libros*, Noviembre 20, 2019, https://www.letraslibres.com/mexico/politica/bolivia-biblias -balas-y-votos.

24   Vladimir Diez Cuellar, "Requiem for the Process of Change in Bolivia," *Toward Freedom*, December 19, 2019, https://towardfreedom.org/story/ requiem-for-the-process-of-change-in-bolivia/.

25   Gloria Carrasco, "Condenan a 10 años de cárcel a Gabriela Zapata, expareja de Evo Morales," *CNN*, May 23, 2017, https://cnnespanol.cnn. com/2017/05/23/condenan-a-10-anos-de-carcel-a-gabriela- zapata-expareja-de-evo-morales/.

26   "Encuesta: Las nueve ciudades capitales rechazan una posible repostulación de Evo Morales," *Los Tiempos*, October 24, 2017, https://www.lostiempos.com/actualidad/pais/20171024/ encuesta-nueve-ciudades-capitales-rechazan-posible-repostulacion-evo.

27   Gabriel Villegas, interview, Cochabamba, October 10, 2019.

28   Thomas Grisaffi, "Democracy or Dictatorship? Illiberal Governance in Bolivia's Coca Growers' Unions," paper presented at the European Association of Social Anthropologists Conference, July 20–24, 2020.

29   Carol Conzelman, "Coca Leaf and Sindicato Democracy in the Bolivian Yungas," PhD diss. University of Colorado Boulder, 2007.

30   Interview, Coroico, October 20, 2018.

31   Jonas Wolff, "Evo Morales and the Promise of Political Incorporation: Advancements and Limits," paper prepared for the 2017 LASA Congress, Lima, Peru, April 29—May 1, 2017, 5.

32   Felipe Quispe Huanca, "Prólogo," in Mamani Ramírez, *Wiphalas, luchas y la nueva nación*, 17; Anna Krausova, "What Social Movements Ask for and How They Ask for It: Strategic Claiming and Framing and the Successes

and Failures of Indigenous Movements in Latin America" (unpublished PhD, Oxford University, 2018), www.academia.edu/38220291.

33  Fernando Molina, *Racismo y poder en Bolivia* (La Paz: Librería Subtterranea, 2021), 141.

34  Pamela Calla, "Epilogue: Making Sense of May 24th in Sucre. Toward an Anti-racist Legislative Agenda," in *Histories of Race and Racism: The Andes and Mesoamerica from Colonial Times to the Present*, Laura Gotkowitz, ed. (Durham: Duke University Press, 2011), 311–20.

35  Personal communication, La Paz, November 16, 2019.

36  Juan Tellez, personal communication, La Paz, April 14, 2019.

37  Fernando Molina, "La rebelión de los blancos: Causas raciales de la caída de Evo Morales," in Mayorga, *Crisis y cambio político en Bolivia*, 155–57; Andrés Calla and Khantuta Muruchi, "Transgressions and Racism: The Struggle over a New Constitution in Bolivia," in Gotkowitz, *Histories of Race and Racism*, 299–310.

38  Interview, La Paz, November 14, 2019.

39  Suárez, "Evo Morales ante la historia," 215.

40  Casimira Rodríguez, interview, Cochabamba, May 2, 2012.

41  Emily Achtenberg, "After the Referendum, What's Next for Bolivia's Progressive Left?," *NACLA*, April 15, 2016, https://nacla.org/blog/2016/04/15/after-referendum-what%E2%80%99s-next-bolivia%E2%80%99s-progressive-left.

42  Linda Farthing, *Bolivia: The Left in Power; State Officials' Perspectives on the Challenges to Progressive Governance* (Amsterdam: Transnational Institute, 2018), https://www.tni.org/en/publication/bolivia-the-left-in-power.

43  Personal communication, La Paz, March 14, 2012.

44  Interview, Betanzos, June 25, 2017.

45  Vicky Ayllón, interview, La Paz, September 26, 2011.

46  Personal communication, Cochabamba, May 22, 2014. For examples of accusations leveled against the MAS for persecution, see: "De rebeldes políticos a perseguidos y privados de Libertad," BolPress, April 22, 2019, https://www.bolpress.com/2019/04/22/de-rebeldes-politicos-a-perseguidos-y-privados-de-libertad/ and articles at https://cedib.org/tag/persecucion-politica/.

47  "Las acusaciones contra Carlos Mesa," *Página Siete*, June 6, 2018, https://www.paginasiete.bo/opinion/editorial/2018/6/6/las-acusaciones-contra-carlos-mesa-182424.html.

48  Farthing, *Bolivia: The Left in Power*, 15.

49  Mauricio Sánchez Patzy, "Corporativismo, disciplina y violencias corporativas en Bolivia," in *¿Todo cambia? Reflexiones sobre el "proceso de cambio" en Bolivia*, Hugo José Suárez, ed. (México: Instituto de Investigaciones Sociales, UNAM, 2018), 135–78.

50  Angus McNelly, "The Incorporation of Social Organizations under the MAS in Bolivia," *Latin American Perspectives* 47, no. 4 (2020): 76–95.

51   In 2007, the Bartolinas broke from the CSTUCB, establishing their own Confederation and in 2009, the CSCB changed their name to the CSCIOB (Union Confederation of Intercultural and Indigenous Communities of Bolivia).

52   Fernando Garcés, *El Pacto de Unidad y el proceso de construcción de una propuesta de constitución política del Estado* (La Paz: Preview Gráfica, 2010).

53   Linda Farthing, "An Opportunity Squandered? Elites, Social Movements, and the Bolivian Government of Evo Morales," in *Pink Tide: Breakthroughs and Shortcomings*, Steve Ellner, ed., Latin American Perspectives in the Classroom (Lanham, MD: Rowman & Littlefield, 2019).

54   Santiago Anria, *When Movements Become Parties: The Bolivian MAS in Comparative Perspective* (Cambridge, UK: Cambridge University Press, 2018).

55   Fernando Mayorga, "Movimientos sociales y participación política en Bolivia," in *Ciudadanía y legitimidad democrática en América Latina*, Isidoro Cheresky, ed. (Buenos Aires: Prometeo, 2011), 9–41.

56   Anna Krausova, "Just Another Protest Cycle? Bolivia's Indigenous Peasant Movement and 'Their' Government," in *Revolutions in Bolivia*, eds. Into A. Goudsmit, Kate Maclean, and Winstons Moore (London: Anglo-Bolivian Society and the Institute of Latin American Studies, University of London, 2018).

57   Jorge León Trujillo and Susan Spronk, "Socialism without Workers? Trade Unions and the New Left in Bolivia and Ecuador," in *Reshaping the Political Arena in Latin America: From Resisting Neoliberalism to the Second Incorporation*, Eduardo Silva and Federico M. Rossi, eds. (Pittsburgh: University of Pittsburgh Press, 2018), 129–56.

58   The relationship between the COB and the Morales government was often stormy. The COB led popular mobilizations against cuts to government fuel subsidies (2010), a reformed labor law that would have required a two-thirds-majority vote for strike action and stripped the right to strike from public sector workers (2010), and even proposed the formation of an independent workers' party to challenge Morales's reelection (2013). But at the end of 2013, the COB adopted a pro-MAS leadership that backed Morales in exchange for a doubling of the end-of-year bonus and job promises. In October 2014, fifteen COB leaders were elected to the Plurinational Legislative Assembly on the MAS ticket. In 2019, the COB joined the protests calling for Morales's resignation, initially joining the opposition alliance CONADE. See Emily Achtenberg, "Why Bolivian Workers Are Marching against Evo Morales," Rebel Currents, *NACLA*, July 5, 2016, https://nacla.org/blog/2016/07/05/why-bolivian-workers-are-marching-against-evo-morales; McNelly, *Social Organizations under the MAS*, 76–95; and Yuri F. Tórrez, "Oposición no partidaria al MAS-IPSP. Antes, durante y después de la crisis de octubre–noviembre," in *Nuevo mapa de actores en Bolivia Crisis, polarización e incertidumbre, 2019–2020*, Jan Souverein and José Luis Exeni Rodríguez, eds. (La Paz: Friedrich Ebert Stiftung, 2020), 35–75.

59   Moira Zuazo, "Bolivia: Social Control as the Fourth State Power
     (1994–2015)," in *Intermediation and Representation in Latin America: Actors
     and Roles beyond Elections*, Gisela Zaremberg, Valeria Guarneros-Meza, and
     Adrián Gurza Lavalle, eds. (London: Palgrave Macmillan, 2017), 95–114.

60   Wolff, "Promise of Political Incorporation," 13.

61   Santiago Anria, "More Inclusion, Less Liberalism in Bolivia," *Journal of
     Democracy* 27, no. 3 (2016): 99–108.

62   Freddy Condo, personal communication, La Paz, February 18, 2017.

63   Moira Zuazo, "¿Los movimientos sociales en el poder? El gobierno del
     MAS en Bolivia," *Nueva Sociedad* 227 (2010): 120–35.

64   Nancy Postero, *The Indigenous State* (Berkeley: University of California
     Press, 2017).

65   Emily Achtenberg, "Rival Factions in Bolivia's CONAMAQ: Internal
     Conflict or Government Manipulation?," *NACLA*, 2014, https://nacla.org/
     blog/2014/2/3/rival-factions-bolivias-conamaq-internal-conflict-or-
     government-manipulation.

66   María Teresa Zegada and George Komadina, *El intercambio político.
     Indígenas/campesinos en el Estado Plurinacional* (Cochabamba and La Paz:
     CERES/Plural Editores, 2017), 72.

67   Oscar Olivera, interview, Cochabamba, February 14, 2017.

68   Laurence Blair, "Understanding the Fires in South America," *NACLA*,
     August 30, 2019.

69   Fernando Molina, "Los incendios en Bolivia golpean a Evo Morales a
     menos de dos meses de las elecciones," *El País*, August 29, 2019, https://
     elpais.com/internacional/2019/08/27/america/1566924897_335190.html.

70   Miguel Urioste, "The Great Soy Expansion: Brazilian Land Grabs in
     Eastern Bolivia," Transnational Institute, Land and Sovereignty Brief no.
     30, September 2013.

71   Blair, "Understanding the Fires in South America."

72   Robert Müller, Pacheco Pablo, and Montero Juan Carlos, "The Context
     of Deforestation and Forest Degradation in Bolivia: Drivers, Agents and
     Institutions," CIFOR Occasional Paper 108, 2014.

73   "Una chuquisaqueña, a los países de la OEA: '¿Dónde estaban todos estos
     años?,'" *Correo del Sur*, December 12, 2019, https://correodelsur.com/
     politica/20191212_una-chuquisaquena-a-los-paises-de-la-oea-donde-
     estaban-todos-estos-anos.html.

74   Juan Rivero, interview, Santa Cruz, October 8, 2019.

75   The fires returned during the next *chaqueo* in August 2020. They were
     severe, but not on the same scale as in 2019.

76   Sergio Martín-Carrillo, "La economía boliviana en 2019," *CELAG*,
     December 16, 2018, https://www.celag.org/la-economia-boliviana-2019/.

77   "Bolivia—Gasto público," Datosmacro, https://datosmacro.expansion.
     com/estado/gasto/bolivia.

78   "Foreign Exchange Reserves in Bolivia Decreased to 3465.31
     USD Million in September from 3753.66 USD Million in May of

2020," *Trading Economics*, https://tradingeconomics.com/bolivia/foreign-exchange-reserves.

79 Miguel Angel Melendres Galvis, "PIB de Tarija, Chuquisaca y Potosí fue negativo en 2019, afectado por hidrocarburos y minerales," *El Deber*, April 23, 2020, https://eldeber.com.bo/economia/pib-de-tarija-chuquisaca-y-potosi-fue-negativo-en-2019-afectado-por-hidrocarburos-y-minerales_176147.

80 Instituto Boliviano de Comercio Exterior, "Bolivia: Exportaciones de Gas Natural," *Boletín Electrónico Bisemanal* 902 (August 17, 2020), https://ibce.org.bo/images/ibcecifras_documentos/Cifras-902-Bolivia-Exportaciones-gas-natural.pdf.

81 Interview, La Paz, October 14, 2019. What came across in this interview was how enormously proud Arce was of how the economic model he had introduced had dramatically improved poor Bolivians' incomes.

82 Fernando Mayorga, interview, Cochabamba, October 11, 2019.

83 Anonymous interview, La Paz, October 19, 2019.

84 Personal communication, Santa Cruz, February 5, 2016.

85 Natalya Naqvi, "State-Directed Credit in a World of Globalised Finance: Developmental Policy Autonomy and Business Power in Bolivia," Oxford Global Economic Governance Working Paper 138, 2018.

86 Jeffery R. Webber, "Bolivia's Passive Revolution," *Jacobin*, October 29, 2015, https://www.jacobinmag.com/2015/10/morales-bolivia-chavez-castro-mas/.

87 These events had striking parallels with those in Venezuela. See Steve Ellner, "Introduction," in *Latin America's Pink Tide: Breakthroughs and Shortcomings*.

88 Atilio Borón, "Foreword," in Hugo Moldiz Mercado, *Golpe de Estado en Bolivia: La soledad de Evo Morales* (La Habana: Ocean Sur, 2020).

89 Borón, "Foreword." The War of the Pacific, which Chile fought against a Peruvian–Bolivian alliance between 1879 and 1884, largely over valuable nitrate (fertilizer) deposits, was disastrous for Bolivia, costing the country its seacoast and considerable national pride. It has claimed a right to access to the sea ever since.

## Chapter 2: Setting the Stage for an Ouster

1 Fernando Mayorga, interview, Cochabamba, October 11, 2019.

2 Rosa Rojas Canaviri, interview, El Alto, October 18, 2019.

3 Marlene Soto, interview, Sucre, March 4, 2018.

4 María Teresa Zegada, "La crisis del sistema de representación política. Los partidos opositores al MAS en el interregno post y preelectoral (2019–2020)," in *Nuevo mapa de actores en Bolivia Crisis, polarización e incertidumbre, 2019–2020*, Jan Souverein and José Luis Exeni Rodríguez, eds. (La Paz: Friedrich Ebert Stiftung, 2020), 35–75.

5 *Cultura política de la democracia en Bolivia, 2014. Hacia una democracia de ciudadanos*, CIUDADANIA (Comunidad de Estudios Sociales y Acción

Pública) / Proyecto de Opinión Pública de América Latina (LAPOP), 2014, 9, http://ciudadaniabolivia.org/sites/default/files/archivos_articulos/Cultura%20Pol%C3%ADtica%20de%20la%20Democracia%20en%20Bolivia,%202014.pdf.

6   Marcelo Arequipa, "El Antimasismo como identidad consolidada," in *Crisis y cambio político en Bolivia. Octubre y noviembre de 2019: La democracia en una encrucijada*, Fernando Mayorga, ed. (La Paz: CESU/Oxfam, 2020), 193–214.

7   Spanish for "town hall," in Bolivia *cabildos* are outdoor public gatherings to rally citizens around a particular agenda.

8   Steve Zambrana, interview, Cochabamba, October 10, 2019.

9   A *pollera* is a wide pleated skirt worn by Indigenous women in the highland and valleys.

10  Ana Maria Nina, interview, La Paz, October 16, 2019.

11  Michael Alvarez, Thad E. Hall, and Susan D. Hyde, *Election Fraud: Detecting and Deterring Electoral Manipulation* (Washington, DC: Brookings Institution Press, 2009).

12  José Luis Andia, "Elecciones y gobierno de transición," in Mayorga, *Crisis y cambio político*, 79–110.

13  Bret Gustafson, personal communication, November 26, 2019.

14  Eliana Quiroz and Wilmer Machaca, "La reconfiguración del espacio político en Internet durante la crisis política de finales de 2019," in Souverein and Exeni Rodríguez, *Nuevo mapa de actores*, 307–46.

15  Ana Maria Copeticón, interview, La Paz, October 21, 2019.

16  Alex Ojeda Copa, "Cámaras de eco y desinformación. Efectos amplificadores de las redes digitales en la polarización social de 2019," in Mayorga, *Crisis y cambio político*, 113–16.

17  Erin Gallagher, "Information Operations in Bolivia," *Medium*, December 30, 2019, https://medium.com/@erin_gallagher/information-operations-in-bolivia-bc277ef56e73.

18  "Crisis y fake news," video, *AJ+ Español*, November 30, 2019, www.youtube.com/watch?v=Vp-gpNYgEwI.

19  José Antonio Quiroga, interview, La Paz, October 20, 2019.

20  Lisbeth Machaca, interview, La Paz, October 15, 2019.

21  José Antonio Quiroga, interview, La Paz, October 20, 2019.

22  Ivon Chávez, interview, La Paz, October 20, 2019.

23  Erika Brockman, "Tentativa de toma gradual del poder: Prorroguismo fallido y transiciones," in Mayorga, *Crisis y cambio político*, 29–60.

24  Linda Farthing, "Evo Morales Wins Bolivia's Election, but Fraud Allegations Tarnish the Victory," *Latino USA*, October 28, 2019, https://www.latinousa.org/2019/10/28/moraleswins/.

25  Evo Morales, speech, La Paz, October 20, 2019.

26  The tweet read: "The Electoral Observation Mission of the Organization of American States (OAS) in #Bolivia calls for respect for the will of the citizenry." The OAS statement from October 21, 2019, is

available at https://www.oas.org/en/media_center/press_release.
asp?scodigo=E-085/19.

27   Kathryn Ledebur, personal communication, Cochabamba, November 14,
     2019.

28   Carlos Mesa, press conference, La Paz, October 24, 2019.

29   Miguel Roca, interview, La Paz, October 26, 2019.

30   They adopted this name after Evo Morales poked fun at their organizing,
     saying that tying a piece of string (*pita*) across the street does not
     constitute a road blockade.

31   Jonas Wolff, "Las élites económicas en la Bolivia Contemporánea," in
     Souverein and Exeni Rodríguez, *Nuevo mapa de actores*, 139–64.

32   Vladimir Diez Cuellar, "Requiem for the Process of Change in Bolivia,"
     *Toward Freedom*, December 19, 2019, https://towardfreedom.org/story/
     requiem-for-the-process-of-change-in-bolivia/.

33   Noah Friedman, personal communication, November 1, 2020.

34   William Wroblewski, personal communication, La Paz, November 16,
     2019.

35   Personal communication, La Paz, November 8, 2019.

36   Brígida Quiroga, interview, La Paz, October 29, 2019.

37   Anonymous interview, La Paz, November 7, 2019.

38   Felipe Tapia, interview, La Paz, November 9, 2019.

39   See Cassandra Garrison, "Bolivian President Morales Calls for New
     Elections after OAS Audit," *Reuters*, November 10, 2019, https://news.
     yahoo.com/bolivian-president-morales-calls-elections-114822561.html.

40   Andia, "Elecciones y gobierno de transición."

41   Andia, "Elecciones y gobierno de transición," 100.

42   Ayelén Oliva, personal communication, Chimoré, November 11, 2020.
     Morales and García Linera spent about a month in Mexico before moving
     to Buenos Aires, Argentina.

43   Guillaume Long and Lola Allen, "Evo Morales's Life Was in Danger,
     and He Almost Didn't Make It Out of Bolivia," Center for Economic
     Research and Policy (CEPR), November 20, 2019, https://cepr.net/
     evo-s-odyssey-how-mexico-got-morales-out-of-bolivia/.

44   "Bolivia Crisis: Evo Morales Says He Fled to Mexico as Life Was at
     Risk," *BBC News*, November 13, 2019, https://www.bbc.com/news/
     world-latin-america-50397922.

45   Diez Cuellar, "Requiem for the Process of Change."

46   Overheard, Plaza San Francisco, La Paz, November 14, 2019.

47   "Deaths in Conflict," Office of the Ombudsman of the Plurinational
     State of Bolivia, https://www.defensoria.gob.bo/contenido/
     muertos-en-los-conflictos.

48   "Enfrentamientos en Montero dejan dos muertos por proyectil
     de arma de fuego y varios heridos," *Los Tiempos*, October 30,

2019, https://www.lostiempos.com/actualidad/pais/20191030/
enfrentamientos-montero-dejan-dos-muertos-proyectil-arma-fuego-varios.

49   "Emboscan a segunda caravana que iba de Potosi a La Paz," *Los
Tiempos*, November 10, 2019, https://www.lostiempos.com/actualidad/
pais/20191110/emboscan-segunda-caravana-que-iba-potosi-paz.

50   Marcelo Blanco, "Cae presunto autor de quema de la casa de Waldo
Albarracin," *Página Siete*, November 26, 2019; Ariel Duranboger, interview,
La Paz, January 7, 2020; Waldo Albarracin, interview, La Paz, December
19, 2019.

51   *Hordas* means "hordes" in English. See Diez Cuellar, "Requiem for the
Process of Change."

52   "Bolivia Out of Control: Looting of Evo Morales' House and Burning
of Houses of Opposition Leaders and Journalists," *Infobae*, November
11, 2019; Waldo Albarracin, interview, La Paz, December 19, 2019;
ArielDuranboger, interview, La Paz, January 7, 2020.

53   GIEI Bolivia, 2021, *Informe sobre los hechos de violencia y vulneración de los
derechos humanos*, Organization of American States, https://gieibolivia.org/
informes/.

54   Anthony Faiola, "Protests, Arson, Looting in Bolivia as Opponents Accuse
Evo Morales of Trying to Steal Election," *Washington Post*, October 22,
2019, https://www.washingtonpost.com/world/the_americas/unrest-
erupts-in-bolivia-as-opponents-accuse-evo-morales-of-trying-to-steal-
election/2019/10/22/214d85f2-f4d4-11e9-b2d2-1f37c9d82dbb_story.
html.

55   "La presidenta del Tribunal Supremo Electoral de Bolivia lamenta el 'acoso'
y niega el 'fraude electoral,'" *Notimérica*, October 23, 2019, https://www.
europapress.es/internacional/noticia-presidenta-tribunal-supremo-electoral-
bolivia-lamenta-acoso-niega-fraude-electoral-20191023053643.html.

56   Ivan Alejandro Paredes Tamayo, "Renuncia Víctor Borda, presidente de la
Cámara de Diputados", *El Deber*, November 11, 2019, https://eldeber.com.
bo/el-deber/renuncia-victor-borda-presidente-de-la-camara-de-diputados
_156188.

57   Maria Fernández, telephone interview, November 14, 2019.

58   Luisa Ayala, personal communication, La Paz, October 14, 2013.

59   Mimi Yagoub, "From Chile to Mexico: Best and Worst of LatAm Police,"
*InSight Crime*, March 20, 2017, https://insightcrime.org/news/analysis/
best-worst-latam-police/.

60   Esther Vallero, interview, La Paz, October 21, 2019.

61   "Lessons from Black October," *Andean Information Network*, 2006, https://
ain-bolivia.org/2006/10/lessons-from-bolivia%e2%80%99s-black-
october-2003/.

62   Gabriela Reyes Rodas, "Motín policial de 2019. Tensiones irresueltas y
reconfiguración político-institucional en Bolivia," in Souverein and Exeni
Rodríguez, *Nuevo mapa de actores*, 201–40.

63   Linda Farthing, "Bolivia Has Been Promised Elections. But Will They Be Fair?," *Guardian*, December 2, 2019.

64   María Victoria Murillo and Steven Levitsky, "La tentación militar en América Latina," *Nueva Sociedad* 285 (January–February 2020).

65   National Endowment for Democracy grants database: search results for Bolivia, 2016–2019, https://www.ned.org/wp-content/themes/ned/search/grant-search.php?organizationName=&region=LATIN+AMERICA+%26+CARIBBEAN &projectCountry=Bolivia& amount= &fromDate=&toDate=&projectFocus[]=&search=&maxCount=25&orderBy=Year&start=1&sbmt=1.

66   "Surgen 16 audios que vinculan presuntamente a cívicos, exmilitares y EEUU en planes de agitación," *ERBOL*, November 3, 2019, https://www.erbol.com.bo/nacional/surgen-16-audios-que-vinculan-c%C3%ADvicos-exmilitares-y-eeuu-en-planes-de-agitaci%C3%B3n.

67   "Statement from President Donald J. Trump regarding the Resignation of Bolivian President Evo Morales," White House briefing, November 11, 2019, https://www.whitehouse.gov/briefings-statements/statement-president-donald-j-trump-regarding-resignation-bolivian-president-evo-morales/.

68   Editorial Board, "A Democratic Breakout in Bolivia," *Wall Street Journal*, November 11, 2020, https://www.wsj.com/articles/a-democratic-breakout-in-bolivia-11573517299; Editorial Board, "Evo Morales Is Gone. Bolivia's Problems Aren't," *New York Times*, November 11, 2019, https://www.nytimes.com/2019/11/11/opinion/evo-morales-bolivia.html.

69   Rafael Bautista, "Bolivia: 'A confesión de golpe, relevo de fase,'" *América Latino en Movimiento*, December 30, 2019, https://www.alainet.org/es/articulo/204026.

70   Jake Johnson, "Global Condemnation of 'Appalling' Coup in Bolivia as Military Forces Socialist President Evo Morales to Resign," *Common Dreams*, November 11, 2019, https://www.commondreams.org/news/2019/11/11/global-condemnation-appalling-coup-bolivia-military-forces-socialist-president-evo.

71   Democratic senators Christopher S. Murphy, Patrick Leahy, Benjamin L. Cardin, Tim Kaine, Bernard Sanders, Chris Van Hollen, and Edward J. Markey to Secretary of State Mike Pompeo, official correspondence, July 7, 2020, available at https://www.murphy.senate.gov/download/2077-bolivia-letter.

72   Janaína Figueiredo, "'Brasil tem as informações em primeira mão,' diz Camacho, o opositor de Evo Morales," *Epoca*, November 14, 2019, https://epoca.globo.com/mundo/brasil-tem-as-informacoes-em-primeira-mao-diz-camacho-opositor-de-evo-morales-1-24081648.

73   Janaína Figueiredo, "Camacho agradece apoio e quer encontrar Bolsonaro," *Epoca*, November 14, 2019, https://epoca.globo.com/mundo/camacho-agradece-apoio-quer-encontrar-bolsonaro-24080798.

74   Felipe Yapur, "Bolivia: Los sospechosos vuelos del avión presidencial de Jeanine Áñez a Brasil," *Página 12*, June 7, 2020, https://www.pagina12.

com.ar/270774-bolivia-los-sospechosos-vuelos-del-avion-presidencial
-de-jea.

75  María Galindo, "'Sedición en la Universidad Católica' o cómo armaron
el golpe los patriarcas," *Muy Waso*, January 29, 2020, https://muywaso.
com/sedicion-en-la-universidad-catolica-o-como-armaron-el-golpe-los-
patriarcas/.

76  Clement Doleac, "Are the Organization of American States' Imperialist
Roots Too Deep to Extirpate Today?," *Council on Hemispheric Affairs*,
December 4, 2014, https://www.coha.org/are-the-organization-of-
american-states-imperialist-roots-too-deep-to-extirpate-with-today/.

77  "Statement of the Group of Auditors Electoral Process in Bolivia," OAS
press release, November 10, 2019, https://www.oas.org/en/media_center/
press_release.asp?sCodigo=E-099/19.

78  "Final Report of the Audit of the Elections in Bolivia: Intentional
Manipulation and Serious Irregularities Made it Impossible to Validate
the Results," OAS, December 4, 2019, www.oas.org/enspa/deco/
Report-Bolivia-2019.

79  María Eugenia Choque, press conference, La Paz, October 24, 2019.

80  The use of state resources in electoral campaigns is a common, if
illegitimate, practice worldwide. See "Abuse of State Resources,"
International Foundation for Electoral Systems, https://www.ifes.org/
issues/abuse-state-resources.

81  *Bolivia 2019: Final Report*, EU Election Expert Mission, https://ec.europa.
eu/info/strategy/relations-non-eu-countries/types-relations-and-
partnerships/election-observation/mission-recommendations-repository/
missions/341.

82  Jack R. Williams and John Curiel, "Analysis of the 2019 Bolivia Election,"
*Center for Economic Policy and Research*, February 27, 2020, https://cepr.net/
report/analysis-of-the-2019-bolivia-election/.

83  Jan Schakowsky, press release, November 25, 2019, https://schakowsky.
house.gov/sites/schakowsky.house.gov/files/OAS%20Boliva_Final.pdf.

84  Ha-Joon Chang et al., "The OAS Has to Answer for Its Role in the
Bolivian Coup," *Guardian*, December 2, 2019, https://www.theguardian
.com/commentisfree/2019/dec/02/the-oas-has-to-answer-for-its-role-
in-the-bolivian-coup.

85  Walter Mebane Jr., "Evidence against Fraudulent Votes Being Decisive in
the Bolivia 2019 Election," November 13, 2019, available at http://www-
personal.umich.edu/~wmebane/Bolivia2019.pdf.

86  Calla Hummel and V. Ximena Velasco-Guachalla, "How to
Detect Election Fraud: The Bolivian Example," *Mischiefs of Faction*,
November 25, 2019, https://www.mischiefsoffaction.com/post/
how-to-detect-election-fraud-the-bolivian-example.

87  Diego Escobari and Gary A. Hoover, "Evo Morales and Electoral Fraud
in Bolivia: A Natural Experiment Estimate," November 2019, available at
https://papers.ssrn.com/sol3/papers.cfm?abstract_id=3492928; Yolanda
Mamani Cayo, "Al menos cinco informes sustentan la denuncia del fraude

electoral de 2019," *Página Siete*, November 22, 2020, www.paginasiete.bo/especial02/2020/11/22/al-menos-cinco-informes-sustentan-la-denuncia-del-fraude-electoral-de-2019-275669.html.

88 John Curiel and Jack R. Williams, "Bolivia Dismissed Its October Elections as Fraudulent. Our Research Found No Reason to Suspect Fraud," *Washington Post,* February 27, 2020, https://www.washingtonpost.com/politics/2020/02/26/bolivia-dismissed-its-october-elections-fraudulent-our-research-found-no-reason-suspect-fraud/.

89 Anatoly Kurmanaev and María Silvia Trigo, "A Bitter Election. Accusations of Fraud. And Now Second Thoughts," *New York Times,* June 7, 2020, https://www.nytimes.com/2020/06/07/world/americas/bolivia-election-evo-morales.html.

90 MPs Manu Pineda, Maria-Manuel Leitão Marques, and Benoît Biteau to Josep Borrell, official correspondence, July 7, 2020, available at https://izquierdaunida.org/wp-content/uploads/2020/07/Carta_Borrell_Bolivia_07_07_2020.pdf.

91 Office of Senator Bernie Sanders, "Sanders, Two Dozen Lawmakers Call for OAS Accountability to Ensure Fair Elections in Bolivia," press release, September 22, 2020, https://www.sanders.senate.gov/press-releases/sanders-two-dozen-lawmakers-call-for-oas-accountability-to-ensure-fair-elections-in-bolivia/.

92 OAS, "Press Release on Disinformation Campaign regarding the Role of the OAS in the Bolivian Elections," June 16, 2020, https://www.oas.org/en/media_center/press_release.asp?sCodigo=E-064/20.

93 See "En Bolivia NO se ha producido ningún golpe de Estado," YouTube video, November 11, 2019, https://www.youtube.com/watch?v=pp0eu7B4d4A.

94 Drew DeSilver, "Despite Apparent Coup in Zimbabwe, Armed Takeovers Have Become Less Common Worldwide," *Fact Tank*, Pew Research Center, November 17, 2017, https://www.pewresearch.org/fact-tank/2017/11/17/egypts-coup-is-first-in-2013-as-takeovers-become-less-common-worldwide/.

95 Octavio Humberto Moreno Velador and Carlos Alberto Figueroa Ibarra, "Golpe de Estado y Neogolpismo en América Latina," *Revista Debates* 13, no. 1 (2019): 150–72.

96 Andia, "Elecciones y gobierno de transición," 100–4.

97 Franz Barrios Suvelza, "Por Qué No Hubo Golpe de Estado en Bolivia," *Página Siete*, November 14, 2019, https://www.paginasiete.bo/opinion/2019/11/14/por-que-no-hubo-golpe-de-estado-en-bolivia-237353.html.

98 Jonas Wolff, "The Turbulent End of an Era in Bolivia: Contested Elections, the Ouster of Evo Morales, and the Beginning of a Transition Towards an Uncertain Future," *Revista Ciencias Políticas* 40, no. 2: 163–86.

99 Eduardo Rodríguez Veltzé, personal communication, La Paz, March 19, 2021.

100 "Eduardo Rodríguez, Veltze, Crisis, Reconciliación y Justicia," *La Razón*, July 25, 2021, https://www.la-razon.com/politico/2021/07/25/crisis-reconciliacion-y-justicia/.

101 Rodríguez Veltzé, personal communication.

102 Murillo and Levitsky, "La tentación militar en América Latina."

103 Bernie Sanders, quoted in People for Bernie Twitter post, November 16, 2019, https://twitter.com/people4bernie/status/1195884845953470465?lang=en.

104 María Galindo, Women's Parliament, La Paz, November 16, 2019.

105 Nelson Peredo, "Rivero se presenta a la Fiscalía y asegura que no hubo vacío de poder en 2019," June 18, 2021, *Los Tiempos*, https://www.lostiempos.com/actualidad/pais/20210618/rivero-se-presenta-fiscalia-asegura-que-no-hubo-vacio-poder-2019.

106 Glenn Greenwald, "Major New Brazil Events Expose the Fraud of Dilma's Impeachment—and Temer's Corruption," *The Intercept*, June 30, 2016, https://theintercept.com/2016/06/30/major-new-brazil-events-expose-the-fraud-of-dilmas-impeachment-and-temers-corruption/.

## Chapter 3: Growth and Successes

1 Juanita Flores, interview, La Paz, January 20, 2018.

2 "Bolivia - Poverty Headcount Ratio at Rural Poverty Line as a Share of Rural Population," World Data Atlas, Knoema.com/atlas/Bolivia/Rural-poverty-rate.

3 Laura Manzaneda, "Ejecutan nuevo hospital y otros 2 siguen sin funcionar," *Los Tiempos*, June 20, 2017, https://www.lostiempos.com/actualidad/local/20170620/ejecutan-nuevo-hospital-otros-2-siguen-funcionar.

4 "New World Bank Country Classifications by Income Level: 2020–2021," *World Bank Data Blog*, https://blogs.worldbank.org/opendata/new-world-bank-country-classifications-income-level-2020.

5 Daniel Moreno, "Polarización y desconfianza social en Bolivia. Una mirada comparada," in *Polarización y conflicto. Midiendo los riesgos de la violencia*, Roberto Laserna, ed., Documentos de Trabajo (Cochabamba: CERES, 2020), 6.

6 Amaru Villanueva Rance, "'Clases a medias': The Changing Contours of Bolivian Middle Classes," in *Revolutions in Bolivia*, Into A. Goudsmit, Kate Maclean, and Winston Moore, eds. (London: Anglo-Bolivian Society and the Institute of Latin American Studies, University of London, 2018).

7 "En 12 años, funcionarios del nivel central aumentaron en un 91,6%", Página Siete, December 6, 2018, https://www.paginasiete.bo/economia/2018/12/9/en-12-anos-funcionarios-del-nivel-central-aumentaron-en-un-916-202566.html

8 In comparison, in 2006 Mexico and Chile both had a Gini of 0.46, and Brazil 0.51. "Bolivia Poverty Rate 1992–2020," *Macrotrends*, https://www.macrotrends.net/countries/BOL/bolivia/poverty-rate; "Bolivia Gini Index," World Bank, https://data.worldbank.org/indicator/SI.POV.GINI?locations=BO.

9　Wendy Hunter and Natasha Borges Sugiyama, "Conditional Cash Transfer Programs: Assessing Their Achievements and Probing Their Promise," *LASA Forum* 43 (2012): 9–10.

10　Kenneth M. Roberts, "The Politics of Declining Inequality," *LASA Forum* 43 (2012): 11–12.

11　Leandro Vergara-Camus and Kay Cristobal, "New Agrarian Democracies: The Pink Tide's Lost Opportunity," *Socialist Register* 54 (2018): 224–43; Luis F. López-Calva and Nora Lustig, "The Decline in Inequality in Latin America: The Role of Markets and the State," *LASA Forum* 43 (2012): 4–6.

12　Interview, Cochabamba, May 16, 2011.

13　Juancito Pinto was a 12-year-old drummer who died in combat during the 1880s War of the Pacific against Chile.

14　Carla Canelas and Miguel Niño-Zarazúa, "Schooling and Labour Market Impacts of Bolivia's Bono Juancito Pinto," WIDER Working Paper 2018/36, March 1, 2018, available at https://ssrn.com/abstract=3152235.

15　Nora Nagels, *The Social Investment Perspective, Conditional Cash Transfer Programmes and the Welfare Mix: Peru and Bolivia* (Cambridge, UK: Cambridge University Press, 2016); Pablo A. Celhay, Julia Johannsen, Sebastian Martinez, and Cecilia Vidal, "Can Small Incentives Have Large Payoffs? Health Impacts of a National Conditional Cash Transfer Program in Bolivia" (CEDLAS, Universidad Nacional de La Plata, 2017).

16　"The Juana Azurduy Voucher Program: Health Services for Mothers and Their Children," *Impacto*, Inter-American Development Bank blog, May 31, 2016, https://blogs.iadb.org/efectividad-desarrollo/en/the-juana-azurduy-voucher-program/.

17　Florinda Vallejo, interview, Shinahota, May 27, 2009.

18　La Época, "Según fuente oficial y la CEPAL, Bolivia tiene la mayor reducción de pobreza extrema de Sudamérica", July 30, 2019, https://www.la-epoca.com.bo/2019/07/30/segun-fuente-oficial-y-la-cepal-bolivia-tiene-la-mayor-reduccion-de-pobreza-extrema-de-sudamerica/.

19　"Bolivia, Human Development Report," UN Development Programme, http://hdr.undp.org/en/countries/profiles/BOL.

20　In comparison, the Gini index in the United States stood at 41.1 in 2016 "Gini Index," World Bank, https://data.worldbank.org/indicator/SI.POV.GINI?view=chart.

21　Fellipe Abreu and Luiz Felipe Silva, "The Three Rs: How Bolivia Combats Illiteracy," *BBC News*, April 21, 2016, https://www.bbc.com/news/world-latin-america-37117243.

22　Abreu and Silva, "The Three Rs."

23　Margarita Pérez, interview, Cochabamba, March 4, 2008.

24　Linda Farthing, "Transforming Public Education in Bolivia," *Education Forum*, June 16, 2017, https://education-forum.ca/2017/06/16/transforming-public-education-in-bolivia/.

25　Igor Ampuero, interview, Cochabamba, March 12, 2017.

26  Mónica Navarro Vásquez, ed., *Entre la teoría y la práctica: Aportes para la construcción de una gestión educativa intra e intercultural en Bolivia* (Cochabamba: PROEIB Andes, 2016).

27  Navarro Vásquez, ed., *Entre la teoría y la práctica.*

28  Wilson Ogeda, interview, Cochabamba, March 12, 2017.

29  "Why Education Reform Alone Won't Save Bolivia's Indigenous Languages," *World Politics Review*, April 24, 2017, https://www.worldpoliticsreview.com/trend-lines/21941/why-education-reform-alone-won-t-save-bolivia-s-indigenous-languages.

30  Jiovanny Samanamud, interview, La Paz, March 16, 2012.

31  Ampuero, interview.

32  Joëtta M. Zoetelief, *Teachers and Intercultural Education Reform in Bolivia: From Discursive Imaginaries to Educational Realities* (Amsterdam: University of Amsterdam, 2014).

33  Ampuero, interview.

34  Farthing, "Transforming Public Education."

35  Mieke T. A. Lopes Cardozo, "Bolivian Teachers' Agency: Soldiers of Liberation or Guards of Coloniality and Continuation?," *Education Policy Analysis Archives* 23, no. 4 (2015): 17, http://dx.doi.org/10.14507/epaa.v23.

36  Marcia Mandepora (ex-rector, UNIBOL Guaraní), interview, Camiri, March 2, 2017.

37  Farthing, "Transforming Public Education."

38  Jaime Zambrana (ex-rector, UNIBOL Chapare), interview, Cochabamba, September 22, 2017; Mandepora, interview.

39  Mandepora, interview.

40  Leni Machis, interview, Warisata, May 9, 2012.

41  Mandepora, interview.

42  Juan Rodríguez, interview, Cuevo, March 1, 2017.

43  Alejandro Izquierdo, Carola Pessino, and Guillermo Vuletin, eds., "Better Spending for Better Lives. How Latin America and the Caribbean Can Do More with Less," *Inter-American Development Bank*, September 2018, https://flagships.iadb.org/sites/default/files/dia/chapters/DIA2018-Better-Spending-for-Better-Lives-Ch-6-Making-Spending-Count-in-Education.pdf.

44  Lykke E. Andersen, "Who Is Being Left Behind by the Education Revolution in Bolivia?," *Southern Voice*, March 13, 2019, http://southernvoice.org/who-is-being-left-behind-by-the-education-revolution-in-bolivia/; Linda Farthing, "Evo's Bolivia: The Limits of Change," *The Next System Project*, 2017, https://thenextsystem.org/learn/stories/evos-bolivia-limits-change.

45  "Bolivia se encamina hacia la salud universal," OPS Bolivia, February 24, 2019, https://www.paho.org/bol/index.php?option=com_content&view=article&id=2209:bolivia-se-encamina-hacia-la-salud-universal&Itemid=481.

46  Juan Carlos León, speech, Cotagaita, March 2, 2019.

47  "People Using at Least Basic Sanitation Services, Rural (% of Rural Population)," *Index Mundi*, January 1, 2020, https://www.indexmundi. com/facts/indicators/SH.STA.BASS.RU.ZS/compare#country=bo.

48  Jason Tockman, "Bolivia Prescribes Solidarity: Health Care Reform under Evo Morales," *NACLA*, 2009, https://nacla.org/news/ bolivia-prescribes-solidarity-health-care-reform-under-evo-morales.

49  Francisco N. Alvarez, Mart Leys, Hugo E. Rivera Mérida, and Giovanni Escalante Guzmán, "Primary Health Care Research in Bolivia: Systematic Review and Analysis," *Health Policy and Planning* 31, no. 1 (2016): 114–28.

50  Alexandra Shand, "An Exploratory Study on Perceptions of the Social Oversight Mechanism and the Results of the Efforts of the Community Representatives in Health Network No. 1, the Municipality of La Paz, Bolivia," MSc thesis, Universidad Autónoma de Tomas Frías, La Paz, 2012.

51  "Health in the Americas," PAHO/WHO, 2017, https://www.paho.org/ salud-en-las-americas-2017/?page_id=95.

52  Chris Hartmann, "Bolivia's Plurinational Healthcare Revolution Will Not Be Defeated," *NACLA*, December 19, 2019, https://nacla.org/ news/2019/12/19/bolivia-plurinational-healthcare-revolution-evo-morales.

53  Brian B. Johnson, "Decolonization and Its Paradoxes: The (Re)Envisioning of Health Policy in Bolivia," *Latin American Perspectives* 37, no. 3 (2010): 139–59.

54  Tockman, "Bolivia Prescribes Solidarity."

55  Johnson, "Decolonization and Its Paradoxes."

56  Daniel Flores Quispe, telephone interview, May 2012.

57  Johnson, "Decolonization and Its Paradoxes."

58  Hernán Vallejos Calle, interview, May 1, 2012.

59  Linda Farthing, "Bolivia Prison Report: Marginal Progress and Unwieldly Challenges," *Andean Information Network*, November 15, 2016, http:// ain-bolivia.org/2016/11/bolivia-prison-report-marginal-progress-and- unwieldly-challenges/.

60  "Bolivia—Gasto público," *Datosmascro*, https://datosmacro.expansion.com/ estado/gasto/bolivia.

61  "Bolivia tiene nivel más alto de reservas internacionales respecto del PIB en Suramérica," *América Economía*, August 24, 2018, https:// www.americaeconomia.com/economia-mercados/finanzas/ bolivia-tiene-nivel-mas-alto-de-reservas-internacionales-respecto-del-pib.

62  Andres Schipani, "After 14 Years, Is Bolivia Falling Out of Love with Evo Morales?," *Financial Times*, October 7, 2019, https://www.ft.com/content/ e16c0c7c-e387-11e9-b112-9624ec9edc59.

63  "¿Cómo funciona el 15% destinado a la compra de productos nacionales?," Doble Aguinaldo program website, https://www.dobleaguinaldo.gob.bo.

64  Wagner A. Kamakura and Jose Alfonso Mazzon, "Measuring the Impact of a Conditional Cash Transfer Program on Consumption Behavior with Propensity Scoring," *Customer Needs and Solutions* 2 (2015): 302–16.

65  McNelly, "Critical Junctures."

66 Silvia Escobar de Pabón, Bruno Rojas, and Carlos Arze, "País sin industrias, país con empleos precarios: Situación de los derechos laborales en Bolivia, 2011–12," *CEDLA*, La Paz, 2014.

67 Jorge León Trujillo and Susan Spronk, "Socialism without Workers? Trade Unions and the New Left in Bolivia and Ecuador," in *Reshaping the Political Arena in Latin America: From Resisting Neoliberalism to the Second Incorporation*, Eduardo Silva and Federico M. Rossi, eds. (Pittsburgh: University of Pittsburgh Press, 2018), 129–56.

68 Angus McNelly, "Labour Bureaucracy and Labour Officialdom in Evo Morales's Bolivia," *Development and Change* 50 (2019): 896–922.

69 "Presidents of Bolivia, Argentina Get Highest Approval Ratings in Latin America World," *Public Opinion*, 2006, http://www.worldpublicopinion. org/pipa/articles/brlatinamericara/242.php?nid=&id=&pnt=242.

70 Fernando Molina, *El pensamiento boliviano sobre los recursos naturales* (La Paz: Pulso, 2009).

71 Vladimir Dennis Díaz Cuellar, *Industrialización y desindustrialización en Bolivia durante el Gobierno del MAS* (Ottawa: Carleton University Press, 2017).

72 Latin America leads world records in constitution writing: the Dominican Republic has had thirty-two documents, and Venezuela twenty-six, since independence from Spain.

73 Fernando Garcés, "The Domestication of Indigenous Autonomies in Bolivia," in *Remapping Bolivia: Resources, Territory and Indigeneity in a Plural National State*, Nicole Fabricant and Bret Gustafson, eds. (Santa Fe, NM: School for Advanced Research Press, 2011), 46–67.

74 "El MAS gana en el país con el 45,7%," *La Razón*, July 4, 2006.

75 Stéphanie Rousseau, "Indigenous and Feminist Movements at the Constituent Assembly in Bolivia: Locating the Representation of Indigenous Women," *Latin American Research Review* 46, no. 2 (2011): 5–28.

76 Miguel Centellas, "Bolivia's New Multicultural Constitution: The 2009 Constitution in Historical and Comparative Perspective," in *Latin America's Multicultural Movements*, Todd Eisenstadt et al., eds. (New York: Oxford University Press, 2013), 88–110.

77 Interview courtesy of Anne Catherine Bajard, Concepción, Santa Cruz, October 6, 2012.

78 Raúl Prada Alcoreza, interview, La Paz, March 27, 2012.

79 Fernando Mayorga, "Referéndum y asamblea constituyente: Autonomías departamentales en Bolivia," *Colombia International* 64 (2006): 50–67.

80 Willem Assies, "Bolivia's New Constitution and Its Implications," in *Evo Morales and the Movimiento al Socialismo in Bolivia* (London: Institute for the Study of the Americas, University of London, 2011), 93–116.

81 "Bolivia: Three Dead in Capital Conflict," *Andean Information Network*, November 26, 2007, http://ain-bolivia.org/2007/11/ bolivia-three-dead-in-capital-conflict/.

82 Democracy Center, "Bolivia's Struggle for a New Constitution," *J'allalla* 2 (2008): 4–6.

83  Salvador Schavelzon, "El nacimiento del Estado Plurinacional de Bolivia: Etnografía de una Asamblea Constituyente," *IWGIA* (2012): 321.

84  Garcés, "Domestication of Indigenous Autonomies."

85  Oscar Vega Camacho, presentation, Latin American Studies Association meetings, San Francisco, May 27, 2012.

86  Garcés, "Domestication of Indigenous Autonomies," 64.

87  Martín Mendoza-Botelho, "Revisiting Bolivia's Constituent Assembly: Lessons on the Quality of Democracy," *Asian Journal of Latin American Studies* 29, no. 1 (2016): 19–55.

88  Jonas Wolff, "Postliberal Democracy Emerging? A Conceptual Proposal and the Case of Bolivia," Peace Research Institute Frankfurt Working Paper No. 11, 2012, https://www.files.ethz.ch/isn/137497/arbeitspapier1112.pdf.

89  Lorenza Fontana, "On the Perils and Potentialities of Revolution: Conflict and Collective Action in Contemporary Bolivia," *Latin American Perspectives* 40, no. 3 (2013): 26–42.

90  John Crabtree, "Bolivia: New Constitution, New Definition," *Open Democracy*, January 22, 2009, http://www.opendemocracy.net/article/bolivia-new-constitution-new-definition.

91  Bret Gustafson and Nicole Fabricant, "Introduction: New Cartographies of Knowledge and Struggle," in *Remapping Bolivia*, 1–25.

92  Rousseau, "Indigenous and Feminist Movements."

93  Nick Buxton, *Constituting Change in a Divided Bolivia* (Amsterdam: Transnational Institute, 2008).

94  Garcés, "Domestication of Indigenous Autonomies," 50–58.

95  "Social control" draws from Indigenous concepts of community discipline and self-discipline to ensure citizen-led transparency in government spending. Centro Latinoamericano de Administración para el Desarrollo, *Bolivia: Garantizada la ética, la transparencia y el control social en la nueva Constitución Política de Bolivia*, 2009.

96  Franco Gamboa Rocabado, "La Asamblea Constituyente en Bolivia: Una evaluación de su dinámica," *Frónesis* 16, no. 3 (2009).

97  Gamboa Rocabado, "Asamblea Constituyente."

98  Salvador Schavelson, "Nacimiento del Estado Plurinacional de Bolivia," 231.

99  Buxton, *Constituting Change in a Divided Bolivia*.

100  Marcos Uzquiano, interview, Rurrenabaque, April 16, 2019.

101  Raúl Prada Alcoreza, interview, La Paz, March 27, 2012.

102  Maxwell A. Cameron and Kenneth E. Sharpe, "Andean Left Turns: Constituent Power and Constitution Making," in *Latin America's Left Turns*, Maxwell A. Cameron and Eric Hershberg, eds. (Boulder, CO: Lynne Rienner, 2010), 61–78.

103  José Bailaba, interview courtesy of Anne Catherine Bajard, Concepción, Santa Cruz, October 6, 2012.

104 "Thousands Protest US Asylum for Sanchez Berzaín," *Andean Information Network*, June 10, 2008, http://ain-bolivia.org/2008/06/ii-18/.

105 "Black October Verdict: All Officials Guilty," *Andean Information Network*, August 30, 2011, http://ain-bolivia.org/2011/08/black-october-verdict -all-officials-guilty/.

106 "FEJUVE El Alto: 'Agenda de Octubre' no va a ser cerrada, sino reforzada," *JORNADA/Atipiri*, 2011.

107 "Morales: Si Shannon coopera con extradición de Goni tendrá trabajo en El Alto," *Hoy Bolivia*, July 23, 2008, http://hoybolivia.com/Noticia. php?IdNoticia=4281.

108 "A Case for Extradition: Gonzalo Sánchez de Lozada and Carlos Sanchez Berzain," *Council on Hemispheric Affairs*, September 3, 2008, http://www. coha.org/a-case-for-extradition-gonzalo-sanchez-de-lozada-and-carlos -sanchez-berzain/comment-page-1/.

109 Linda Farthing and Benjamin H. Kohl, *Evo's Bolivia: Continuity and Change* (Austin: University of Texas Press, 2014).

110 Linda Farthing, "How US Civil Law Is Being Used to Bring Human- Rights Abuses to Court," *The Nation*, April 27, 2018, https://www. thenation.com/article/archive/how-us-civil-law-is-being-used-to-bring -human-rights-abuses-to-court/.

111 "Morales toma juramento a los 16 ministros que integran el 'nuevo Gabinete del pueblo,'" *El País*, January 23, 2006, https://elpais.com/ internacional/2006/01/23/actualidad/1137970802_850215.html.

112 Personal communication, La Paz, April 4, 2019.

113 "29 Institutos de Lengua y Cultura preservan y promueven sus lenguas originarias," *Avanzamos* 6, no. 48 (2018), https://www.minedu.gob.bo/ index.php?option=com_k2&view=item&id=476:29-institutos-de-lengua- y-cultura-preservan-y-promueven-sus-lenguas-originarias&Itemid=889.

114 Garcés, "Domestication of Indigenous Autonomies," 50–58.

115 Chuck Sturtevant, "Evo Morales Champions Indigenous Rights Abroad, but in Bolivia It's a Different Story," *The Conversation*, February 27, 2015.

116 Linda Farthing, "Indigenous Justice or Western Justice in Bolivia?," *Indian Country Today*, December 15, 2016, https://indiancountrytoday.com/ archive/indigenous-justice-western-justice-bolivia.

117 Farthing, "Indigenous Justice," 2016.

118 "Bolivia: 51 Per Cent of Women Elected to Parliament," *Institute for Democracy and Electoral Assistance*, March 8, 2015, https://www.idea.int/ news-media/news/bolivia-51-cent-women-elected-parliament%C2%A0.

119 Andres Schipani, "Bolivian Women Spearhead Morales Revolution," *BBC News*, February 11, 2010, http://news.bbc.co.uk/2/hi/americas/8498081. stm.

120 "Situación de mujeres en Bolivia," *Observatorio de Género*, March 8, 2019, http://www.coordinadoradelamujer.org.bo/observatorio/archivos/ destacados/boletin8mcompressed_86.pdf.

121 Monica Novillo, interview, La Paz, October 2015.

122 Rachel B. Vogelstein and Alexandra Bro, "Women's Power Index," *Council on Foreign Relations*, September 18, 2020, https://www.cfr.org/article/womens-power-index.

123 Linda Farthing, "Parity at a Price," *Ms.*, Summer 2015.

124 Jessy López, interview, La Paz, February 22, 2015.

125 Linda Farthing, "Bolivian Women Win Legislative Parity," *Herizons*, Fall 2015.

126 Fabiola Alvelais et al., "No Justice for Me: Femicide and Impunity in Bolivia," International Human Rights Clinic, Harvard Law School, 2019, hrp.law.harvard.edu/wp-content/uploads/2019/03/No-Justice-for-Me.pdf.

127 Sofia Silvestre, interview, La Paz, February 22, 2015.

128 Alvelais et al., "No Justice for Me."

129 Emily Achtenberg, "For Abortion Rights in Bolivia, a Modest Gain," *NACLA*, February 27, 2014, https://nacla.org/blog/2014/2/28/abortion-rights-bolivia-modest-gain.

130 Anonymous interview, La Paz, March 18, 2018.

131 Ineke Dibbits and Ximena Pabón, *Granizadas, bautizos y despachos. Aportes al debate sobre el aborto desde la provincia Ingavi* (La Paz: Conexión, 2013).

132 Julia Mamani, personal communication, La Paz, October 15, 2017.

133 Shawnna Mullenax, "De Jure Transformation, De Facto Stagnation: The Status of Women's and LGBT Rights in Bolivia," in *Seeking Rights from the Left: Gender, Sexuality, and the Latin American Pink Tide*, Elisabeth Jay Friedman, ed. (Durham: Duke University Press, 2018), 173–99.

134 "Bolivia," OutRight Action International, https://outrightinternational.org/region/bolivia.

135 David Aruquipa, telephone interview, December 20, 2020.

136 Simon Teagal, "A Surprising Move on LGBT Rights From a 'Macho' South American President," *Pulitzer Center*, July 17, 2016, https://pulitzercenter.org/reporting/suprising-move-lgbt-rights-macho-south-american-president.

137 "Bolivia promulgó una polémica ley de identidad de género," May 21, 2016, *Infobae*, https://www.infobae.com/2016/05/21/1813270-bolivia-promulgo-una-polemica-ley-identidad-genero/.

138 David Aruquipa, telephone interview.

139 David Aruquipa and Guido Monaño, interview, La Paz, March 27, 2021.

140 Gonzalo Colque, Efraín Tinta, and Esteban Sanjinés, *Segunda reforma agraria: Una historia que incomoda* (La Paz: Tierra, 2016); Louca Lerch, "The Geopolitics of Land: Population, Security and Territory Viewed from the International Financing of the Land Survey in Bolivia (1996–2013)," *Journal of Latin American Geography* 13, no. 1 (2014): 137–68.

141 Emily Achtenberg, "Bolivia: The Unfinished Business of Land Reform," *NACLA*, March 31, 2013, https://nacla.org/blog/2013/3/31/bolivia-unfinished-business-land-reform.

142 Penelope Anthias, *Limits to Decolonization: Indigeneity, Territory, and Hydrocarbon Politics in the Bolivian Chaco* (Ithaca, NY: Cornell University Press, 2017).

143 Miguel Urioste, "La 'revolución agraria' de Evo Morales. Desafíos de un proceso complejo," *Nueva Sociedad* 223 (2009): 113–27.

144 Lee MacKey, "Legitimating Foreignization in Bolivia: Brazilian Agriculture and the Relations of Conflict and Consent in Santa Cruz, Bolivia," paper presented at the International Conference on Global Land Grabbing, Brighton, UK, April 6–8, 2011, https://www.future-agricultures.org/wp-content/ uploads/pdf-archive/Lee%20Mackey.pdf.

145 Colque, Tinta, and Sanjinés, *Segunda reforma agraria.*

146 Bolivia Information Forum, Bulletin 35, *Ten Years On: The Morales Government in Perspective,* (2016).

147 Colque, Tinta, and Sanjinés, *Segunda reforma agraria.*

148 Marilyn Carayuri, interview, Santa Cruz, April 17, 2012.

149 Marcos Uzquiano, interview, Rurrenabaque, April 16, 2019.

150 Colque, Tinta, and Sanjinés, *Segunda reforma agraria.*

151 "ONDCP Releases Data on Coca Cultivation and Cocaine Production in Bolivia," White House briefing, November 13, 2020, https://www.whitehouse.gov/briefings-statements/ ondcp-releases-data-coca-cultivation-cocaine-production-bolivia/.

152 Jorge Chambi, interview, Oruro, February 22, 2017.

153 Jamie Doward, "Bolivians Demand the Right to Chew Coca Leaves," *Guardian,* January 13, 2013, https://www.theguardian.com/world/2013/ jan/13/bolivia-drugs-row-chew-coca.

154 Wilson Bernal, interview, La Paz, March 16, 2018.

155 Thomas Grisaffi, "Rethinking Drugs Policy in Latin America," in *South America, Central America and the Caribbean 2016,* Jacqueline West, ed. (London: Routledge, 2015).

156 Known as the Cato Accord, the permitted plot is 1,600 square meters in the Chapare and 2,500 in the Yungas (because of differences in yield between the two coca growing regions). Linda Farthing and Kathryn Ledebur, *Habeas Coca: Bolivia's Community Coca Control,* Lessons for Drug Policy Series, Open Society Foundations, July 2015, https://www.opensocietyfoundations.org/ uploads/dd3082d5-1bab-4fa0-9cb5-273a921ea32b/habeas-coca-bolivias-community-coca-control-20150706.pdf.

157 Emilio Flores, interview, Shinahota, Cochabamba, January 30, 2014.

158 Thomas Grisaffi, Linda Farthing, and Kathryn Ledebur, "Integrated Development with Coca in the Plurinational State of Bolivia: Shifting the Focus from Eradication to Poverty Alleviation," *UNODC Bulletin on Narcotics* 61 (2017), https://www.unodc.org/documents/data-and-analysis/bulletin/2017/Bulletin_on_Narcotics_V1705843.pdf.

159 OAS, *The Drug Problem in the Americas: 2013,* available at fileserver.idpc.net/ library/OAS-Analytical%20Report_The-drug-problem-in-the-Americas.pdf.

160 UNDP, *Development Dimensions of Drug Policy: Innovative Approaches*, June 2019, https://www.undp.org/content/dam/undp/library/people/health/Development_Dimensions_of_Drug_Policy.pdf.

161 White House Presidential Determination, September 14, 2012.

162 Ricardo Hegedus, interview, El Alto, January 24, 2014.

163 Felipe Cáceres, interview, La Paz, February 3, 2014.

164 Ministerio de Gobierno, *Estudio Integral de la Demanda de la Hoja de Coca en Bolivia*, Estado Plurinacional de Bolivia, 2014, https://studylib.es/doc/5560705/estudio-integral-de-la-demanda-de-la-hoja-de-coca-en-bolivia.

165 Kathryn Ledebur, interview, Cochabamba, April 20, 2017.

166 Lucio Mendoza, interview, Coroico, La Paz, October 16, 2014.

167 Christian Oporto, interview, El Alto, January 24, 2014.

## Chapter 4: Challenges and Missteps

1 Freddy Condo, personal communication, La Paz, February 18, 2017.

2 Brígida Quiroga, telephone interview, November 14, 2019.

3 Miguel A. Centeno, Atul Kohli, and Deborah J. Yashar, eds., *States in the Developing World* (Cambridge, UK: Cambridge University Press, 2017), 14.

4 Rossana Barragán, "Hegemonías y 'ejemonías': Las relaciones entre el estado central y las regiones (Bolivia, 1825 to 1952)," *Iconos* 34 (2009): 39–51.

5 Marco Just Quiles, *Fragmented State Capacity: External Dependencies, Subnational Actors, and Local Public Services in Bolivia*, Springer Fachmedian Weisbaden (2019).

6 Koldo Echebarría and Juan Carlos Cortázar, "Public Administration and Public Employment Reform in Latin America," in *The State of State Reform in Latin America*, Eduardo Lora, ed. (Washington, DC: The Inter-American Development Bank and Stanford University Press, 2007).

7 Claudia Peña Claros, interview, La Paz, April 12, 2018.

8 Just Quiles, *Fragmented State Capacity*.

9 María Teresa Zegada and George Komadina, *El intercambio político: Indígenas/campesinos en el Estado Plurinacional* (Cochabamba and La Paz: CERES / Plural Editores).

10 Alberto Borda, interview, Cochabamba, March 7, 2018.

11 Linda Farthing, *Bolivia: The Left in Power: State Officials' Perspectives on the Challenges to Progressive Governance in Bolivia* (Amsterdam: Transnational Institute, 2018), https://www.tni.org/files/publication-downloads/bolivia.pdf.

12 Just Quiles, *Fragmented State Capacity*, 262–63.

13 Ximena Soruco, Daniela Franco, and Mariela Durán, *Composición social del Estado Plurinacional: Hacia descolonización de la burocracia* (La Paz: Centro de Investigación Social, 2014).

14 Anonymous interview, La Paz, April 9, 2012.

15  Farthing, *Bolivia: The Left in Power.*

16  Mark Goodale, *A Revolution in Fragments: Traversing Scales of Justice, Ideology and Practice in Bolivia* (Durham: Duke University Press, 2019), 29.

17  Alberto Borda, interview, Cochabamba, March 14, 2018.

18  Casimira Rodríguez Romero, interview, Cochabamba, March 12, 2018.

19  Claudia Peña Claros, interview, La Paz, March 20, 2018.

20  Mauricio Becerra R., "Félix Cárdenas, viceministro de Descolonización de Bolivia: 'Todos los Estados de este continente son coloniales,'" *Red de Noticias e Información sobre Pueblos Indígenas,* Derechos Humanos, April 15, 2011.

21  Jenny Ybarnegaray Ortiz, "Feminismo y descolonización. Notas para el debate," *Nueva Sociedad* 234 (July–August 2011).

22  Marcia Mandepora, interview, Camiri, Santa Cruz, March 2, 2017.

23  Ricardo Aguilar Agramont, "La descolonización aún se encuentra en el plano discursivo," *La Razón,* August 26, 2012, http://www.larazon. com/suplementos/animal_politico/descolonizacionencuentra-plano-discursivo_0_1675632467.html.

24  Ybarnegaray Ortiz, "Feminismo y descolonización."

25  Marilyn Carayuri, interview, Santa Cruz, April 17, 2012.

26  Jaime Zambrana, interview, Cochabamba, September 22, 2017.

27  Eija Ranta, *Vivir Bien as an Alternative to Neoliberal Globalization: Can Indigenous Terminologies Decolonize the State?* (London: Routledge, 2018).

28  Juan N. Téllez, "El Vivir Bien en el contexto de desarrollo de Bolivia Observatorio de Desarrollo," *Observatorio del Desarollo* 2, no. 6 (2014).

29  Mandepora, interview.

30  Jessica Locke, "Buddhist Modernism Underway in Bhutan: Gross National Happiness and Buddhist Political Theory," *Religions* 11, no. 6 (June 2020).

31  Fernando Huanacuni Mamani, *Vivir Bien/Buen Vivir: Filosofía, políticas, estrategias y experiencias regionales* (La Paz: CAOI, 2010).

32  Marcia Mandepora, "Bolivia's Indigenous Universities," *ReVista,* Fall 2011, https://revista.drclas.harvard.edu/book/bolivias-indigenous-universities.

33  "7 principios del Mandar Obedeciendo," *Huizache,* November 28, 2016, http://www.huizache.org/posts/7-principios-del-mandar-obedeciendo.

34  Shannon Speed, *Rights in Rebellion: Indigenous Struggle and Human Rights in Chiapas* (Stanford: Stanford University Press, 2008), 170.

35  Petronila Mamani, interview, El Alto, October 14, 2019.

36  Nancy Postero and Jason Tockman, "Self-Governance in Bolivia's First Indigenous Autonomy: Charagua," *Latin America Research Review,* 2020, https://larrlasa.org/articles/10.25222/larr.213/.

37  Thomas Grisaffi, "Democracy or Dictatorship? Illiberal Governance in Bolivia's Coca Growers' Unions," paper presented at the EASA Biennial Virtual Conference, July 20–24, 2020.

38  The *ayllu* is an Andean form of social organization that reflects a combination of both kinship and territorial ties that has survived in

some parts of the Andes. Ayllu membership generally includes a service requirement involving rotating leadership, participatory decision making through communal consensus, and mechanisms to ensure a relatively equitable distribution of resources. See Simón Yampara Huarachi, "The Ayllu and Territoriality in the Andes," Sue Iamamoto, trans., *Alternautas*, May 22, 2017, http://www.alternautas.net/blog/2017/5/22/ the-ayllu-and-territoriality-in-the-andes.

39   Angus McNelly, "Labour Bureaucracy and Labour Officialdom in Evo Morales's Bolivia," *Development and Change* 50, no. 4 (October 2018).

40   Benjamin H. Kohl, Feliciano Muruchi Poma, and Linda Farthing, *From the Mines to the Streets: A Bolivian Activist's Life* (Austin: University of Texas Press, 2012).

41   Centro de Investigaciones, *Revista Traspatios 2: La transformación del Estado y del campo político en Bolivia* (La Paz: Plural Editores, 2011).

42   Bruno Fornillo, "Encrucijadas del cogobierno en la Bolivia actual. Un análisis sociopolítico de la experiencia del Movimiento al Socialismo en el poder (2006–7)," Programa Regional de Becas, *CLACSO*, 2008, https://www.scribd.com/document/166479429/Bolivia-EL-MAS-en-El-Poder.

43   Fernando Mayorga, "Movimientos sociales y participación política en Bolivia," in *Ciudadanía y legitimidad democrática en América Latina*, Isidoro Cheresky, ed. (Buenos Aires: Promoteo, 2011), 19–41, http://biblioteca.clacso.edu.ar/clacso/gt/20120329050824/cheresky.pdf.

44   Moira Zuazo, "Bolivia: Social Control as the Fourth State power (1994–2015)," in *Intermediation and Representation in Latin America: Actors and Roles beyond Elections*, Gisela Zaremberg, Valeria Guarneros-Meza, and Adrián Gurza Lavalle, eds. (London: Palgrave Macmillan, 2017), 95–114.

45   Rafael Puente, "¿Qué hacer para reconstituir el sujeto del proceso?," *La Época*, August 8, 2018, https://www.la-epoca.com.bo/2011/06/22/ que-hacer-para-reconstituir-el-sujeto-del-proceso/.

46   Centro de Investigaciones, *Revista Traspatios 2*.

47   Jonas Wolff, "Evo Morales and the Promise of Political Incorporation: Advancements and Limits," paper prepared for the 2017 LASA Congress, Lima, Peru, April 29—May 1, 2017, 5; Moira Zuazo, "¿Los movimientos sociales en el poder? El gobierno del MAS en Bolivia," *Nueva Sociedad* 227 (May–June 2010).

48   Jimmy Osorio, "La participación y el control social ahora," *La Razón*, September 29, 2015, http://www.la-razon.com/suplementos/animal_ politico/participacion-control-social-ahora_0_1915008539.html; "Cartilla Control Social 2015," Banco Central de Bolivia, https://www.bcb.gob.bo/?q=content/cartilla-control-social-2015.

49   Carlos Böhrt Irahola, Fernando García Yapur, and Alberto García Orellana, eds., "La autonomía indígena originaria en el 'Pacto de Unidad' y el proceso constituyente," in *Diversidad institucional: Autonomías Indígenas y Estado Plurinacional en Bolivia* (La Paz: United Nations Development Program, 2018), 184; Jason Tockman, personal communication, November 8, 2020.

50  "Protocolos autonómicos de consulta previa: Nuevos caminos para la libre determinación de los pueblos indígenas en América Latina," IWGIA, 2019, https://www.iwgia.org/images/documentos/Protocolos_autonomicos_de_Consulta_Previa.pdf.

51  Milton Chacay Guayupan, interview, Cuevo, Santa Cruz, November 6, 2017.

52  Gonzalo Vargas, interview, La Paz, November 22, 2017.

53  Postero and Tockman, "Self-Governance."

54  José Luis Exeni, "Bolivia: Las autonomías frente al estado plurinacional," in ¿Cómo transformar? Instituciones y cambio social en América Latina y Europa, Miriam Lang, Belén Cevallos, and Claudia López, eds. (Quito: Fundación Rosa Luxemburgo / Ediciones Abya Yala, 2015), 145–190.

55  Vargas, interview.

56  They are, however, Paraguay's largest.

57  José Fernando Menacho Amosquivar, interview, Charagua, November 7, 2017.

58  Chacay Guayupan, interview.

59  Pabel Camilo López Flores y Gaya Makaran, "Autonomía indígena en disputa: Entre la reconstitución comunitaria y la tutela estatal. La experiencia guaraní de Huacaya en Bolivia," Revista Crítica de Ciências Sociais 121 (2020): 49–70.

60  Marianela Baldelomar Davalos, interview, Charagua, November 7, 2017.

61  Centro de Investigación y Promoción del Campesinado, Compendio de Leyes Autonómicas Charagua Iyambae 2017–2018, 2018.

62  Postero and Tockman, "Self-Governance."

63  Baldelomar Davalos, interview.

64  Chacay Guayupan, interview.

65  Asier de Bringas, "Autonomías indígenas en América Latina: Una mirada comparada a partir de las dificultades para la construcción de un derecho intercultural," Journal of Self-Government 8 (December 2018): 101–38.

66  Baldelomar Davalos, interview.

67  Linda Farthing and Nicole Fabricant, "Introduction: Open Veins Revisited: Charting the Social, Economic, and Political Contours of the New Extractivism in Latin America," Latin American Perspectives 45, no. 5 (2018): 4–17.

68  Brent Z. Kaup, "A Neoliberal Nationalization? The Constraints on Natural-Gas-Led Development in Bolivia," Latin American Perspectives 37, no. 3 (2010): 123–38.

69  Luis Tapia and Marxa Chávez, Producción y reproducción de desigualdades. Organización social y poder político (La Paz: CEDLA, 2020), 78–79.

70  Eduardo Gudynas, The New Extractivism of the 21st Century: Ten Urgent Theses about Extractivism in Relation to Current South American Progressivism (Washington, DC: American Policy Center, 2010).

71  Steve Ellner, "Introduction," Latin American Extractivism Dependency, Resource Nationalism, and Resistance in Broad Perspective (Lanham, MD:

Rowman & Littlefield, 2020), 1–28. Resource nationalism is a commitment to gain greater control or value from a country's natural resources for the benefit of its citizens.

72  Alfredo Macías Vázquez and Jorge García-Arias, "Financialization, Institutional Reform, and Structural Change in the Bolivian Boom (2006–2014)," *Latin American Perspectives* 46, no. 2 (2019): 47–64.

73  Tapia and Chávez, *Producción y reproducción de desigualdades.*

74  Manuel de la Fuente, "Extractivismo y conflictos en Bolivia," in *Lógicas de Desarrollo, extractivismo y cambio climático,* Manuel De La Fuente, Tania Ricaldi A., and Angél Saldomando, eds. (Cochabamba: CESU, 2017), 233–58.

75  Steve Ellner, "Introduction," in Ellner, *Latin American Extractivism.*

76  Skyrocketing investment made China Bolivia's largest creditor by 2015.

77  Álvaro García Linera, "Geopolitics of the Amazon," Richard Fidler, trans., *Climate and Capitalism,* January 13, 2013, http://climateandcapitalism.com/wp-content/uploads/sites/2/2013/01/Geopolitics-of-the-Amazon-A4.pdf.

78  Herbert S. Klein, *The American Finances of the Spanish Empire: Royal Income and Expenditures in Colonial Mexico, Peru, and Bolivia, 1680–1809* (Albuquerque: University of New Mexico Press, 1998).

79  Although mining, by then dominated by tin, was nationalized after the 1952 revolution through pressure from organized miners, the state-owned Bolivian Mining Corporation (COMIBOL) was highly inefficient and driven by patronage. In 1985, a plunge in world tin prices brought about the state mining sector's almost-total demise and massive mine closures. Many of the nearly thirty thousand miners who lost their jobs migrated to poor neighborhoods in major cities, or to the coca growing Chapare. Others swelled the ranks of so-called cooperative mines. Rather than cooperatives as commonly understood, these are small, frequently precarious, and often family-run businesses, many of which require high degrees of self-exploitation. Leadership of their miners' organization is concentrated in a wealthy few, who subcontract day laborers and resist unionization. The country's mining communities remain among the poorest and most environmentally degraded. See John Crabtree, Jenny Pearce, and Gavan Duffy, *The Great Tin Crash: Bolivia and the World Tin Market* (London: Latin America Bureau, 1987); and Linda Farthing, "Bolivia's Dilemma: Development Confronts the Legacy of Extraction," *NACLA,* September 1, 2009, https://nacla.org/article/bolivia%E2%80%99s-dilemma-development-confronts-legacy-extraction.

80  Fernando Molina, *El pensamiento boliviano sobre los recursos naturales* (La Paz: Pulso, 2009).

81  Benjamin Kohl and Linda Farthing, "Material Constraints to Popular Imaginaries: The Extractive Economy and Resource Nationalism in Bolivia," *Political Geography* 31, no. 4 (May 2012): 225–35.

82  "Mining in Bolivia," US Government Export Assistance, July 12, 2019, https://www.export.gov/apex/article2?id=Bolivia-Mining.

83 Thomas Graham, "Gold Fever Grips Bolivia, but at What Cost?," *World Politics Review*, September 16, 2019, https://www.worldpoliticsreview.com/articles/28191/gold-fever-grips-bolivia-but-at-what-cost.

84 "Cooperativistas de Bolivia: 'Estimado Evo, salga por la puerta grande de su Palacio,'" *ANF*, October 26, 2019, https://www.noticiasfides.com/nacional/politica/cooperativistas-de-bolivia-estimado-evo-salga-por-la-puerta-grande-de-su-palacio-401935.

85 See Kevin Young, "From Open Door to Nationalization: Oil and Development Visions in Bolivia, 1952–1969," *Hispanic American Historical Review* 97 (2017): 95–129.

86 Gustafson, *Bolivia in the Age of Gas*.

87 Emily Achtenberg, "Industrializing Bolivia's Gas in Bolivia, Not Brazil," *NACLA*, March 5, 2013, https://nacla.org/blog/2013/5/23/industrializing-bolivia%25E2%2580%2599s-gas-bolivia-not-brazil.

88 Mat Youkee, "Foreign Firms Show Renewed Interest in Bolivia's Gas Fields," *Americas Quarterly*, August 2017.

89 Gustafson, *Bolivia in the Age of Gas*.

90 David Hill, "Bolivia Opens Up National Parks to Oil and Gas Firms," *Guardian*, June 5, 2015, https://www.theguardian.com/environment/andes-to-the-amazon/2015/jun/05/bolivia-national-parks-oil-gas.

91 Lisbet Christoffersen, "Amazonian Erasures: Landscape and Myth-Making in Lowland Bolivia," *Rural Landscapes: Society, Environment, History* 5, no. 1 (2018): 3.

92 Gustafson, *Bolivia in the Age of Gas*, 242. The Áñez government announced two years later that it was searching for gas to extract through fracking in the Chaco region. See "Bolivia: Tres claves para entender la polémica por el fracking en el Chaco," *Mongabay*, August 10, 2020, https://es.mongabay.com/2020/08/bolivia-fracking-chaco/.

93 Luis Arce, interview, La Paz, October 17, 2019.

94 Carlos Ramos, interview, Cochabamba, March 12, 2011.

95 M. J. Osorio, "Clientes deben sacar hierro de El Mutún por su cuenta," *Los Tiempos*, March 6, 2011, available at http://hemeroteca.correodelsur.com/2011/0306/74.php.

96 Prasenjit Bhattacharya, "Jindal Steel Exits Bolivia Project," *Wall Street Journal*, July 17, 2012, https://www.wsj.com/articles/SB10001424052702303754904577532592283910030.

97 "China Sinosteel comienza a trabajar en El Mutún," *BNamericas*, January 20, 2019, https://www.bnamericas.com/es/noticias/china-sinosteel-comienza-a-trabajar-en-el-mutun.

98 "China Enters Bolivia's Steel Industry," *Diálogo Chino*, July 22, 2015, https://dialogochino.net/en/extractive-industries/3016-china-enters-bolivias-steel-industry/.

99 Laura Manzaneda, "La producción de urea en Bulo es incierta," *Los Tiempos*, October 10, 2017, https://www.lostiempos.com/actualidad/economia/20171010/produccion-urea-bulo-bulo-es-incierta.

100  Laura Manzaneda, "Bulo Bulo cumple 7 meses sin operar y no hay señales de su reanudación," *Los Tiempos,* May 16, 2020, https://www.lostiempos.com/actualidad/economia/20200516/bulo-bulo-cumple-7-meses-operar-no-hay-senales-su-reanudacion.

101  *Correo del Sur,* La planta de amoniaco y urea reanuda labores, September 6, 2021, https://correodelsur.com/economia/20210906_la-planta-de-amoniaco-y-urea-reanuda-labores.html.

102  "Bolivia to Invest in Billion-Dollar Lithium Deal with ACI Systems," *Reuters,* April 21, 2018, https://in.reuters.com/article/us-bolivia-lithium/bolivia-to-invest-in-billion-dollar-lithium-deal-with-aci-systems-idINKBN1HS0RW.

103  Matthew Eisler, "Bolivian Lithium: Why You Should Not Expect Any 'White Gold Rush' in the Wake of Morales Overthrow," *The Conversation,* November 15, 2019, https://theconversation.com/bolivian-lithium-why-you-should-not-expect-any-white-gold-rush-in-the-wake-of-morales-overthrow-127139.

104  Laura Millan Lombrana, "Bolivia's Almost Impossible Lithium Dream," *Bloomberg,* December 3, 2018, https://www.bloomberg.com/news/features/2018-12-03/bolivia-s-almost-impossible-lithium-dream#:~:text=Bolivia%E2%80%99s%20Almost%20Impossible%20Lithium%20Dream%20One%20of%20the,the%20mineral%20needed%20to%20power%20electric%20cars.%20By.

105  Tom Perreault, 2020, Bolivia's High Stakes Lithium Gamble, Summer 2020 | NACLA — Report on the Americas, 165-172.

106  Ivan Penn and Eric Lipton, "The Lithium Gold Rush: Inside the Race to Power Electric Vehicles," *New York Times,* May 6, 2021, https://www.nytimes.com/2021/05/06/business/lithium-mining-race.html.

107  Postero and Tockman, "Self-Governance."

108  TIPNIS—*Territorio Indígena Parque Nacional Isiboro Sécure* (Indigenous Territory of Isiboro-Sécure National Park).

109  Penelope Anthias, "Indigenous Peoples and the New Extraction: From Territorial Rights to Hydrocarbon Citizenship in the Bolivian Chaco," *Latin American Perspectives* 45, no. 5 (2018): 136–53.

110  Gisela Zaremberg and Marcela Torres Wong, "Participation on the Edge: Prior Consultation and Extractivism in Latin America," *Journal of Politics in Latin America* 10, no. 3 (2018): 29–58.

111  Almut Schilling-Vacaflor and Jessika Eichler, "The Shady Side of Consultation and Compensation: 'Divide-and-Rule' Tactics in Bolivia's Extraction Sector," *Development and Change* 48, no. 6 (November 2017): 1439–63.

112  José Luis Montero, interview, Camiri, Santa Cruz, March 2, 2017.

113  Riccarda Flemmer and Almut Schilling-Vacaflor, "Unfulfilled Promises of the Consultation Approach: The Limits to Effective Indigenous Participation in Bolivia's and Peru's Extractive Industries," *Third World Quarterly* 37, no. 1 (2016): 172–88.

114  Michael Dougherty, "How Does Development Mean? Attitudes toward Mining and the Social Meaning of Development in Guatemala," *Latin American Perspectives* 46, no. 2 (2019): 161–81.

115  CONAMAQ and CIDOB, *La "Consulta Previa" en opinión de los pueblos indígenas*, December 9, 2013, https://es.slideshare.net/somossur/00-texto-consulta.

116  Zaremberg and Torres Wong, "Participation on the Edge."

117  Schilling-Vacaflor and Eichler, "The Shady Side of Consultation and Compensation."

118  Jessika Eichler, "Symposium: Prior Consultation in Latin America—The Case of Bolivia: Legal Anthropological Experience in the Field of Indigenous Peoples," October 5, 2015, *Völkerrechtsblog*, https://voelkerrechtsblog.org/articles/mini-symposium-prior-consultation-in-latin-america-the-case-of-bolivia/.

119  Penelope Anthias, "Indigenous Peoples and the New Extraction."

120  Schilling-Vacaflor and Eichler, "The Shady Side of Consultation and Compensation."

121  Marianela Baldelomar Davalos, interview, Charagua, March 4, 2017.

122  Evo Morales, "Declaración Universal de los Derechos de la Madre Tierra," April 22, 2009, UN General Assembly, https://www.un.org/esa/socdev/unpfii/documents/MEDSE_Morales_es.pdf.

123  LIDEMA, "Las 10 prioridades ambientales para Bolivia en 2020," available at https://cebem.org/wp-content/uploads/2020/01/Las-10-prioridades-ambientales-para-Bolivia-en-2020_f.pdf.

124  Ben Mckay and Gonzalo Colque, "Bolivia's soy complex: the development of 'productive exclusion,'" *The Journal of Peasant Studies*, 43:2, (August 2015), 583–610.

125  Laetitia Perrier Bruslé and Pierre Gautreau, "Forest Management in Bolivia under Evo Morales: The Challenges of Post-neoliberalism," *Political Geography* 68 (January 2019): 110–21.

126  Nelson Peredo, "Evo pide defender madre tierra, pero impulsa 10 acciones que la destruyen," *Los Tiempos*, September 25, 2019, https://www.lostiempos.com/actualidad/pais/20190925/evo-pide-defender-madre-tierra-pero-impulsa-10-acciones-que-destruyen.

127  Miguel Urioste, "The Great Soy Expansion: Brazilian Land Grabs in Eastern Bolivia," *Land and Sovereignty*, Brief No. 30, September 2013.

128  Marcos Uzquiano, interview, Rurrenabaque, April 16, 2019.

129  Farthing, "Bolivia's Dilemma."

130  Marcos Uzquiano, interview.

131  Lisa Friedman, Nadja Popovich, and Henry Fountain, "Who's Most Responsible for Global Warming?," *New York Times*, April 26, 2018, https://www.nytimes.com/2018/04/26/climate/countries-responsible-global-warming.html; Anne-Sophie Brändlin, "The Global Injustice of the Climate Crisis," *Deutsche Welle*, August 28, 2019, https://www.dw.com/

en/the-global-injustice-of-the-climate-crisis-food-insecurity-carbon-
emissions-nutrients-a-49966854/a-49966854.

132   Kevin Muñoz, "Corrupted Idealism: Bolivia's Compromise between
Development and the Environment," *Truthout*, July 5, 2015, https://
truthout.org/articles/corrupted-idealism-bolivia-s-compromise-between-
development-and-the-environment/.

133   Sara Shahriari, "Whiteout: The End of the Andean Glacier?," *Bolivian
Express*, October 22, 2014, https://bolivianexpress.org/blog/posts/
whiteout-the-end-of-the-andean-glacier.

134   Cody Eaton, "Betanzos: Confronting Climate Change," SIT Independent
Study Project (ISP) Collection, Fall 2017, https://digitalcollections.sit.edu/
isp_collection/2693/.

135   Linda Farthing, "Bolivia's Disappearing Lake," *Earth Island Journal*,
February 1, 2017, https://www.earthisland.org/journal/index.php/
articles/entry/bolivias_disappearing_lake/.

136   Raúl Quispe, interview, El Alto, March 10, 2017.

137   IACHR, Informe No. 113/20, Petición 211–12, April 24, 2020, http://
www.oas.org/es/cidh/decisiones/2020/boad211-12es.pdf.

138   Rob Albro, "Evo Morales's Chaotic Departure Won't Define His
Legacy," *Foreign Policy*, November 22, 2019, https://foreignpolicy.
com/2019/11/22/evo-morales-departure-bolivia-indigenous-legacy/.

139   Thomas Graham, "The Dirty Business behind Bolivia's Clean
Energy Plans," *World Politics Review*, July 19, 2019, https://www.
worldpoliticsreview.com/articles/28048/the-dirty-business-behind-
bolivia-s-clean-energy-plans.

140   Hayley Stuart, "What Does Bolivia's Transition in Government Mean for
the Chepete-Bala Dam Proposals?," *The Hidden Crisis in Bolivia*, December
19, 2019, https://www.hiddencrisisbolivia.org/new-blog/what-does-
bolivias-transition-in-government-mean-for-the-chepete-bala-dam-
proposals.

141   "Planta solar de Oruro inicia producción de energía eléctrica con
50MW," *Opinión*, September 19, 2019, https://www.opinion.com.bo/
articulo/pais/planta-solar-oruro-inicia-produccion-energia-electrica-
50mw/20190919155044727172.html.

142   Linda Farthing, "Pollution Levels in Bolivia Plummet on Nationwide
Car-Free Day," *Guardian*, September 3, 2017, https://www.theguardian.
com/cities/2017/sep/03/bolivia-car-free-day-pollution.

143   Álvaro García Linera, interview, La Paz, October 16, 2019.

144   Fernando Mayorga, interview, Cochabamba, October 8, 2019.

145   John D. French, "Understanding the Politics of Latin America's Plural
Lefts (Chávez/Lula): Social Democracy, Populism and Convergence on
the Path to a Post-neoliberal World," *Third World Quarterly* 30, no. 2
(2009): 349–70; Cas Mudde and Cristóbal Rovira Kaltwasser, *Populism: A
Very Short Introduction* (Oxford: Oxford University Press, 2017).

146 Francisco Panizza, *Contemporary Latin America: Development and Democracy beyond the Washington Consensus* (London: Zed, 2009), 192–94.

147 Juan Pablo Luna, "¿Participación versus representación? Partidos políticos y democracia en la Región Andina," in *Democracia en la Región Andina: Diversidad y desafíos*, Juan Pablo Luna and Maxwell A. Cameron, eds. (Lima: IEP Instituto de Estudios Peruanos, 2010), 373–420.

148 John Crabtree, "The MNR, the MAS and the Meaning of Populism in Bolivia," in *Revolutions in Bolivia*, Into A. Goudsmit, Kate Maclean, and Winston Moore, eds. (London: Anglo-Bolivian Society and the Institute of Latin American Studies, University of London, 2018).

149 Manuel Suárez, "Evo Morales antes la historia," in *Crisis y cambio político en Bolivia. Octubre y noviembre de 2019: La democracia en una encrucijada*, Fernando Mayorga, ed. (La Paz: CESU/Oxfam, 2020), 220; Francisco Panizza, *Populism and the Mirror of Democracy* (London and New York: Verso, 2005).

150 Suárez, "Evo Morales antes la historia," 220.

151 Fernando Mayorga, *Mandato y contingencia. Estilo de gobierno de Evo Morales* (Buenos Aires: CLACSO / Friedrich-Ebert-Stiftung, 2020).

152 Mayorga, *Mandato y contingencia*.

153 Personal communication, La Paz, November 19, 2020.

154 Jaime Zambrana, interview, Cochabamba, September 22, 2017.

155 Maristella Svampa and Pablo Stefanoni, "Entrevista a Álvaro García Linera: 'Evo simboliza el quiebre de un imaginario restringido a la subalternidad de los indígenas,'" in *Reinventando la nación en Bolivia*, Pablo Stefanoni and Hervé Do Alto, eds. (La Paz: CLACSO / Plural, 2007), 147–72.

156 Hervé Do Alto, "Un partido campesino en el poder: Una mirada sociológica del MAS boliviano," *Nueva Sociedad* 234 (2011), http://www.nuso.org/revista.php?n=234.

157 Jonas Wolff, "Political Incorporation in Measures of Democracy: A Missing Dimension (and the Case of Bolivia)," *Democratization* 25, no. 4 (2018): 692–708.

158 David Aruquipa, interview, La Paz, November 20, 2017.

159 Pablo Solón, "Bolivia's Process of Change Needs a Change in Course," Richard Fidler, trans., *LINKS: International Journal of Socialist Renewal*, 2016, http://links.org.au/solon-bolivia-process-change-vivir-bien-extractivism.

## Chapter 5: "Black November"

1 Some of the names and identifying characteristics of people interviewed in this chapter were changed at their request.

2 Matthew Bristow and John Quigley, "Senator Brandishing Giant Bible Assumes Bolivia Presidency," *Bloomberg*, November 11, 2019, https://www.bloomberg.com/news/articles/2019–11–11/bolivia-faces-power-vacuum-and-more-chaos-after-morales-quits.

3    "Stand-In President 'Brings Back Bible' to Bolivian Politics,"
     *France24*, November 14, 2019, https://www.france24.com/
     en/20191114-stand-in-president-brings-back-bible-to-bolivian-politics.

4    Sylvia Colombo, "Déjà vu en Bolivia: Áñez quiere ser como Evo," *New
     York Times*, February 3, 2020, https://www.nytimes.com/es/2020/02/03/
     espanol/opinion/bolivia-evo-anez.html.

5    Brígida Quiroga, interview, La Paz, November 14, 2019.

6    Jon Lee Anderson, "The Fall of Evo Morales," *The New Yorker*, March
     16, 2020, https://www.newyorker.com/magazine/2020/03/23/
     the-fall-of-evo-morales.

7    Albert Bender, "Interim Bolivian President's Racist Remarks Hit Close to
     Home in Nashville," *Tennessean*, March 9, 2020, https://www.tennessean.
     com/story/opinion/2020/03/09/interim-bolivian-president-jeanine-anez-
     recalls-painful-past-remarks/4982763002/.

8    Jeanine Áñez Chavez (@JeanineAnez), Twitter post, November 6, 2019,
     3:56 AM, available at https://web.archive.org/web/20191113024420/
     https://twitter.com/JeanineAnez/status/1192048025998446593?s=.

9    Cindy Forster, "Bolivia's Post-coup President Has Unleashed a
     Campaign of Terror," *Jacobin*, May 30, 2020, https://www.jacobinmag.
     com/2020/05/bolivia-coup-jeanine-anez-evo-morales-mas.

10   Anatoly Kurmanaev, "In Bolivia, Interim Leader Sets Conservative,
     Religious Tone," *New York Times*, November 16, 2019, https://www.
     nytimes.com/2019/11/16/world/americas/bolivia-anez-morales.html.

11   Morales had appointed Indigenous Bolivians to fourteen of the sixteen
     posts in his first cabinet. Anatoly Kurmanaev and Clifford Krauss, "Ethnic
     Rifts in Bolivia Burst into View with Fall of Evo Morales," *New York
     Times*, November 17, 2019, https://www.nytimes.com/2019/11/15/world/
     americas/morales-bolivia-Indigenous-racism.html.

12   "El senador Arturo Murillo será sentenciado por falsificar libreta militar,"
     *El Deber*, November 20, 2015, https://eldeber.com.bo/bolivia/el-senador-
     arturo-murillo-sera-sentenciado-por-falsificar-libreta-militar_16568.

13   Anahí Cazas, "Murillo sobre aborto: Suicídense, pero no maten una vida
     ajena," *Página Siete*, December 8, 2017, https://www.paginasiete.bo/
     sociedad/2017/12/8/murillo-sobre-aborto-suicdense-pero-maten-vida-
     ajena-162346.html.

14   "Ministro de Jeanine Áñez afirma que irá 'a la cacería' de exfuncionario de
     Evo Morales," *La República*, November 14, 2019, https://larepublica.pe/
     mundo/2019/11/14/jeanine-anez-bolivia-arturo-murillo-ira-a-la-caceria-
     juan-ramon-quintana-y-raul-garcia-linera-evo-morales-video-atmp/.

15   "Luis Fernando Camacho confesó: 'Fue mi padre quien cerró con los
     militares,'" *Página 12*, December 29, 2019, https://www.pagina12.com.
     ar/238942-luis-fernando-camacho-confeso-fue-mi-padre-quien-cerro-con-l.

16   Camacho told the press, "Coordinating [the military mutiny] was
     Fernando López, current minister of defense. That is why he is a minister,"
     https://www.youtube.com/watch?v=4uuiF0_8N4E.

17 "Justiniano atribuye su destitución a razones políticas y asegura sentirse sorprendido," *Los Tiempos*, December 4, 2019, https://www.lostiempos.com/actualidad/pais/20191204/justiniano-atribuye-su-destitucion-razones-politicas-asegura-sentirse.

18 The Spanish name for the group—which grew to five thousand strong by December 2019—is *Resistencia Juvenil Cochala* (Cochabamba Youth Resistance). It has strong parallels to Santa Cruz's *Unión Juvenil Crucenista* (Santa Cruz Youth Union), which was founded in 1957. The Cochabamba group, which is often seen on motorcycles, comprises part of an estimated twenty thousand paramilitaries in Bolivia. María Mena M., "Resistencia Cochala crece y busca pasar de grupo de choque a cívico," *Página Siete*, December 9, 2019, https://www.paginasiete.bo/nacional/2019/12/9/resistencia-cochala-crece-busca-pasar-de-grupo-de-choque-civico-239882.html.

19 *Indio* (Indian) is a derogatory slur in Bolivia. Interview, Sacaba, November 15, 2019.

20 Isaac Bigio, "La Guaidó boliviana," *Bolpress*, November 14, 2019, https://www.bolpress.com/2019/11/14/la-guaido-boliviana/.

21 "La jura como presidenta de Jeanine Áñez confirma la deriva ultraderechista de la revuelta contra Morales," *El Salto*, November 13, 2019, https://www.elsaltodiario.com/bolivia/jura-presidenta-jeanine-anez-confirma-deriva-ultraderechista-revuelta-contra-evo-morales.

22 Anonymous interview, La Paz, November 13, 2019.

23 Paola Paniagua, interview, La Paz, January 15, 2020.

24 Salvatierra had announced her resignation as president of the Senate on November 10, 2019, and requested asylum at the Mexican embassy. However, she later insisted that although her resignation letter had been presented, it was never accepted by the Senate, and therefore was not valid. Nonetheless, the Senate confirmed she had resigned November 14, and another young woman, Eva Copa, a MAS senator from El Alto, took her place. Jeanine Áñez later declared that Carlos Mesa was instrumental in preventing Salvatierra from taking office. See Rubén Atahuichi, "Nueve momentos: Carlos Mesa fue el factor clave de la sucesión de Jeanine Áñez," *La Razón*, June 14, 2021, www.la-razon.com/nacional/2021/06/14/nueve-momentos-carlos-mesa-fue-el-factor-clave-de-la-sucesion-de-jeanine-anez.

25 "Bolivian Senate's Leader Attacked by Police and Coup Supporters," *Telesur*, November 13, 2019, https://www.telesurenglish.net/news/Bolivian-Senates-Leader-Attacked-By-Police-and-Coup-Supporters-20191113-0009.html.

26 "Golpe en Bolivia: Áñez asumió rodeada de militares mientras reprimen en las calles de La Paz," *La Izquierda Diario*, November 13, 2019, http://laizquierdadiario.com/Video-El-Alto-Bolivia-cabildo-popular-contra-la-derecha-golpista.

27 Interviews, El Alto, May 20, 2020.

28 Interview, El Alto, December 6, 2019.

29 Iván Apaza, "La crisis política y la revuelta aymara," in *Wiphala, crisis y memoria. Senkata, no te merecen* (El Alto: Jichha, 2020), 62–66.

30 Fernanda Rojas, "Bolivia: Bloqueo total y divisiones en el partido de Evo Morales," *La Tercera*, November 21, 2019, https://www.latercera.com/la-tercera-pm/noticia/bolivia-bloqueo-total-y-divisiones-en-el-partido-de-evo-morales/909873/.

31 Iveth Saravia, interview, El Alto, May 20, 2020.

32 Margarita Solís, interview, Sacaba, January 21, 2020.

33 Richard Cayo, interview, Sacaba, December 10, 2019.

34 Abel Colque, interview, Sacaba, December 10, 2019; Wilmer Vedia, interview, Cochabamba, January 20, 2020.

35 Colque, interview.

36 Edwin Alejo Morales, interview, Sacaba, January 21, 2020.

37 Ambrosio Yucra Aguilar, interview, Cochabamba, November 16, 2020.

38 Sheila Pérez, interview, Sacaba, January 21, 2020; Carla Sánchez, interview, Sacaba, January 20, 2020.

39 Pérez, interview.

40 Antonio Cruz Ramírez, interview, Sacaba, December 10, 2019.

41 Julia Vallejas, interview, Sacaba, January 20, 2020; Vitalino Montaño Chocaya, interview, Sacaba, January 20, 2020.

42 Abraham Cuiza, interview, Sacaba, December 10, 2019.

43 Vallejas, interview.

44 Dionisio Gamarra, interview, Cochabamba, November 16, 2019.

45 Rodolfo Larico Quispe, interview, Cochabamba, November 16, 2019.

46 Colque, interview, Sacaba, December 10, 2019.

47 Marco Paz Fernández, interview, Sacaba, January 21, 2020.

48 Vladimir Pérez, interview, Chapare, May 10, 2021. Nine civilians who were shot on November 15 died that day or in the following days. A tenth, Julio Pinto, died six months later from his injuries. See "Fallece Julio Pinto, la décima víctima de los enfrentamientos en Huayllani," *La Opinión*, June 11, 2020, https://www.opinion.com.bo/articulo/cochabamba/fallece-julio-pinto-decima-victima-enfrentamientos-huayllani/20200611121012772285.html. Right-wing vigilantes killed another civilian a few days prior to the mass violence in Sacaba. The most comprehensive data collection was carried out by the Ombudsman's Office (Defensoría del Pueblo), which concluded that the number of wounded reached 124. "Afectación a la Integridad," Defensoria del Pueblo, https://www.defensoria.gob.bo/contenido/afectacion-a-la-integridad.

49 David Inca, interview, El Alto, April 16, 2020.

50 Anderson, "The Fall of Evo Morales."

51 Plurinational State of Bolivia, Supreme Decree 4078, November 14, 2019.

52 Center for Justice and Accountability, *International Human Rights and Humanitarian Law Experts Urge the Bolivian Government and Armed Forces to Abide by their International Law Obligations*, November 27, 2019, https://

cja.org/wp-content/uploads/2019/11/Command-Responsibility-Use-of-Force-and-Invalid-Immunity-laws-in-BoliviaExec-summary.pdf.

53  "Gobierno aprueba decreto que transfiere Bs 34,7 millones para las FFAA," *Opinión*, November 18, 2019, https://www.opinion.com.bo/articulo/pais/gobierno-anez-aprueba-decreto-transfiere-bs-347-millones-ffaa/20191118211652737418.html.

54  Saravia, interview.

55  *Cholitas* refers to women who wear the wide skirt, the *pollera*, and bowler hats, and have long braids, all of which are associated with highland Indigenous identity.

56  Saravia, interview.

57  "Bolivia: Campesinos de los Yungas se adhirieron a la marcha contra el gobierno interino," *Infobae*, November 11, 2019, https://www.infobae.com/america/america-latina/2019/11/18/bolivia-campesinos-de-los-yungas-se-adhirieron-a-la-marcha-contra-el-gobierno-interino/.

58  "Golpe en Bolivia."

59  Paola Febrero, interview, El Alto, January 29, 2020.

60  Saravia, interview.

61  Erika Mamani, interview, El Alto, May 20, 2020.

62  David Laura, interview, Senkata, December 8, 2019.

63  Vladimir Apaza, interview, Senkata, December 12, 2019; Yosimar Choque Flores, interview, Senkata, December 8, 2019.

64  Apaza, interview.

65  Eulogio Vasquez Cuba, interview, Senkata, January 18, 2020.

66  Choque Flores, interview.

67  Gloria Quisbert, interview, Senkata, May 20, 2020.

68  Apolinar Colque Choque, interview, Senkata, December 12, 2019.

69  Mariela Mamani, interview, Senkata, December 6, 2019.

70  Anonymous interview, La Paz, January 25, 2020.

71  Anonymous interview, El Alto, January 16, 2020.

72  Vásquez Cuba, interview.

73  Permanent Assembly of Human Rights in El Alto and Achacachi (APDH), "Letter to Minister of the Interior, Concerning the Protections of Articles 13, 24, and 113 of the Political Constitution of the State," February 13, 2020.

74  Interview with anonymous government official, Senkata, January 17, 2020.

75  "Minister of Defense on Senkata: 'Not One Projectile Came from the Army,'" *Correo del Sur*, November 11, 2019, https://correodelsur.com/politica/20191119_ministro-de-defensa-sobre-senkata-no-salio-un-solo-proyectil-del-ejercito.html. See also "Minister Fernando López Julio Gives A Press Conference," YouTube video, November 19, 2019, https://www.youtube.com/watch?v=BLCDd_aJu0I.

76  Father Gechi Revelin, public sermon, Senkata, November 19, 2020.

77  Choque Flores, interview.

78  Gloria Quisbert, telephone interview, May 18, 2020.

79  In August 2020, OAS secretary general Luis Almagro refused to renew the mandate of Paulo Abrão as executive secretary of the IACHR, citing sixty-one workplace complaints by staff. IACHR commissioners, who had previously unanimously approved his extension, complained that Almagro's action "breaks with a 20-year practice of respecting the IACHR's decision to appoint its own Executive Secretary and thus makes it difficult to obtain truth, justice, and reparation." UN High Commissioner for Human Rights Michelle Bachelet and the NGO Human Rights Watch also objected. "IACHR Announces Decision to Open Selection Process for the Executive Secretary Position and Thanks Secretary Paulo Abrão's Administration," September 18, 2020, http://www.oas.org/en/iachr/media_center/PReleases/2020/224.asp.

80  Public testimony, Senkata, November 22, 2019.

81  Public testimony, Senkata, November 22, 2019.

82  Ricardo Leclere, interview, Sacaba, March 4, 2020; "Bolivia: Familias de víctimas de Senkata rechazan la indemnización del gobierno de facto," *Tiempo*, December 7, 2019, https://www.tiempoar.com.ar/nota/bolivia-familias-de-victimas-de-senkata-rechazan-la-indemnizacion-del-gobierno-de-facto.

83  Gregoria Siles, interview, Cochabamba, December 9, 2019.

84  María Javiera, interview, Cochabamba, December 9, 2019.

85  Bruno Santana, interview, Sacaba, December 10, 2019.

86  During peaceful protests by local residents in Zona Sur on November 10 and 11, 2019, security forces killed five people, according to witness interviews and the December 10 IACHR report; see IACHR press release, December 10, 2019, https://www.oas.org/en/iachr/media_center/PReleases/2019/321.asp. Others were seriously injured by live rounds reportedly shot by the police.

87  "Fallecidos en conflictos," Defensoría del Pueblo, https://www.defensoria.gob.bo/contenido/muertos-en-los-conflictos.

88  César Sánchez, "El Gobierno dice que pedir la renuncia de Arturo Murillo es un 'exceso,'" *Oxígeno*, November 25, 2019, http://www.oxigeno.bo/pol%C3%ADtica/39740.

## Chapter 6: "Dicta-Suave": A Soft Dictatorship

1   "Eduardo Rodríguez Veltzé," Barcelona Centre for International Affairs, https://www.cidob.org/biografias_lideres_politicos/america_del_sur/bolivia/eduardo_rodriguez_veltze.

2   Kathryn Ledebur, personal communication, October 19, 2020.

3   Pedro Brieger, "Entrevista a Eduardo Rodríguez Veltzé, Expresidente de Bolivia," *NODAL*, February 10, 2020, https://www.nodal.am/2020/02/eduardo-rodriguez-veltze-expresidente-de-bolivia-este-gobierno-tenia-un-proposito-explicito-de-conducir-un-tiempo-mucho-mas-plural-e-independiente-pero-ahora-esta-tenido-de-sus-propios-int/.

4     Benjamin Dangl, "State Violence in Áñez's Bolivia: Interview with Human Rights Lawyer David Inca Apaza," *NACLA*, May 29, 2020, https://nacla. org/news/2020/05/29/state-violence-bolivia-interview.

5     Carlos Romero, interview, La Paz, January 15, 2020.

6     "Gobierno de Bolivia irá por diputados 'subversivos' leales a Evo," *La Jornada*, November 17, 2019, https://web.archive.org/ web/20200105055703/https://www.jornada.com.mx/ultimas/ mundo/2019/11/17/gobierno-de-bolivia-ira-por-diputados-201csubversivos201d-leales-a-evo-285.html.

7     "Murillo advierte con 'perseguir' personalmente a jueces y fiscales que beneficien a 'delincuentes,'" *Página Siete*, February 11, 2020, https://www. paginasiete.bo/nacional/2020/2/11/murillo-advierte-con-perseguir-personalmente-jueces-fiscales-que-beneficien-delincuentes-246387.html.

8     "Gobierno investiga a 592 ex autoridades del gobierno de Morales por presunto desvío de bienes," *SOL*, January 8, 2020, http://sol.bo/gobierno-investiga-a-592-exautoridades-del-gobierno-de-morales-por-presunto-desvio-de-bienes/.

9     Human Rights Watch, *Justice as a Weapon*, September 11, 2020, https://www.hrw.org/report/2020/09/11/justice-weapon/ political-persecution-bolivia.

10    "Torrico: Si me detienen por masista, me van a tener que dar cadena perpetua," *Erbol*, February 6, 2020, https://erbol.com.bo/seguridad/ torrico-si-me-detienen-por-masista-me-van-tener-que-dar-cadena-perpetua.

11    Human Rights Watch, *Justice as a Weapon*.

12    "Denuncian a Evo Morales por 'genocidio y terrorismo' en una Bolivia convulsionada," *Clarín*, August 10, 2020, https://www.clarin. com/mundo/denuncian-evo-morales-genocidio-terrorismo-bolivia-convulsionada_0_4bwLDY9vI.html.

13    "Evo Morales: Exiled Bolivian Ex-president Accused of Rape," *BBC News*, August 21, 2020, https://www.bbc.com/news/ world-latin-america-53858091.

14    Linda Farthing, "Amid Repression and Scrutiny of the OAS, Bolivia Staggers Toward an Election Rerun," *World Politics Review*, June 25, 2020, https://www.worldpoliticsreview.com/articles/28866/amid-repression-and-scrutiny-of-the-oas-bolivia-staggers-toward-an-election-rerun.

15    "Mexico Calls Amplified Police Presence at Bolivia Embassy a 'Siege,'" *New York Times*, December 24, 2019, https://www.nytimes. com/2019/12/24/world/americas/bolivia-police-mexico.html.

16    Valeria Silva Guzmán La Paz, "Notas para la memoria y la justicia," *La Razón*, November 28, 2020, https://www.la-razon.com/voces/2020/11 /28/notas-para-la-memoria-y-la-justicia/.

17    "Envían a la cárcel a la niñera de los hijos del exministro Quintana," *Radiofides*, February 12, 2020, https://www.radiofides.com/es/2020/02 /12/envian-a-la-carcel-a-la-ninera-de-los-hijos-del-exministro-quintana/.

18 "Fiscalía sindica al primo y 'mano derecha' de Morales," *Los Tiempos*, December 21, 2020, https://www.lostiempos.com/actualidad/pais/20191221/fiscalia-sindica-al-primo-mano-derecha-morales.

19 "Albarracín pide la liberación de Patricia Hermosa, apoderada de Evo," *Alerta Bolivia*, June 11, 2020, https://alertabolivia.com/albarracin-pide-la-liberacion-de-patricia-hermosa-apoderada-de-evo/.

20 Urooba Jamal, "Canadian Charged with Sedition and Terrorism in Bolivia," *Vice*, August 27, 2020, https://www.vice.com/en/article/pky8k8/canadian-juan-tellez-charged-with-sedition-and-terrorism-in-bolivia.

21 Karla Zabludovksy, "She Survived a Mob Attack and Became a Symbol of Bolivia's Political Crisis," *Buzzfeed News*, December 21, 2019, https://www.buzzfeednews.com/article/karlazabludovsky/bolivia-mayor-patricia-arce?bftwnews&utm_term=4ldqpgc#4ldqpgc.

22 Patricia Arce, interview, Vinto, February 27, 2020.

23 "IHRC Grants Precautionary Measures in Favor of María Patricia Arce Guzmán, Mayor of the Municipality of Vinto, in Bolivia," IHRC, December 27, 2019, https://www.oas.org/es/cidh/prensa/comunicados/2019/339.asp.

24 Patricia Arce, telephone interview, April 27, 2020.

25 "Denuncian que la alcaldesa de Vinto planificó un autoatentado," *Opinión*, January 16, 2020, https://www.opinion.com.bo/articulo/cochabamba/denuncian-alcaldesa-vinto-planifico-autoatentado/20200116005353746240.html.

26 Patricia Arce, telephone interview, April 18, 2020.

27 Patricia Arce, telephone interview, April 27, 2020.

28 Fabiola Alvelais et al., "They Shot Us Like Animals: Black October and Bolivia's Interim Government," International Human Rights Clinic, Harvard Law School, and University Network for Human Rights, 2020, http://hrp.law.harvard.edu/wp-content/uploads/2020/07/Black-November-English-Final_Accessible.pdf.

29 "Bolivia: La ministra de comunicación acusó de sedición a periodistas extranjeros," *La Nación*, November 14, 2019, https://www.lanacion.com.ar/el-mundo/bolivia-ministra-comunicacion-acuso-sedicion-periodistas-extranjeros-nid2306534.

30 Fernando Molina and Susana Bejarano, "La transformación restauradora del campo mediático. El alineamiento de los medios de comunicación con el bloque de poder postevista en noviembre de 2019," in *Nuevo mapa de actores en Bolivia Crisis. Polarización e incertidumbre, 2019–2020*, Jan Souverein and José Luis Exeni Rodríguez, eds. (La Paz: Friedrich Ebert Stiftung, 2020), 164–200.

31 "Ministro López dice que 'terrorismo' también es 'comunicacional y digital,'" *El Día*, November 21, 2019, http://m.eldia.com.bo/articulo.php?articulo=Ministro-López-dice-que--terrorismo--también-es--comunicacional-y-digital-&id=1&id_articulo=291719.

32 "Canciller: Actores internacionales intentan desestabilizar el gobierno de Jeanine Áñez," *Agencia Boliviana de Información*, March 10, 2020, https://www1.abi.bo/abi_/?i=446617.

33 "Bolivian TV Operator Shuts Down RT Spanish Broadcasts," *RT*, November 27, 2019, https://www.rt.com/news/474513-rt-spanish-bolivia-taken-off-air/; "Bolivia: Coup-Born Government Takes TeleSUR Spanish Off the Air," *Telesur*, November 22, 2019, https://www.telesurenglish.net/news/Bolivia-Coup-Born-Government-Takes-TeleSUR-Spanish-Off-The-Air-20191122-0001.html.

34 Wilma Pérez, "Las 53 radios comunitarias suspenden informativos," *La Razón*, December 17, 2019, https://web.archive.org/web/20200323010952/http://www.la-razon.com/sociedad/radios-comunitarias-suspenden-informativos_0_3277472233.html.

35 Humberto Pacosillo, interview, El Alto, January 9, 2020; "Lizárraga advierte Kawsachun Coca que la libertad de expresión tiene límites," *Página Siete*, January 8, 2020, https://www.paginasiete.bo/nacional/2020/1/8/lizarraga-advierte-kawsachun-coca-que-la-libertad-de-expresion-tiene-limites-242837.html; Facebook post, Radio Kawsachun Coca, January 7, 2020, https://www.facebook.com/RadioKawsachunCoca/posts/146541763466035.

36 Anonymous interview, La Paz, January 15, 2020.

37 Jon Queally, "Police in Bolivia Pepper Spray Journalist 'On Purpose' During Live Coverage of Anti-Coup Protests," *Common Dreams*, November 16, 2019, https://www.commondreams.org/news/2019/11/16/police-bolivia-pepper-spray-journalist-purpose-during-live-coverage-anti-coup; Andrea Tapia, interview, El Alto, January 10, 2020.

38 Sebastián Moro, "Un golpe de estado en marcha en Bolivia," *Página 12*, November 10, 2019, https://www.pagina12.com.ar/230124-un-golpe-de-estado-en-marcha-en-bolivia.

39 Leny Chuquimia, "El misterio ronda la muerte de periodista argentino afín a Evo," *Página Siete*, February 6, 2020, https://www.paginasiete.bo/nacional/2020/2/26/el-misterio-ronda-la-muerte-de-periodista-argentino-afin-evo-247789.html.

40 Human Rights Watch, *Justice as a Weapon*.

41 Paulo Cuiza, "Periodistas critican detención de 'guerrero digital' Jara y ven violación de derechos," *La Rázon*, April 30, 2020, https://www.la-razon.com/sociedad/2020/04/30/periodistas-critican-detencion-de-guerrero-digital-jara-y-ven-violacion-de-derechos/.

42 Juan Cristóbal Soruco, personal communication, May 21, 2020.

43 Anonymous interview, La Paz, January 15, 2020.

44 "La política internacional de Áñez," *Latinoamérica Piensa*, November 15, 2019, https://latinoamericapiensa.com/la-politica-internacional-de-anez-anuncio-la-salida-de-bolivia-del-alba-de-la-unasur-y-rompio-relaciones-con-venezuela/21065/.

45 Anonymous interview, December 24, 2019.

46  Sputnik, "Cancillería boliviana da marcha atrás en orden de vestimenta formal y occidental," *El País*, December 9, 2019, https://www.elpais. cr/2019/12/09/cancilleria-boliviana-da-marcha-atras-en-orden-de-vestimenta-formal-y-occidental/.

47  Jim Wyss, "Bolivia's New Government Expels Cuban Officials, Recalls Its Diplomatic Staff from Venezuela," *Miami Herald*, November 15, 2019, https://www.miamiherald.com/news/nation-world/world/americas/article237405369.html.

48  Carlos de la Rocha, interview, La Paz, January 11, 2020.

49  Eduardo Tzompa, "Gobierno interino de Bolivia expulsa a 725 cubanos y al cuerpo diplomático de Nicolás Maduro," *La Gran Época*, November 15, 2019, https://es.theepochtimes.com/gobierno-interino-de-bolivia-expulsa-a-725-cubanos-y-al-cuerpo-diplomatico-de-nicolas-maduro_559283.html.

50  Norberto Paredes, "How Venezuelans Are Becoming the Scapegoat throughout the Protests in South America," *BBC Mundo*, November 28, 2019, https://www.bbc.com/mundo/noticias-america-latina-50559187.

51  "Tuto Quiroga sobre López Obrador: 'Es un cobarde matoncito,'" *Opinión*, December 26, 2019, https://www.opinion.com.bo/articulo/escenario-politico1/tuto-quiroga-lopez-obrador-es-cobarde-matoncito/20191226171133742996.html.

52  "Dirigentes de Vox viajaron a Bolivia y cuestionaron la explicación del gobierno español sobre los incidentes en la embajada mexicana," *Infobae*, January 2, 2020, https://www.infobae.com/america/america-latina/2020/01/02/dirigentes-de-vox-viajaron-a-bolivia-y-cuestionaron-la-explicacion-del-gobierno-espanol-sobre-los-incidentes-en-la-embajada-mexicana/.

53  Raphael Ahren, "Interim Government Announces Renewal of Diplomatic Ties with Israel," *Times of Israel*, November 28, 2019, https://www.timesofisrael.com/bolivias-interim-government-announces-renewal-of-diplomatic-ties-with-israel/.

54  Monica Machicao, "Bolivian Minister Seeks Israel Help in Fighting Alleged Leftist 'Terrorism,'" December 6, 2020, https://www.reuters.com/article/us-bolivia-politics-security-idUSKBN1YA28V.

55  "Áñez elimina exigencia de visas para israelíes y estadounidenses," *Erbol*, December 11, 2019, https://erbol.com.bo/nacional/añez-elimina-exigencia-de-visas-para-israel%C3%ADes-y-estadounidenses.

56  "Congratulations to Bolivian Senator Áñez for Assuming the Role of Interim President," US Department of State, November 13, 2019, https://www.state.gov/congratulations-to-bolivian-senator-anez-for-assuming-the-role-of-interim-president/.

57  "Donald Trump declaró su apoyo a Jeanine Áñez en Bolivia en su misión de 'asegurar una transición democrática pacífica a través de elecciones libres,'" *Infobae*, December 17, 2019, www.infobae.com%2Famerica%2Feeuu%2F2019%2F12%2F17%2Fdon

ald-trump-declaro-su-apoyo-a-jeanine-anez-en-bolivia-en-su-mision-
de-asegurar-una-transicion-democratica-pacifica-a-traves-de-elecciones-
libres%2F.

58  Daniel Ramos and Mitra Taj, "Bolivia Reforges U.S. Ties as Political
    Alliances Redrawn," *Reuters*, November 27, 2019, https://www.reuters.
    com/article/us-bolivia-politics-idUSKBN1Y11QS.

59  "Presidential Determination on Waiving a Restriction on United
    States Assistance to Bolivia," US Presidential Memoranda, January 6,
    2020, https://www.whitehouse.gov/presidential-actions/presidential-
    determination-waiving-restriction-united-states-assistance-bolivia/.

60  Cindy Forster, "Bolivia's Post-coup President Has Unleashed a
    Campaign of Terror," *Jacobin*, May 30, 2020, https://www.jacobinmag.
    com/2020/05/bolivia-coup-jeanine-anez-evo-morales-mas.

61  "Gobierno asciende por decreto a militares de las FFAA," *Página Siete*, July
    15, 2020, https://www.paginasiete.bo/nacional/2020/7/15/gobierno-
    asciende-por-decreto-militares-de-las-ffaa-261434.html.

62  Nelson Peredo, "Sustituyen la escuela antiimperialista por héroes de
    Ñancahuazú," *Los Tiempos*, January 16, 2020, https://www.lostiempos.
    com/actualidad/pais/20200116/sustituyen-escuela-antiimperialista
    -heroes-nancahuazu.

63  "Ejecutivo transfirió Bs 506 millones a gobierno y defensa en plena
    cuarentena," *Página Siete*, June 5, 2020, https://www.paginasiete.bo/
    economia/2020/6/5/ejecutivo-transfirio-bs-506-millones-gobierno-
    defensa-en-plena-cuarentena-257512.html.

64  "Ministro advierte con privatizar empresas estatales
    deficitarias," *Los Tiempos*, December 12, 2019, https://
    www.lostiempos.com/actualidad/economia/20191212/
    ministro-advierte-privatizar-empresas-estatales-deficitarias.

65  "Murillo insiste en privatización de Elfec, motivo del alejamiento de
    Cabrera y Ortiz," *Página Siete*, September 28, 2020, https://www.
    paginasiete.bo/sociedad/2020/9/28/murillo-insiste-en-privatizacion-de-
    elfec-motivo-del-alejamiento-de-cabrera-ortiz-269651.html.

66  "Trabajadores de Sabsa denuncian que se pretende privatizar los
    aeropuertos internacionales," *Los Tiempos*, September 22, 2019,
    https://www.lostiempos.com/actualidad/economia/20200922/
    trabajadores-sabsa-denuncian-que-se-pretende-privatizar-aeropuertos.

67  Tom Phillips, "New Bolivian Interior Minister Vows to Jail
    Evo Morales for Rest of his Life," *Guardian*, November 24,
    2019, https://www.theguardian.com/world/2019/nov/24/
    bolivia-evo-morales-vow-jail-rest-life-arturo-murillo.

68  "Entel ofrece desde hoy la promoción mega pitita," *Página Siete*, December
    21, 2019, https://www.paginasiete.bo/economia/2019/12/21/entel-
    ofrece-desde-hoy-la-promocion-mega-pitita-241098.html.

69  Avivah Wittenberg-Cox, "8 (More) Women Leaders Facing the
    Coronavirus Crisis," *Forbes*, April 22, 2020, https://www.forbes.com/

sites/avivahwittenbergcox/2020/04/22/8-more-women-leaders-facing-the-coronavirus-crisis/#1ac083ed288f.

70   "Encuesta Ciesmori: El 63% de consultados aprueba la gestión de Áñez en la pandemia," *ANF*, May 6, 2020, https://www.noticiasfides.com/nacional/politica/encuesta-ciesmori-el-63-de-consultados-aprueba-la-gestion-de-anez-en-la-pandemia-de-covid-19-404669.

71   "IMF: Bolivia Has World's Largest Informal Economy," *Financial Tribune*, January 29, 2018, https://financialtribune.com/articles/world-economy/81033/imf-bolivia-has-world-s-largest-informal-economy.

72   Bolivia Information Forum, *Bolivia in Times of Coronavirus*, Special Bulletin, April 28, 2020, https://ymlp.com/zn4N0k.

73   "Lockdowns Leave Poor Latin Americans with Impossible Choice: Stay Home or Feed Families," *Guardian*, April 21, 2020, https://www.theguardian.com/world/2020/apr/21/latin-america-coronavirus-lockdowns-low-income.

74   Oishimaya Sen Nag, "The Poorest Countries in South America," *World Atlas*, October 22, 2019, https://www.worldatlas.com/articles/the-poorest-countries-in-south-america.html.

75   Ciesmori, Facebook post, April 28, 2020, https://www.facebook.com/ciesmori/videos/927264104382786/.

76   Farthing, "Bolivia Staggers towards Election Re-run."

77   Fabiola Alvelais et al., "No Justice for Me: Femicide and Impunity in Bolivia," International Human Rights Clinic, Harvard Law School, 2019, http://hrp.law.harvard.edu/wp-content/uploads/2019/03/No-Justice-for-Me.pdf.

78   Micaela Villa, "La Defensoría del Pueblo recibió 52 denuncias de violencia contra la mujer en 38 días," *La Rázon*, April 27, 2020, https://www.la-razon.com/ciudades/2020/04/27/defensoria-del-pueblo-recibio-52-denuncias-violencia-contra-mujer-38-dias/.

79   Tapia Callao, "Bloqueadores de K'ara K'ara piden desde agua hasta renuncia de Áñez," *Los Tiempos*, May 13, 2020, https://www.lostiempos.com/actualidad/cochabamba/20200513/bloqueadores-kara-kara-piden-agua-renuncia-anez.

80   COVID-19 deaths worldwide per one million population as of October 30, 2020, by country, *Statista*, https://www.statista.com/statistics/1104709/coronavirus-deaths-worldwide-per-million-inhabitants/.

81   Amy Booth, "Bolivia's School Closures Will Deepen Divide of Who Gets to Study," *NACLA*, September 22, 2020, https://nacla.org/news/2020/09/23/bolivia's-school-closures-will-deepen-divide-who-gets-study.

82   "Bolivia's Health Minister Held for 'Ventilator Corruption,'" *Al Jazeera*, May 23, 2020, https://www.aljazeera.com/news/2020/5/23/bolivias-health-minister-held-for-ventilator-corruption.

83   Pablo Solón, "Why Lucho and David Won the Bolivian Elections," *Systemic Alternatives*, October 19, 2020, https://systemicalternatives.org/2020/10/19/why-lucho-david-won-the-bolivian-elections/.

84  Yvette Sierra Praeli, "A Million Hectares Ablaze as Forest Fires Sweep through Bolivia," *Monga Bay*, November 20, 2020, https://news. mongabay.com/2020/11/a-million-hectares-ablaze-as-forest-fires-sweep-through-bolivia/.

85  Yuri Flores, "Hasta abril se triplica la exportación de carne," *La Razón*, June 17, 2020, https://www.la-razon.com/financiero/2020/06/17/ hasta-abril-se-triplica-la-exportacion-de-carne/.

86  "Ante el tráfico de tierras en la gestión de Jeanine Áñez," *Tierra*, November 3, 2020, https://ftierra.org/index.php/tema/tierra-territorio/964-pronunciamiento-2020-ante-el-trafico-de-tierras-en-la-gestion-de-jeanine-anez.

87  "Áñez posesionó a 36 ministros en 10 meses," *El Deber*, September 30, 2020, https://eldeber.com.bo/usted-elige/anez-posesiono-a-36-ministros -en-10-meses_202582.

88  Fernando Molina, "La cuarentena desata protestas en barrios populares de Bolivia," *El País*, April 2, 2020, https://elpais.com/ internacional/2020-04-03/la-cuarentena-desata-protestas-en-barrios-populares-de-bolivia.html.

89  Tapia Callao, "Bloqueadores de K'ara K'ara piden desde agua."

90  "Ocho puntos de bloqueos y protesta están activos en el país," *Correo del Sur*, May 19, 2020, https://correodelsur.com/sociedad/20200519_ocho-puntos-de-bloqueos-y-protesta-estan-activos-en-el-pais.html.

91  "RJC amenaza con tomarse la atribución de desbloquear el ingreso a K'ara K'ara," *Opinión*, May 19, 2020, https://www.opinion.com.bo/articulo/ cochabamba/rjc-amenazan-tomarse-atribucion/20200519191434768514. html.

92  Ivan Alejandro Paredes Tamayo, "Gobierno dice que caerá 'todo el peso de la ley' a dirigentes de K'ara K'ara y anuncia un detenido tras emboscada," July 4, 2020, *El Deber*, https://eldeber.com.bo/coronavirus/gobierno-dice-que-caera-todo-el-peso-de-la-ley-a-dirigentes-de-kara-kara-y-anuncia-un-detenido-tras-_188695.

93  *Red Uno*, Issa: "Accionan un plan subversivo en K'ara K'ara", May 20, 2020

94  *Opinión*, Ministros de Áñez ante la tensión: Murillo abraza el "diálogo"; Mercado no quiere debates en la pandemia, May 19, 2020. https://www. opinion.com.bo/articulo/pais/ministros-anez-tension-murillo-abraza-dialogo-mercado-quiere-debates-pandemia/20200519021258768355. html.

95  "Bonos de emergencia COVID-19 representan Bs 4.860 millones," *El Estado Digital*, April 20, 2020, https://www.elestadodigital.com /2020/04/20/bonos-de-emergencia-covid-19-representan-bs-4 -860-millones/.

96  "Murillo: 'La mayoría de los chapareños son presos de dirigentes y narcotraficantes,'" *Erbol*, April 24, 2020, https://erbol.com.bo/nacional/ murillo-%E2%80%9Cla-mayor%C3%ADa-de-los-chapare%C3%B1os-son-presos-de-dirigentes-y-narcotraficantes%E2%80%9D. Murillo was later accused of ties to drug traffickers himself. "Gobierno procesa a Murillo

y Montero y defiende a Aguilera en caso del narco Lima Lobo," *Agencia de Noticias Fides*, May 7, 2021, https://www.noticiasfides.com/nacional/seguridad/gobierno-procesa-a-murillo-y-montero-y-saca-cara-por-aguilera-en-caso-del-narco-lima-lobo-409593.

97 Thomas Grisaffi, "Challenging Myths about Chapare Coca Paste Production," *NACLA*, July 22, 2014, https://nacla.org/news/2014/7/22/challenging-myths-about-chapare-coca-paste-production.

98 Miguel Angel Melendres Galvis, "Productores de Chapare denuncian que el Gobierno los dejó sin combustible," *El Deber*, April 20, 2020, https://eldeber.com.bo/pais/productores-de-chapare-denuncian-que-el-gobierno-los-dejo-sin-combustible_175607.

99 "Denuncian muerte de 11 millones de peces por cierre de surtidores en el trópico," *La Rázon*, April 25, 2020, https://www.paginasiete.bo/sociedad/2020/4/25/denuncian-muerte-de-11-millones-de-peces-por-cierre-de-surtidores-en-el-tropico-253745.html.

100 Adrónico Ródriguez, Twitter post, April 21, 2020, https://twitter.com/AndronicoRod/status/1252716960162422784.

101 "Gobierno habla de encapsular el Chapare y pide a cocaleros que se disculpen con la Policía," *Página Siete*, April 19, 2020, https://www.paginasiete.bo/seguridad/2020/4/19/gobierno-habla-de-encapsular-el-chapare-pide-cocaleros-que-se-disculpen-con-la-policia-253099.html.

102 Guadalupe Tapia, Morales dice que ingreso de la Policía al Chapare puso en riesgo salud de sus pobladores, 18 de abril, 2020, *La Razón*.

103 Lorena Amurrio Montes, "Trópico de Cochabamba: Falta de gasolina paraliza al agro y productores migran de rubro," *Los Tiempos*, May 5, 2020, https://www.lostiempos.com/actualidad/economia/20200515/tropico-cochabamba-falta-gasolina-paraliza-al-agro-productores-migran.

104 Leonardo Loza, telephone interview, June 19, 2020.

105 Iván Bustillos, "Según UNODC, en 2019 el cultivo de hoja coca en el país subió en 10%," *La Rázon*, July 29, 2020, https://www.la-razon.com/nacional/2020/07/29/segun-unodc-en-2019-el-cultivo-de-hoja-coca-en-el-pais-subio-en-10/.

106 Alba Silva, "La pandemia disparó el precio de la hoja de coca y miles de trabajadores se quedan sin ese insumo," *Télam*, July 18, 2020, https://www.telam.com.ar/notas/202007/491217-la-pandemia-disparo-el-precio-de-la-hoja-de-coca-y-miles-de-trabajadores-se-quedan-sin-ese-insumo.html.

107 Andean Information Network, *Bolivia and Peru: Coca Farmers in the Time of Covid-19*, AIN / University of Reading, May 11, 2020, https://research.reading.ac.uk/coca-cocaine-bolivia-peru/wp-content/uploads/sites/127/Unorganized/Bolivia-and-Peru_-Coca-Farmers-in-the-Time-of-Covid-19-copy.pdf.

108 Interview courtesy of Thomas Grisaffi, July 23, 2020.

109 Carlos Corz, EEUU dice que Bolivia incumplió compromisos antidroga y le pide reducir cultivos de coca ilegales, *La Rázon*, September 15, 2021, https://www.la-razon.com/nacional/2021/09/15/

eeuu-dice-que-bolivia-incumplio-compromisos-antidroga-y-le-pide-
reducir-cultivos-de-coca-ilegales/.

110 UNODC, Coca Crop Monitoring Survey Report, 2020.

111 Neveen Mimica, Twitter post, May 3, 2018, https://twitter.com/
mimicaeu/status/992191946008551424.

112 Consilium, *European Union Drugs Strategy, 2013–2020*, 2020, https://www.
consilium.europa.eu/media/30727/drugs-strategy-2013_content.pdf.

113 Kathryn Ledebur, Linda Farthing, and Tom Grisaffi, "Bolivia Reverses
Years of Progress with New Draconian Cocaine Policy, Supported by the
EU," *The Conversation*, September 7, 2020, https://theconversation.com/
bolivia-reverses-years-of-progress-with-new-draconian-cocaine-policy-
supported-by-the-eu-144386.

114 Ledebur, Farthing, and Grisaffi, "Bolivia Reverses Years of Progress."

115 María Mena M., "Resistencia Cochala crece y busca pasar de grupo de
choque a cívico," *Página Siete*, December 9, 2019, https://www.paginasiete.
bo/nacional/2019/12/9/resistencia-cochala-crece-busca-pasar-de-grupo-
de-choque-civico-239882.html.

116 Fernando Molina, "La 'redención' del MAS y el mal momento de la
oposición en Bolivia," *Nueva Sociedad*, May 2021, https://nuso.org/
articulo/la-redencion-del-mas-y-el-mal-momento-de-la-oposicion
-en-bolivia.

117 Anonymous anti-Morales protest organizer, personal communication, July
21, 2020.

118 William Wroblewski, personal communication, October 30, 2020.

119 Brett Heinz, "Why a DC Public Relations Firm Pretended to Be
Bolivian on Facebook," *CEPR*, October 5, 2020, https://cepr.net/
why-a-dc-public-relations-firm-pretended-to-be-bolivian-on-facebook/.

120 Craig Timberg and Elizabeth Dwoskin, "Washington Firm Ran Fake
Facebook Accounts in Venezuela, Bolivia and Mexico, Report Finds,"
*Washington Post*, September 4, 2020, https://www.washingtonpost.com/
technology/2020/09/04/facebook-bolivia-cls/.

121 Interview, Sacaba, January 21, 2020.

122 Farthing, "Bolivia Staggers towards an Election Re-run."

123 Rolando Borda Padilla, telephone interview, October 22, 2020.

124 Porfirio Ramírez, interview, Sacaba, January 21, 2020.

125 Abel Colque, interview, Sacaba, December 10, 2019.

126 Anonymous interview, Senkata, December 6, 2019.

127 "70 mil uniformados, entre policías y militares, ejecutan acciones de
seguridad ciudadana en todo el país," *ATB Digital*, January 16, 2020,
https://www.atb.com.bo/seguridad/70-mil-uniformados-entre-
polic%C3%ADas-y-militares-ejecutan-acciones-de-seguridad-ciudadana-
en-todo-el-pa%C3%ADs.

128 Gloria Quisbert, telephone interview, May 18, 2020.

129 Rubén Atahuichi, "Áñez dece que venció a los violentos 'autodenominados'
movimientos sociales," *La Rázon*, March 5, 2020, www.la-razon.

com/nacional/2020/03/05/anez-dice-que-vencio-a-los-violentos-autodenominados-movimientos-sociales.

130 "Bolivia: Jornalista é torturado após filmar bombas de gás atingindo crianças em escolas de El Alto," *Nodal*, March 18, 2020, https://www.nodal.am/2020/03/bolivia-jornalista-e-torturado-apos-filmar-bombas-de-gas-atingindo-criancas-em-escolas-de-el-alto/.

131 Plurinational State of Bolivia, Supreme Decree 4200, March 21, 2020, available at https://boliviaemprende.com/wp-content/uploads/2020/03/D.S.-4200-1.pdf-1.pdf.

132 "Quien desinforme será llevado a hospitales para atender a enfermos con Covid-19, advirtió Arias," *Urgente*, March 27, 2020, https://urgente.bo/noticia/quien-desinforme-será-llevado-hospitales-para-atender-enfermos-con-covid-9-advirtió-arias.

133 Cristian J. Tejada, Twitter post, December 19, 2019, https://twitter.com/TejadaTejadaC/status/1259870531865784320.

134 Joanna Slater, Anthony Faiola, and Niha Masih, "Under the Cover of Coronavirus, Governments Punish Adversaries and Reward Friends," *Washington Post*, April 30, 2020, https://www.washingtonpost.com/world/under-the-cover-of-coronavirus-governments-punish-enemies-and-reward-friends/2020/04/29/a232cfc0-83ee-11ea-81a3-9690c9881111_story.html.

135 "Núñez sobre el Decreto Aprobado: Los periodistas tienen que estar tranquilos," *Página Siete*, May 11, 2020, https://www.paginasiete.bo/nacional/2020/5/11/nunez-sobre-decreto-aprobado-los-periodistas-tienen-que-estar-tranquilos-255162.html.

136 Edison Lanza, Twitter post, May 11, 2020, https://twitter.com/EdisonLanza/status/1260036192822796288.

137 "Elecciones 2020: El MAS le saca un 15% de ventaja a Carlos Mesa," *El Deber*, March 15, 2020, https://eldeber.com.bo/169559_encuesta-elecciones-2020-el-mas-le-saca-un-15-de-ventaja-a-carlos-mesa.

138 Fernando Mayorga, "Elecciones ya: ¿El MAS recupera la iniciativa?," *Nueva Sociedad*, June 2020, https://nuso.org/articulo/bolivia-de-la-pandemia-las-elecciones/.

139 Bolivia Information Forum, Bulletin 50, *Elections, Democracy and Covid-19*, July 3, 2020, https://twitter.com/Boliviainfo/status/1314285731284758529.

140 "Reunión del TSE con Sectores Sociales no Frena Movilizaciones Anunciadas por la COB," *Fides*, July 30, 2020, https://www.noticiasfides.com/nacional/politica/reunion-del-tse-con-sectores-sociales-no-frena-movilizaciones-anunciadas-por-la-cob-405707?.

141 Fernando Mayorga, "El MAS-IPSP ante un nuevo contexto político: De 'partido de gobierno' a 'instrumento político' de las organizaciones populares," in Souverein and Exeni Rodríguez, *Nuevo mapa de actores*, 1–35.

142 "Al menos 7.000 camiones están varados en carreteras por bloqueos," *Red Uno*, August 7, 2020, https://www.reduno.com.bo/noticias/al-menos-7-000-camiones-estan-varados-en-carreteras-por-bloqueos-20208782455.

143   "Tránsito reporta el levantamiento gradual de puntos de bloqueo en el
      país," *Los Tiempos*, August 14, 2020, https://www.lostiempos.
      com/actualidad/pais/20200814/transito-reporta-levantamiento-gradual
      -puntos-bloqueo-pais.

144   Laurence Blair and Cindy Jiménez Bercerra, "Bolivia Protesters Bring
      Country to Standstill over Election Delays," *Guardian*, August 9, 2020,
      https://www.theguardian.com/world/2020/aug/09/bolivia-protesters-
      bring-country-to-standstill-over-election-delays-covid-19-evo-morales.

145   Philip Reeves, "'We Can't Stand It Anymore': Bolivian Protesters Demand
      Quick Elections," *NPR*, August 11, 2020, https://www.npr.org
      /2020/08/11/901334859/we-cant-stand-it-anymore-bolivian-protesters
      -demand-quick-elections.

146   María Silvia Trigo and Anatoly Kurmanaev, "Bolivia under Blockade
      as Protesters Choke Access to Cities," *New York Times*, August 7, 2020,
      https://www.nytimes.com/2020/08/07/world/americas/bolivia-
      roadblock-blockade.html.

147   Yolanda Mamani Cayo, "Gobierno y el MAS se Enjuician por Bloqueos y
      Muertos Covid," *Página Siete*, August 19, 2020, https://www.paginasiete.
      bo/nacional/2020/8/19/gobierno-el-mas-se-enjuician-por-bloqueos-
      muertos-covid-265014.html.

148   Rafael Bautista, "Del Estado de excepción al Estado de rebelión en
      Bolivia," *Observatorio Plurinacional de Aguas*, August 15, 2020, https://oplas.
      org/sitio/2020/08/15/rafael-bautista-del-estado-de-excepcion-al-estado
      -de-rebelion-en-bolivia/.

## Chapter 7: The "Process of Change" Revived?

1   "Luis Arce Promises to 'Rebuild' Bolivia after Huge Election Win," *Al
    Jazeera*, October 23, 2020, https://www.aljazeera.com/news/2020/10/23/
    final-count-gives-big-victory-for-luis-arce-in-bolivia-election.

2   Iván Bustillos, "El TREP, la otra suspensión que generó la anulación de las
    elecciones de 2019," *La Razón*, October 18, 2020, https://www.la-razon.
    com/nacional/2020/10/18/el-trep-la-otra-suspension-que-genero-la-
    anulacion-de-las-elecciones-de-2019/.

3   Patricia Arce, personal communication, October 18, 2020.

4   Jihan Abdalla, "Luis Arce Presumed Winner of Bolivia Presidential
    Election," October 19, 2020, https://www.aljazeera.com/
    news/2020/10/19/luis-arce-presumed-winner-of-bolivia-presidential
    -election.

5   Interview, La Paz, October 19, 2020.

6   Ollie Vargas, Twitter post, October 19, 2020, https://twitter.com/
    OVargas52/status/1318057172308283392.

7   Bernie Sanders, Twitter post, October 19, 2020, https://twitter.com/
    SenSanders/status/1318297125357342720.

8   Interview, Cochabamba, November 15, 2020.

9   Bolivia Information Forum, *General Elections 18 October 2020*, Special
    Bulletin, October 19, 2020, https://ymlp.com/zkIqLn.

10  See, for example, Teddy Rivero, Twitter post, October 14, 2020, available at https://archive.vn/Ebg8E and https://archive.vn/C1yfz.

11  "El ministro del Interior de Bolivia acusó de mentiroso a Fagioli: 'Jamás se detuvo a ningún diputado argentino,'" *Clarín*, October 17, 2020, https://www.clarin.com/politica/ministro-interior-bolivia-acuso-mentiroso-fagioli-jamas-detuvo-diputado-argentino-_0_sKUSq6iyN.html.

12  Doug Hertzler, personal communication, October 19, 2020.

13  Pablo Ortiz et al., "¿Por qué volvió a ganar el MAS? Lecturas de las elecciones bolivianas," *Nueva Sociedad*, October 2020, https://nuso.org/articulo/Bolivia-Luis-Arce-Evo-Morales/.

14  OACNUDH Bolivia, Twitter post, October 7, 2020, https://twitter.com/Oacnudh_BO/status/1313839761019330561.

15  Julie Turkewitz, "From Bolivia, Lessons for a Successful Election," *New York Times*, October 29, 2020, https://www.nytimes.com/2020/10/29/world/americas/Bolivia-election-explainer-lessons.html.

16  Pablo Stefanoni, "A New MAS Era in Bolivia," *NACLA*, October 21, 2020, https://nacla.org/news/2020/10/24/new-mas-era-bolivia.

17  Interview, La Paz, November 2, 2020.

18  Interview, La Paz, November 2, 2020.

19  Eliana Uchani, "Cívicos refutan resultados y políticos piden pruebas de fraude," *Periódico Bolivia*, October 23, 2020, https://www.periodicobolivia.com.bo/civicos-refutan-resultados-y-politicos-piden-pruebas-de-fraude/.

20  Laurence Blair and Ryan Grim, "Bolivian Ex-Minister of Defense Plotted a Second Coup Using U.S. Mercenaries," *Intercept*, June 17, 2021, http://theintercept.com/2021/06/17/bolivia-coup-plot-mercenaries.

21  Gabriel Hetland, "Bolivia's Electoral Victory: What Challenges Lie Ahead for MAS?," panel discussion, NACLA/Center for Latin American Studies, New York University, November 16, 2020.

22  Jake Johnson, "The MAS Received More Votes in Almost All of the OAS's 86 Suspect Precincts in 2020 than in 2019," *CEPR*, October 21, 2020, https://cepr.net/data-from-bolivias-election-add-more-evidence-that-oas-fabricated-last-years-fraud-claims/.

23  Claudia Torrens and Débora Rey, "Almagro defiende labor electoral en Bolivia ante críticas," *AP News*, October 22, 2020, https://apnews.com/article/noticias-0b4cba3314f7e34c4fa85e27da8efe7e.

24  Ortiz et al., "¿Por qué volvió a ganar el MAS?"

25  Bolivia Information Forum, *General Elections II*, Special Bulletin, October 28, 2020, available at https://ymlp.com/z3jYfk.

26  Stefanoni, "A New MAS Era."

27  "El MAS cambia 2/3 por mayoría absoluta; se activan las alarmas," *Opinión*, October 28, 2020, https://www.opinion.com.bo/articulo/escenario-politico1/mas-cambia-2-3-mayoria-absoluta-activan-alarmas/20201028005715793207.html.

28  Eva Copa, personal communication, El Alto, November 1, 2020.

29 "Arrecia presión y críticas contra el MAS; rechazan anulación de 2/3," *Opinión*, October 28, 2020, https://www.opinion.com.bo/articulo/ escenario-politico1/arrecia-presión-criticas-mas-rechazan-anulac ion-2-3/20201028234551793353.html.

30 Gloria Quisbert, personal communication, Senkata, November 1, 2020.

31 Eva Copa, personal communication.

32 The speech is available on YouTube: https://www.youtube.com/ watch?v=cn3qRLnzuTU.

33 Stefanoni, "A New MAS Era in Bolivia."

34 Kathryn Ledebur, personal communication, October 24, 2020.

35 Pablo Solón, "Why Lucho and David Won the Bolivian Elections," *Systemic Alternatives*, October 2020, https://systemicalternatives.org/2020/10/19/ why-lucho-david-won-the-bolivian-elections/.

36 Wilmer Machaca, interview, November 10, 2020; see Jichha website, http://jichha.blogspot.com/.

37 Laurence Blair and Cindy Jiménez Bercerra, "Bolivia in Danger of Squandering Its Head Start over Coronavirus," *Guardian*, July 3, 2020, https://www.theguardian.com/world/2020/jul/03/ bolivia-coronavirus-pandemic.

38 Ortiz et al., "¿Por qué volvió a ganar el MAS?"

39 María Silvia Trigo and Anatoly Kurmanaev, "Bolivia under Blockade as Protesters Choke Access to Cities," *New York Times*, August 7, 2020, https://www.nytimes.com/2020/08/07/world/americas/bolivia-roadblock-blockade.html.

40 Juan Rivero, interview, Santa Cruz, October 8, 2019.

41 Ortiz et al., "¿Por qué volvió a ganar el MAS?"

42 "Exdiputada del MAS denuncia la quema de objetos de su domicilio," *La Razón*, November 18, 2020, https://www.paginasiete.bo/ sociedad/2020/11/18/exdiputada-del-mas-denuncia-la-quema-de-objetos-de-su-domicilio-275287.html.

43 "Arce cierra campaña en El Alto con mensajes para policías de base, soldados y periodismo," *Erbol*, October 14, 2020, https://erbol.com.bo/ el-ánfora-1/arce-cierra-campaña-en-el-alto-con-mensajes-para-policías-de-base-soldados-y-periodismo.

44 Fernando Molina, "Los primeros pasos de Luis Arce en el laberinto boliviano," *Nueva Sociedad*, December 2020, https://nuso.org/articulo/ luis-arce-Evo-Morales-Bolivia/.

45 Government official, personal communication, La Paz, March 8, 2021.

46 Miguel Gómez and Miguel Lazcano, "Novillo: 'Militares golpistas' hicieron desaparecer información sobre los operativos en Sacaba y Senkata," *La Razón*, March 12, 2021, https://www.la-razon.com/nacional/2021/03/12/ novillo-revela-que-militares-golpistas-hicieron-desaparecer -informacion-sobre-los-operativos-en-sacaba-y-senkata/?amp=1&__ twitter_impression=true.

47 "Camacho en cabildo: 'La única vez que volvamos a La Paz será para derrotar a un gobierno tirano,'" *La Razón*, March 16, 2021, https://www.la-razon.com/nacional/2021/03/15/camacho-en-cabildo-la-unica-vez-que-volvamos-a-la-paz-sera-para-derrotar-a-un-gobierno-tirano/.

48 "México pide a Almagro evitar posicionamiento en asuntos de Bolivia," *La Jornada*, March 16, 2021, https://www.jornada.com.mx/notas/2021/03/16/politica/mexico-pide-a-almagro-evitar-posicionamiento-en-asuntos-de-bolivia/.

49 "Bolivia le iniciará un juicio a Luis Almagro," *Pagina 12*, March 17, 2021, https://www.pagina12.com.ar/329862-bolivia-le-iniciara-un-juicio-a-luis-almagro.

50 Jin Wu et al., "The Pandemic's Hidden Toll: Half a Million Deaths," *New York Times*, February 9, 2021, https://www.nytimes.com/interactive/2020/04/21/world/coronavirus-missing-deaths.html.

51 Bolivia Information Forum, Bulletin 51, *Arce's First 100 Days*, February 27, 2021, https://ymlp.com/zYSdo3.

52 Molina, "Los primeros pasos de Luis Arce."

53 Rogelio Mayta, Twitter post, April 14, 2021, https://twitter.com/RogelioMayta_Bo/status/1382535551098744832

54 "Bolivia organiza foro internacional sobre patentes," *Página Siete*, May 8, 2021, https://www.paginasiete.bo/sociedad/2021/5/8/bolivia-organiza-foro-internacional-sobre-patentes-294368.html.

55 Bolivia Information Forum, *Arce's First 100 Days*.

56 *EFE*, "Arce anuncia el hallazgo de un nuevo campo de gas en el sureste de Bolivia," December 24, 2020, https://www.msn.com/es-es/noticias/internacional/arce-anuncia-el-hallazgo-de-un-nuevo-campo-de-gas-en-el-sureste-de-bolivia/ar-BB1cd2VV.

57 Daniel Ramos, "As Bolivia Election Nears, Could 'Evonomics' Make a Comeback?," Reuters, October 8, 2020, https://www.reuters.com/article/us-bolivia-election-economy-analysis/as-bolivia-election-nears-could-evonomics-make-a-comeback-idUSKBN26T2CD.

58 "La deuda interna se disparó en 38,1% en medio de pandemia," *Página Siete*, November 15, 2020, https://www.paginasiete.bo/economia/2020/11/15/la-deuda-interna-se-disparo-en-381-en-medio-de-pandemia-274968.html.

59 Luis Arce, interview, La Paz, October 17, 2019.

60 Juan Carlos Pinto Quintanilla, telephone interview, October 20, 2020. Sadly, Juan Carlos died of COVID-19 in January 2021.

61 Jeffery R. Webber, *The Last Day of Oppression, and the First Day of the Same: The Politics and Economics of the New Latin American Left* (Chicago: Haymarket Books, 2017).

62 Craig Johnson, "What Should Bolivia Do Now with Its Coup Plotters?," *Jacobin*, October 24, 2020, https://www.jacobinmag.com/2020/10/bolivia-coup-mas-evo-morales-elections-arce-anez.

63 Jesus Reynaldo Alanoca Paco, "Piden la detención preventiva del exdirector de Migración por facilitar la salida de Murillo y

López," *El Deber*, November 20, 2020, https://eldeber.com.bo/pais/
aprehenden-al-exdirector-de-migracion-marcel-rivas_209293.

64    "La compra de gases pasó por cuatro entidades y fue autorizada
      por Añez," *Página Siete*, May 28, 2021, https://www.paginasiete.bo/
      seguridad/2021/5/28/la-compra-de-gases-paso-por-cuatro-entidades-
      fue-autorizada-por-anez-296398.html; Fernando Molina, "La 'redención'
      del MAS y el mal momento de la oposición en Bolivia," *Nueva Sociedad*,
      May 2021, https://nuso.org/articulo/la-redencion-del-mas-y-el-mal-
      momento-de-la-oposicion-en-bolivia/?utm_source=email&utm_
      medium=email&utm_campaign=email.

65    Rogelio Mayta, speech, La Paz, November 23, 2020.

66    GIEI Bolivia, 2021, *Informe sobre los hechos de violencia y vulneración de los
      derechos humanos*, Organization of American States, https://gieibolivia.org/
      informes/.

67    Francisco Adolfo Garcia Jerez and Juliane Muller, "Between Two Pasts:
      Dictatorships and the Politics of Memory in Bolivia," *Latin American
      Perspectives* 202, vol. 42, no. 3 (May 2015): 120–39.

68    Ayelén Oliva, "Evo Morales: La historia de su regreso a Bolivia (y nuevos
      detalles de su partida hace un año)," *BBC News Mundo*, November 22,
      2020, https://www.bbc.com/mundo/noticias-america-latina-55025234.

69    Anonymous interview, Potosí Department, November 10, 2020.

70    Personal communication, Chimoré, November 11, 2020.

71    Personal communication, Chimoré, November 11, 2020.

72    "Futuro de Evo y exministros ponen en aprietos a Arce y Choquehuanca,"
      *Los Tiempos*, September 25, 2020, https://www.lostiempos.com/
      actualidad/pais/20200925/futuro-evo-exministros-ponen-aprietos
      -arce-choquehuanca.

73    "Choquehuanca dice que 'el entorno' del gobierno de Evo no debe
      volver," *Página Siete*, September 21, 2020, https://www.paginasiete.bo/
      nacional/2020/9/21/choquehuanca-dice-que-el-entorno-del-gobierno-
      de-evo-no-debe-volver-268813.html.

74    Pinto Quintanilla, telephone interview.

75    Fernando Molina, "Evo Morales se libera de su 'entorno' y acicala al
      gobierno para lograr la reelección," *Nueva Sociedad*, January 2017, https://
      nuso.org/articulo/evo-morales-se-libera-de-su-entorno-y-acicala-al-
      gobierno-para-lograr-la-reeleccion/.

76    Julie Turkewitz, "In Election, Bolivia Confronts Legacy of Ousted Socialist
      Leader," *New York Times*, October 18, 2020, https://www.nytimes.
      com/2020/10/18/world/americas/bolivia-election-evo-morales.html.

77    Amy Booth, "'It Will Be My Government': Bolivia's New Socialist
      President-Elect Says, 'No Role' for Evo Morales," *Vice*, October 23, 2020,
      https://www.vice.com/en/article/k7aq79/it-will-be-my-government-
      bolivias-new-socialist-president-elect-says-no-role-for-evo-morales.

78    Angelica Johan, telephone interview, December 15, 2020.

79 Fernando Garcia Yapur, "Reconfiguraciones del MAS en Bolivia," *NUSO*, February 2021. https://nuso.org/articulo/las-reconfiguraciones-del-mas-en-bolivia/?utm_source=email&utm_medium=email.

80 Garcia Yapur, "Reconfiguraciones."

81 Manuel Canelas, "Elecciones regionales en Bolivia: Un mapa para armar," *Nueva Sociedad*, March 2021, https://nuso.org/articulo/elecciones-bolivia-Evo-Arce.

82 Leny Chuquimia, "Mapa azul: MAS ganó 240 de las 336 alcaldías, 13 más que en 2015," *Página Siete*, March 22, 2021, https://www.paginasiete.bo/nacional/2021/3/22/mapa-azul-mas-gano-240-de-las-336-alcaldias-13-mas-que-en-2015-288209.html.

83 Bolivia Information Forum, *Arce's First 100 Days*.

84 Marxa Chávez, "Bolivia's Electoral Victory: What Challenges Lie Ahead for MAS?," panel discussion, NACLA/Center for Latin American Studies, New York University, November 16, 2020.

85 Rolando Borda-Padilla, telephone interview, October 21, 2020.

86 Amy Booth, personal communication, October 19, 2020.

87 Julieta Paredes, "Para 'vivir bien,'" *La Razón*, November 15, 2020, https://www.la-razon.com/voces/2020/11/15/para-vivir-bien/.

88 Pinto Quintanilla, telephone interview.

89 Frank O. Mora and Brian Fonseca, "They're Back. But It's Not Like Before," *Americas Quarterly* 14, no. 1 (2020): 3–19. Organizations and trade blocs such as the OAS, the Southern Common Market (MERCOSUR), the Union of South American Nations (UNASUR), and the Community of Latin American and Caribbean States (CELAC) have provided some pushback against overt military coups.

90 Octavio Humberto Moreno Velador and Carlos Alberto Figueroa Ibarra, "Golpismo y neogolpismo en América Latina. Violencia y conflicto político en el siglo veintiuno," *Iberoamérica Social: Revista red de estudios sociales*, no 3 (2019), http://dialnet.unirioja.es/servlet/articulo?codigo=7108225.

91 Moreno Velador and Figueroa Ibarra, "Golpismo y neogolpismo."

92 Nicole Fabricant, "A Realigned Bolivian Right: New 'Democratic' Destabilizations," *NACLA*, February 24, 2011, https://nacla.org/article/realigned-bolivian-right-new-'democratic'-destabilizations.

93 Personal communication, October 18, 2020.

94 Lorena Pérez, personal communication, December 24, 2020.

95 Personal communication, December 7, 2000.

96 Fabricant, "Realigned Bolivian Right."

97 Silvina Romano, Tamara Lajtman, Aníbal García Fernández, and Arantxa Tirado, "EE. UU. y la construcción del golpe en Bolivia," *CELAG*, November, 2019, available at https://i2.wp.com/thegrayzone.com/wp-content/uploads/2019/11/Screen-Shot-2019-11-11-at-3.10.01-PM.png?w=665&ssl=1.

98   Benjamin Dangl, "The Dark Side of Bolivia's Half Moon," *Upside Down World*, January 24, 2007, https://upsidedownworld.org/archives/bolivia/the-dark-side-of-bolivias-half-moon/.

99   "What Is FIDH," FIDH, https://www.fidh.org/en/about-us/What-is-FIDH/.

100  Maria Galindo, telephone interview, November 30, 2020.

101  Anonymous interview, La Paz, November 15, 2019.

102  Ben Dangl, "Lessons from Latin America," *The Nation*, March 23, 2009, https://www.thenation.com/article/archive/lessons-latin-america/.

103  Gabriel Hetland, "Bolivia Reclaimed Its Democracy, but Big Challenges Remain for the Victorious Socialists," *Washington Post*, October 20, 2020, https://www.washingtonpost.com/opinions/2020/10/20/bolivia-reclaimed-its-democracy-big-challenges-remain-victorious-socialists/.

104  Nicole Fabricant, "Bolivia Has Provided Us a Radical Vision of Hope," *Jacobin*, October 24, 2020, https://jacobinmag.com/2020/10/bolivia-luis-arce-evo-morales-elections-mas.

105  Donatella della Porta, "Protest Cycles and Waves," in *Wiley-Blackwell Encyclopedia of Social and Political Movements*, David. A. Snow et al., eds. (Hoboken, NJ: Wiley & Sons, 2013).

106  Linda Farthing, "Opportunity Squandered? Elites, Social Movements, and the Bolivian Government of Evo Morales," in *Latin America's Pink Tide: Breakthroughs and Shortcomings*, Steve Ellner, ed. (Lanham, MD: Rowman & Littlefield, 2019).

107  Ton Salman, "Social Movements in a Split: Bolivia's Protesters after Their Triumph," *International Journal of Sociology and Anthropology* 2, no. 7 (August 2010): 140–48.

108  Dangl, "Lessons from Latin America."

109  Alina Duarte, "Bolivia y la autocrítica necesaria: 'No basta con tener el gobierno, hay que tener el poder popular,'" *COHA*, November 11, 2020, https://www.coha.org/bolivia-y-la-autocritica-necesaria-no-basta-con-tener-el-gobierno-hay-que-tener-el-poder-popular/.

110  Anonymous interview, Santa Cruz, March 12, 2018.

111  Lorenza Fontana, "On the Perils and Potentialities of Revolution: Conflict and Collective Action in Contemporary Bolivia," *Latin American Perspectives* 40, no. 3 (2013): 26–42.

112  Anonymous interview, pro-Morales demonstration, El Alto, November 14, 2020.

113  Tom Kruse, interview, April 12, 2018.

114  Julia Goldenberg, "Los dilemas del MAS boliviano: Atrincheramiento o renovación; una entrevista con Fernando Mayorga," *Nueva Sociedad*, May 2016, https://nuso.org/articulo/el-proceso-boliviano-es-el-unico-en-el-que-el-liderazgo-se-produjo-de-abajo-hacia-arriba/.

115  Miriam Chávez, telephone interview, October 21, 2020.

116  Solón, "Why Lucho and David Won the Bolivian Elections."

117  "Exfuncionarios del MAS buscan retomar sus pegas por la fuerza,"
     *La Razón*, November 11, 2020, https://www.paginasiete.bo/
     nacional/2020/11/11/exfuncionarios-del-mas-buscan-retomar-sus-pegas-
     por-la-fuerza-274542.html.

118  Hervé Do Alto and Pablo Stefanoni, "El MAS: Las ambivalencias de la
     democracia corporativa," in *Mutaciones del campo político en Bolivia*, Alberto
     García and Fernando García, eds. (La Paz: PNUD Bolivia, 2010), 305–34.

119  Noele Illien, "Plan to Hold Corporations Liable for Violations Abroad
     Fails in Switzerland," *New York Times*, November 29, 2020, https://www.
     nytimes.com/2020/11/29/world/europe/switzerland-votereferendum-
     corporate-responsibility.html

120  Miranda Sheild Johansson, "Taxing the Indigenous: A History of Barriers
     to Fiscal Inclusion in the Bolivian Highlands," *History and Anthropology* 29,
     no. 1 (2018): 83–100.

121  Wilmer Machaca, interview, November 10, 2020.

122  Fabricant, "Radical Vision of Hope."

123  Julieta Paredes, "Para vivir bien."

# INDEX

# ABOUT HAYMARKET BOOKS

Haymarket Books is a radical, independent, nonprofit book publisher based in Chicago.

Our mission is to publish books that contribute to struggles for social and economic justice. We strive to make our books a vibrant and organic part of social movements and the education and development of a critical, engaged, international left.

We take inspiration and courage from our namesakes, the Haymarket martyrs, who gave their lives fighting for a better world. Their 1886 struggle for the eight-hour day—which gave us May Day, the international workers' holiday—reminds workers around the world that ordinary people can organize and struggle for their own liberation. These struggles continue today across the globe—struggles against oppression, exploitation, poverty, and war.

Since our founding in 2001, Haymarket Books has published more than five hundred titles. Radically independent, we seek to drive a wedge into the risk-averse world of corporate book publishing. Our authors include Noam Chomsky, Arundhati Roy, Rebecca Solnit, Angela Y. Davis, Howard Zinn, Amy Goodman, Wallace Shawn, Mike Davis, Winona LaDuke, Ilan Pappé, Richard Wolff, Dave Zirin, Keeanga-Yamahtta Taylor, Nick Turse, Dahr Jamail, David Barsamian, Elizabeth Laird, Amira Hass, Mark Steel, Avi Lewis, Naomi Klein, and Neil Davidson. We are also the trade publishers of the acclaimed Historical Materialism Book Series and of Dispatch Books.